THE PENGUIN GUIDE TO LITERATURE IN ENGLISH

BRITAIN AND IRELAND

Ronald Carter
and John McRae

To Jeremy and Jane
'For love that time was
not as love is nowadays.'
Malory, *Le Morte d'Arthur*

PENGUIN ENGLISH

D0278419

PENGUIN BOOKS

UK | USA | Canada | Ireland | Australia
India | New Zealand | South Africa

Penguin Books is part of the Penguin Random House group of companies
whose addresses can be found at global.penguinrandomhouse.com.

 Penguin
Random House
UK

First published in Great Britain by Penguin Books 1996
Second edition published by Pearson Education 2001
Published in Penguin Books 2016
001

Typeset by Ferdinand Pageworks
Printed in China by C&C Offset

A CIP catalogue record for this book is available from the British Library

ISBN: 978–0–141–98516–9

www.greenpenguin.co.uk

 Penguin Random House is committed to a
sustainable future for our business, our readers
and our planet. This book is made from Forest
Stewardship Council® certified paper.

Our thanks go to Jeremy Hunter and Michael Nation for providing throughout the long gestation of this book friendship, support and eagle-eyed advice. Their contribution is more substantial than we may sometimes, in a note such as this, dare admit it to be. We would also like to add our thanks to Helen Parker for her advice and support in the production of the second edition.

RAC and JM, Nottingham, 1996 and 2000

PICTURE ACKNOWLEDGEMENTS
The publishers make grateful acknowledgement to the following for permission to reproduce the illustrations and photographs in this book:

p. viii: *Decrees of Kings of Anglo-Saxon and Norman England* (Cott Vit A XIII f.3v), illustration of 'William killing Harold at the Battle of Hastings,' 14th century manuscript, British Library, London/courtesy of the Bridgeman Art Library; p. 5: page from *Beowulf*, Anglo-Saxon manuscript (CAD 1000, Cott MS), British Library, London/courtesy of The Mansell Collection; p. 7: Theuet, illustration of The Venerable Bede from *Les vrais portrait et vies des hommes illustre*, 1584, courtesy of The Mansell Collection; p. 8: page from the *Luttrel Psalter*, 14th century manuscript, British Library, London/courtesy of Weidenfeld & Nicolson Ltd, Library & Archives; p. 9: illustration of 'King Arthur and the Knights of the Round Table with the Holy Grail' from *Le Roman de Lancelot du Lac*, 14th century manuscript, Bibliotheque Nationale, France/courtesy of The Mansell Collection; p. 12: portrait of Geoffrey Chaucer, courtesy of the National Portrait Gallery, London; p. 15 photograph of a scene from Harrison Birtwistle's modern opera *Sir Gawain and the Green Knight*, © Clive Barda/Performing Arts Library; p. 16: photograph of a scene from Mystery Plays performed at the Theatre Royal, York, © Susan Lund/BTA/MSI; p. 18: Aubrey Beardsley, illustration from *Le Morte d'Arthur* by Sir Thomas Malory, from the Dent Edition, 1927, courtesy of The Mansell Collection; p. 20: engraving by F. Bartolozzi, from a drawing by B. West, *An Indian Cacique of the Island of Cuba addressing Columbus concerning the future of the state*, 1794, courtesy of the Hulton Deutsch Collection Ltd; p. 24: photograph of Paul Scofield as Hamlet at the Phoenix Theatre, 1955, © Mander & Mitchenson Theatre Collection; p. 26: portrait of William Shakespeare, courtesy of the National Portrait Gallery, London; p. 28: drawing of The Globe Theatre, 1965, © C. Walter Hodges; p. 37: Inigo Jones, border of the scene for *The Temple of Love*, inscribed 'for the Queenes Masque of Indianes, 1634,' Devonshire Collection, Chatsworth, reproduced by permission of the Chatsworth Settlement Trustees, photograph courtesy of The Courtauld Institute of Art; p. 40: advertisement for *A Game at Chess*, 1624, British Museum, London/courtesy of Weidenfeld & Nicolson Ltd, Library and Archives; p. 43: Walter Crane, illustration of The Red Cross Knight from Book I of *The Faerie Queene*, courtesy of The Mansell Collection; p. 51: title page from *A True Revelation of Such Occurrances and Accidents of Note as Have Happened in Virginia* by John Smith, published 1608, British Library, London/courtesy of Weidenfeld & Nicolson Ltd, Library and Archives; p. 53: Francis Bacon, Viscount St Albans, courtesy of the National Portrait Gallery, London; p. 54: *The Royal Oak Tree (English Revolution)*, engraving, 1651, British Library, London/courtesy of The Bridgeman Art Library; p. 59: Gustave Dore, illustration of The Fall of Satan from Book VI of *Paradise Lost*, from the 1882 edition published by Cassell, Peter, Galpin & Co; p. 61: Henry C. Selous, engraving of Christian and Hopeful escaping from the Giant Despair, an illustration from *The Pilgrim's Progress* by John Bunyan, from the 1844 edition published by M. M. Holloway; p. 63: attributed to J. Stuysmans, portrait of John Wilmot, 2nd Earl of Rochester, National Portrait Gallery, London/courtesy of Weidenfeld & Nicolson Ltd, Library and Archives; p. 64: (left) title page from *Heroic Stanzas* by John Dryden, 1659; (right) title page from *To His Sacred Majesty* by John Dryden, 1660; p. 68: The Drury Lane Theatre, 1776, courtesy of The Mander & Mitchenson Theatre Collection; p. 72: J. Fittler, engraving of Aphra Behn from a portrait by Mary Beale, courtesy of The Mander & Mitchenson Theatre Collection; p. 74: C. Lovat Fraser, advertisement for *The Beggar's Opera* by John Gay at the Lyric Theatre, Hammersmith, in a private collection/courtesy of The Bridgeman Art Library; p. 75: photograph of Athene Seyler as Mrs Malaprop in *The Rivals* at the Saville Theatre, 1956, © The Mander & Mitchenson Theatre Collection; p. 76: Jacques Louis David (grisaille sketch), *The Oath of the Tennis Court, 20 June, 1789*, in the collection of the Chateau de Versailles, France, courtesy of Giraudon/Bridgeman Art Library; p. 79: engraving of Mary de la Riviere Manley, Bodleian Library, Oxford/courtesy of the National Portrait Gallery, London; p. 80: an illustration from *Robinson Crusoe* by Daniel Defoe from a French edition, 1784, courtesy of The Mansell Collection; p. 83: Rex Whistler, illustration from *Gulliver's Travels* by Jonathan Swift, Cresset Press edition, photograph © Alan G. Thomas/courtesy of Weidenfeld & Nicolson Ltd, Library and Archives; p. 88: T. Higham, after J. Martin, engraving of the south front of Fonthill Abbey, courtesy of The Mansell Collection; p. 91: Lady Mary Wortley Montagu, gravure after a miniature in a private collection, courtesy of The Mansell Collection; p. 92: an illustration from *Elegy Written in a Country Churchyard* by Thomas Gray, courtesy of The Mansell Collection; p. 97: page from the first edition of *The Tatler*, courtesy of The Mansell Collection; p. 101: David Roberts (1796–1864), *Ruins of the Roman Capitol*, Wolverhampton Art Gallery, Staffordshire/courtesy of The Bridgeman Art Library; p. 102: Caspar David Friedrich (1774–1840), *The Wanderer Over the Sea of Clouds*, 1818,

Contents

Introduction

This book will show you a new world, the world of literature – of stories, plays, poems, songs – all of them telling us what it is like to be a human being.

Writers talk about the same themes all through the centuries and all over the world: love and war, life and death, men and women, kings and ordinary people, the world around them, nature and society, the things they believe in, and the things they are worried about.

But each piece of literature is different because of the time and the place in which it was written, and because of the person who wrote it. A man, a woman, English, Scottish, Irish, or from some other place – these differences have an effect on what the person writes, and how they write.

The readers are different too: the readers at the time the text was written are different from us reading the text today. Each reader uses his or her knowledge and experience to understand the text. If we have different knowledge or experience we may see the text differently.

This book will help you to understand all kinds of writing in the history of literature in English. It is a long history, and an exciting one, because the points of view of the writers are so varied and because the ways they write can be as exciting as what they write about.

Like literature, language also changes over time. You will learn about the history of the English language, as well as about its literature. The book will give you a lot to enjoy and a lot to remember – there are lots of quotations which you can keep in your mind forever.

Ronald Carter and John McRae
University of Nottingham

William the Conqueror killed King Harold at the Battle of Hastings, 1066.

1 The Beginnings of English: Old and Middle English 600–1485

Setting the Scene

The first literature in English goes back to the period between about AD 410 and 1066. These are Anglo-Saxon times and are known as the early medieval period. In 410 the Romans left Britain, and in 1066 the Norman Conquest began the late medieval period of history.

It was a time of wars and invasions – Britain was invaded by many peoples from Europe: Angles, Saxons, Jutes, Vikings and finally Normans. These invasions left many traces in the form of castles and towns, as well as in culture and language. The language known as Old English is the language of the first literature in English. But it was a long time before it was actually written down: the first stories and poems were spoken, and we do not know exactly when these stories were first told. There were two cultures through the Anglo-Saxon period: the Christian culture, which had arrived in England in 597 with Saint Augustine, and the heroic culture, of leaders and heroes who defended their lands against invaders.

The Norman Conquest at the Battle of Hastings in 1066 was the last successful invasion of Britain. The Normans took power, and William the Conqueror became King of England. William tried to bring peace to the country after many centuries of wars and invasions but did not always succeed. The Normans brought with them many French influences, and the French language began to mix with Old English into a more modern language. Scandinavian influences were also strong and Latin was still the language of the Church, so there were many influences on English language and culture. Out of these influences a new national identity began to develop. Parts of France remained British until as late as 1558;

1

Wales was part of the Kingdom of England from 1282. Scotland was the main enemy for another three hundred years, and many wars against the Scots were fought in the fourteenth and fifteenth centuries.

The first parliament was in 1265, and English became the language of national law in 1362. The Magna Carta of 1215 reduced the power of the king, giving more power and property rights to the aristocrats. The city of London became the capital of the country, and the local southern dialect of English became the main spoken form of English, although local dialects remained strong, as they still do today. Trade with Europe became more important. A new class of traders and merchants grew up, as trade between nations replaced war.

Old English

PERSONAL AND RELIGIOUS VOICES

The language of the earliest English literature came from many different places. The literature itself and its subjects were influenced by different countries, and by different places, peoples and cultures, but the question of what is English about English literature is still a big question today, as more and more writers use the English language. The subjects of the first literature are subjects which are familiar even now: war, religion, personal sadness and happiness. It was the Christian monks in the monasteries who first wrote down the words of the early literature – they were the only people who could read and write, and for many centuries they guarded culture and learning. But only a few fragments remain of all the writing that the monks kept. They reflect the two cultures, of Christianity and of heroic actions, with the occasional personal voice coming through. Most of the texts from this period are anonymous, but one or two names are attached to texts. The very first fragment is called 'Caedmon's Hymn'. There is a legend that Caedmon was a shepherd in Northumbria, in the far north of England, and the voice of God came to him, so his 'Hymn' is the first song of praise in English literature. Of course, the monks at nearby Whitby soon heard of this poetic shepherd, and in about 670, Caedmon entered their monastery, and his short poem entered history:

> Nu we sculon herigean   heofonrices Weard,
> Meotodes meahte   ond his modgeþanc

> Now we must praise   of heaven's kingdom the Keeper
> Of the Lord the power   and his wisdom

Two features of most Old English poetry are immediately clear: the gap in the middle of each line, called the caesura, which modern editors use to show the rhythm of the verse, and the alliteration (the letter 'h' in the first line). Both of these influence the *sound* of the poem, reminding us that the poetry was spoken long before it was written down.

Another name from the early medieval period is Deor, but we know nothing about him. We do not know the author of the poem *Deor's Lament* but the narrator, Deor, is a writer and singer of songs who has no job, and he thinks of other unfortunate men, returning always to the refrain:

> Þæs ofereode;   þisses swa mæg

> Of that there was an end;   so there may be of this.

This is not only a poem about a man who is searching for work, but one of the first texts to talk of the passing of time, and of personal suffering. *Deor's Lament* is probably from the beginning of the eighth century, many years after Caedmon. Another important name from these centuries is Cynewulf, and he brings together the other two names. He may also have come from Northumbria, and two of the texts he wrote are found in a book called the *Exeter Book*, where *Deor's Lament* is also written. The *Exeter Book*, and a similar book written in England but now kept in Vercelli in Italy, the *Vercelli Book*, are among the few examples which remain of the work of monks in preserving texts from the Dark Ages. Cynewulf's four poems are all religious in tone, and celebrate the lives of saints and other similar topics.

Beowulf and Long Poems

Several poems are preserved in the *Exeter Book*. Two other personal but anonymous poems are: *The Wanderer* and *The Seafarer* [sailor]. These are elegiac poems – the speaker is always alone, and his memory becomes very important. They are memories of old legends, old battles and old heroes. Although we know very little about the period, we do find ideas and themes which are common in all literature, and memories are a major part of the writing.

Among the anonymous religious texts which remain, the best known is *The Dream of the Rood*. The word rood means cross in Old English. This poem is found not only in the *Vercelli Book*, but also on a standing stone in Ruthwell in southern Scotland. The poem is also important for two reasons: it is the first of a kind of poem which became very popular in later literature, the dream-vision; and *The Dream of the Rood* shows a great range of words to describe the cross of Christ, and a range of images which later poems developed.

The main heroic text is called *Beowulf*, the name of the hero of the long anonymous poem. It describes events which are part of the period's memory: invasions and battles, some historic, some legendary. The poem is set around the sixth century, but was probably not written down until the eighth century. Beowulf is the first hero in English literature, the man who can win battles and give safety to his people over a long period of time.

The Battle of Maldon is another long poem about battles and heroes. But it is much more factual, describing a real battle rather than retelling a fictional story of war. Both *The Battle of Maldon* and *Beowulf* are written in rich and powerful language, full of new words, new tones and new rhythms, and with many images of light, colour and action. *Beowulf*, which is about 3,000 lines, is a story about a brave young man from southern Sweden. Beowulf goes to help Hrothgar, King of the Danes, who cannot defend himself or his people against a terrible monster called Grendel. One night Beowulf attacks Grendel and pulls off the arm of the monster. Grendel returns to the lake where he lives, but dies there. Beowulf is then attacked by the mother of Grendel and Beowulf follows her to the bottom of the lake and kills her, too.

A page from the heroic poem Beowulf. *This page was written in about the year AD 1000.*

Fifty years later, Beowulf has to defend his own people against a dragon which breathes fire. Although he kills the dragon, Beowulf himself is injured in the fight and dies. The poem has a sad ending, but the poem is a statement of heroic values and Beowulf dies a hero. Here Wiglaf reminds Beowulf of his greatest days:

> Leofa Biowulf,   læst eall tela,
> swa ðu on geoguðfeore   geara gecwæde,
> þæt ðu ne alæte   be ðe lifigendum
> dom gedreosan

> Beloved Beowulf, keep well the vow that you swore
> long ago in the days of your youth, not to allow your
> glory to diminish as long as you lived.

When Beowulf dies, Wiglaf has to continue the example for the next generation.

The *Beowulf* story is part myth, part history, but the hero is remembered as the man who can win battles and give safety to his people over a long period of time. Questions of the passing of time through the generations, and of what it means to be a human being, are central. A new translation of *Beowulf* came out in 1999 and was a great popular success. It was written by the Irish Nobel Prize winner, Seamus Heaney, and the translation won the Whitbread Book of the Year prize. This new *Beowulf* shows that a text can speak across centuries and can reach new readers more than a thousand years after it was first written.

PROSE

Many of the earliest books were histories, rather than imaginative writings. They give us a lot of the information we have of this period. Bede, known as the Venerable Bede, was a monk who lived between 673 and 735. He wrote many books, mostly about the Bible, but he is remembered also for his *History of the English Church and People* written in Latin and completed about 731.

The Venerable Bede

One of the first books of history was *The Anglo-Saxon Chronicle* [chronicle = record of events]. It was written over a long period of time, and tells the history of England from the beginning of Christian times, around AD 600, to 1154, with details of invasions and battles. Some of it is in poetry, and it is very important for our knowledge of the history and the language of Old English. King Alfred the Great was probably one of the people who helped to put the *Chronicle* together. His reign, from 871 to 899, was a time of great literary production. Alfred ordered many translations of religious and historical texts, and helped to bring the West Saxon dialect into a strong position as the language of literature and history. Aelfric, a monk from Winchester in the south of England, was an important translator as well as a writer. His works include *Catholic Homilies* [homilies = religious talk] (990–2), and *Lives of the Saints* (993–8). He uses real spoken English, and all the features of Old English literature are found in his work. Aelfric is the greatest figure in Old English prose. He brought excellence of style into the language, and wide knowledge to all his works.

The themes of Old English literature are security, both for the individual and society, and in religious faith. This literature gave comfort, or provided reflection. Usually the poems were sung in the hall of a castle, and these songs and poems were passed on from generation to generation before they were written down. In this way, the spoken tradition led to the first tradition of written literature. At the same time, Old English was beginning to develop into a different language, called Middle English, closer to the English we know today.

Middle English 1150–1485

In Middle English literature the hero of earlier times now became the man of romance, as love poetry began to come in, first of all from the south of France. Women began to appear more in poetry, usually

In Middle English literature love poetry began to come in and women appear more. A page from the Luttrel Psalter, 14th century.

as objects of desire and perfection, but later also as very human
beings with feelings of their own. The literature of Europe,
particularly France and Italy, began to influence English writers, and
there was a clear desire to begin a purely English tradition in
literature and in history. However, wars and tragedies still took
place. There was still to be the Hundred Years War between France
and England (1337–1453), as well as the Wars of the Roses between
the royal houses of Lancaster and York for the throne of England.
And in the mid-fourteenth century [mid = middle] the Black Death
brought illness and death to millions of people all through the
country. There were social problems, too, with the Peasants' Revolt
of 1381.

The first histories, by the Venerable Bede (eighth century),
Nennius (ninth century) and Geoffrey of Monmouth (about 1136),
created a sense of national historical and mythical identity. The
name of King Arthur became important as a figure from the dark
past of history, and he later became a symbol of English history for
many centuries. Layamon, one of the first authors to see himself as
a writer of history, put together *Brut* (late twelfth century), an epic
history which took British history right back to classical Greek and
Roman sources. *Brut* brought together many themes and figures
which returned in later literature, and is an important text in the

*King Arthur and the
Knights of the Round
Table. Arthur became a
symbol of English history.*

THE LEGEND OF KING ARTHUR

The story of King Arthur and the Knights of the Round Table is the greatest national myth in English. There probably was a real King Arthur somewhere in south-west England around the year 500; he may have died in a battle against the Saxons in 537. About 200 years later the story begins to appear in the spoken tradition in Wales. Characters such as the magician Merlin, Lancelot and Guinevere, and features like the sword in the stone (Excalibur, which only the hero can pull out) begin to appear. Later, other myths, like the Holy Grail, a religious symbol of perfection, became part of the Arthurian legend. The myth returns again and again in English literature, especially in times of crisis or war. Arthur and his court appear in the fourteenth-century manuscript of an earlier Welsh story from the spoken tradition: *Kulhwch and Olwen*. This was later included in *The Mabinogion* (nineteenth century).

1130s Geoffrey of Monmouth's Latin text, *Historia Regum Britanniae* – a prose romance rather than a history – includes most of the legends and figures at Arthur's court. An Old English translation, by Robert Wace, was completed about 1155.

1170–90 The French romances of Chrétien de Troyes mixed the legends of King Arthur and the Holy Grail. Welsh versions of scenes from his works were also collected in *The Mabinogion*.

c. 1200 Layamon's *Brut* used many sources, including Wace, to retell Old English history in chivalric style.

1300s At the same time as England's involvement in the Hundred Years War, many Arthurian stories were produced: Sir Gawain was usually the most heroic knight, as in the most famous of fourteenth-century romances, *Sir Gawain and the Green Knight*. Two romances, however, placed Lancelot at the centre of the story.

c. 1430 First Arthurian romance by a named author, *Launfal Miles* by Thomas Chestre, based on an earlier telling of the story.

1485 Caxton printed Sir Thomas Malory's romance *Le Morte d'Arthur*, probably written around 1470.

1590–96 Edmund Spenser, in *The Faerie Queene*, used features of the Arthurian legend to praise Queen Elizabeth I.

1660s John Milton, wishing to write an English epic poem, famously considered King Arthur before choosing the Biblical story of Adam and Eve (*Paradise Lost*).

1842 Alfred Tennyson included many poems inspired by Arthurian legend in his *Poems*. Later he published *Idylls of the King* (1859–85) in several books.

1932 John Cowper Powys's novel *A Glastonbury Romance*.

1937 T. H. White's children's story *The Sword in the Stone* (filmed by Walt Disney); this was republished in 1958, with the addition of three more Arthurian stories, as *The Once and Future King*. This became the stage and film musical *Camelot* in the 1960s. Another successful film about King Arthur, *Excalibur*, followed in the early 1980s.

history of writing in English, just at the time when English was developing as a language and a culture. The popular culture of ballads and songs grew at the same time as the first great masterpieces of English literature were written. There was also a major text for women, but written by a man, *The Ancrene Riwle* or *The Ancrene Wisse*. It is a book of advice for women who want to join the religious life (the title means rules or wisdom for nuns). It was probably written about 1220, and is considered one of the greatest prose works in Middle English.

CHAUCER

One of the best-known names in English literature is Geoffrey Chaucer. He saw himself as the first great poet of the nation and the language, and he remains the reference point which other writers have used through the centuries. Chaucer was influenced by many kinds of writing, and used many European models. For example, his first poems were dream poems, using the Old English model; *Troilus and Criseyde* (about 1385) uses a story from classical Greek times; and *The House of Fame* (1370s) shows the influence of the Latin poet Ovid and the Italian poet Dante (1265–1321). Chaucer was a European in his views and experience, but his ambition was to make the literature of English the equal of any other European writing. *The Canterbury Tales* [tales = stories] (1387–1400) is Chaucer's best-known work, and the first major work in English literature. It is a series (never completed) of linked stories. The stories are told by a group of people on their way from an inn in Southwark to the cathedral of Saint Thomas à Becket in Canterbury. There are many aspects to *The Canterbury Tales*, both secular and religious. The time is spring (April) when the world comes to life again after the long winter; and the people are from every level of society, except the highest and the lowest – a wide range of the new middle class, including a knight, a nun, the wife of Bath, several religious figures and tradesmen. And the stories which they tell are also very different – some are classical, some modern, some moral, some the opposite. Chaucer took the idea of a linked series of stories from the Italian writings of Boccaccio, but he sets them clearly in the here and now of late fourteenth-century England. He had planned for 120 stories,

Geoffrey Chaucer

but only twenty-four of them were written. However, *The Canterbury Tales* is still the great mirror of its times, and a great collection of comic views of the life it describes.

For example, a nun is clearly more fond of love than of religion:

> That of hir smylyng was ful symple and coy;
> . . .
> And she was all conscience and tendre herte.

> Who in her way of smiling was very unaffected[1] and modest;
> . . .
> And all was sentiment and tender heart.
>
> ('The Prioress's[2] Tale')

[1]without false emotions [2]nun's

The knight is seen as a figure from a past age who does not fit in very well with the new modern society. Chaucer uses irony to describe him as 'a verray parfit gentil knight' [parfit = perfect, gentil = gentle] – completely perfect and gentle are high moral values which are difficult to keep. In his story, self-interest is one of the main themes:

> And therefore, at the kynges court, my brother,
> Ech man for hymself, ther is noon oother.

> And therefore, at the king's court, my brother,
> Each man for himself, there is no other way.
>> ('The Knight's Tale')

Chaucer is describing a society that is changing, and its people and their values are changing, too. Again and again the stories and the story-tellers contrast old ways of behaving and of thinking with more modern attitudes. So religion is less important than enjoying life, and making money is a new ambition:

> But al be that he was a philosophre,
> Yet hadde he but litel gold in cofre;

> But although he was a philosopher,
> Nevertheless he had only a little gold in his coffer.
>> ('General Prologue'[1])

[1]introduction

Some of the ideas in *The Canterbury Tales* sound very modern, and show that Chaucer was interested in wider themes:

> What is this world? what asketh men to have?
> Now with his love, now in his colde grave
> Allone, withouten any compaignye.

What is this world? what do men ask for?
Now with his love, now in his cold grave
Alone, without any companionship.

('The Knight's Tale')

Many of the other writers of the Middle English period reflect such themes of love and death, although only Chaucer gives such a wide picture of the society.

POETRY, PROSE AND DRAMA

John Gower wrote a great many books, in Latin and in French as well as in English. His most famous is *Confessio Amantis*, the confession of a lover. At the end the lover says he will give up love – but only because he is getting too old. Again, there is irony in Gower, and the subject matter is clearly very far from the heroism of Old English: emotions and human weakness are becoming more common themes in literature. William Langland, in *Piers Plowman*, uses the dream-vision form to write a long series of dream stories. It is a view of the whole country of England, and is a kind of early satire on the new society and how it could be different. Again, the old values of religious idealism are in contrast with the new views of human ambition and desire.

Many anonymous texts in Middle English explore these contrasts – *Winner and Waster* shows even in its title the kind of conflict it describes. *Pearl* and *Sir Gawain and the Green Knight* are the best known of the anonymous texts. The first is a dream a father has of his daughter who died. She is now perfect, in heaven, and the father can see how far she is from the human level.

Sir Gawain is one of the Knights of the Round Table, from the court of King Arthur, and is expected to be brave, honest and honourable. One evening a huge green man enters the court and challenges a knight to cut his head off. But the knight must have his own head cut off one year later. Gawain accepts the challenge and cuts off the head of the green man. A year later Sir Gawain is looking for the Green Knight when he arrives at a castle. The lord of the castle has a beautiful wife who tempts Gawain. She gives him a magic belt which will save his life. When Gawain finally

Sir Gawain and the Green Knight. A scene from the modern opera by Harrison Birtwistle.

meets the Green Knight he uses the belt. He deceives the knight and he does not accept the challenge with true bravery. The Green Knight is really the lord of the castle and when Sir Gawain accepts that he is not an ideal brave hero he is forgiven by the Green Knight. Gawain returns to the court of King Arthur and is praised for his bravery. Gawain is, in fact, a kind of anti-hero, and the poem is an ironic questioning of the value of the historical myths of heroism in those changed times, much as Chaucer questioned the old-fashioned values of his knight.

A mystery play shows the events of the Bible. Here the Devil is talking to Jesus Christ.

Medieval literature questions its society, making its readers think about the times they live in, as well as giving us a picture of the fast-changing society of the time. The main writing of this period was in poetry, but the tradition of drama was beginning in this time, too.

The original medieval dramas were set in and around the church at festival times, and they showed scenes from the Bible for an audience who perhaps could not understand the Latin of the Bible. The plays were called mystery or miracle plays because they showed the mysterious or miraculous events of the Bible and the saints' lives.

The plays were usually performed on moving carts, by the businessmen of the city, and the texts which remain are often called by the name of the group of businessmen which first performed them (the Fishers and Mariners [sailors] for example). Groups of these plays remain from the cities of York, Wakefield and Chester in particular, and all have local differences in the stories they tell and the way they are told. Many of the theatrical effects were very impressive – *Hell's Mouth* is the most famous example. These plays are an important step towards the great theatrical period at the end of the sixteenth century.

Influenced by the work of Chaucer in England, two writers in Scotland produced some major poetry. They came to be known as the Scottish Chaucerians, although the language they used was Scots rather than English. The names of these writers, the first great figures in Scottish literature, are Robert Henryson and William Dunbar. It is interesting that the King of Scotland, King James I (1394–1437) was also an important poet. His *Kingis Quair* [King's Book] (*c.* 1425) is a book of love poetry written in the verse form which, because of his use of it, came to be known as 'rhyme-royal'.

The major event in literary terms in the fifteenth century was the invention of printing, by Gutenberg (1398–1468), in Germany. The first books to be printed were Bibles, but when William Caxton and later his assistant, Wynken de Worde, brought printing to England in the 1470s, they began to print literary works, the first of which was a story of King Arthur and the Knights of the Round Table, called *Le Morte d'Arthur* by Sir Thomas Malory, published in 1485. The author had died several years before Caxton published the book – and it is not even certain who Malory was. The book is based on a Middle English alliterative poem in dialect from the century before, but Malory's telling of the story is the one which has remained popular ever since. Lancelot and Guinevere, the search for the Holy Grail, and the myth of King Arthur from the Dark Ages, one thousand years before, reached many new readers in published form, and the story, already familiar, became a part of the English national consciousness. It is almost the national myth, and has remained popular until the present day.

The final figure in the late medieval period is John Skelton, a very individual poet who wrote short rapid lines of poetry about such subjects as drinking alcohol, a pet bird and low life. Here his pet bird, a sparrow, complains about cats:

An illustration by Aubrey Beardsley for a nineteenth-century edition of Le Morte d'Arthur, *by Sir Thomas Malory.*

> Vengeance[1] I ask and cry
> By way of exclamation[2]
> On the whole nation
> Of cats wild and tame:[3]
> God send them sorrow and shame!
>   ('Phyllyp Sparrow')

[1] revenge   [2] cry   [3] domesticated

Skelton's humour, as well as his poetic style, are unique. He and his poetry are difficult to describe, and not many critics have written about him in literary history. But he brings together many of the themes of the Middle English period: humour, and a different view on the values of the time, new verse forms and play with language and style, and a strong sense of English identity.

In the Renaissance new worlds were discovered and new ways of seeing and thinking developed. In 1492 Christopher Columbus was the first European to discover America.

2 The Renaissance 1485–1649

Setting the Scene

Renaissance means rebirth. From about 1500 to 1600 the world was reborn in many ways. The Renaissance began in Italy, especially in art and architecture, in the fifteenth century. As England became the most powerful nation in Europe in the late sixteenth century, new worlds were discovered and new ways of seeing and thinking developed. Columbus was the first European to discover America in 1492; Copernicus and Galileo later made important discoveries about the stars and planets; Ferdinand Magellan sailed all round the world. The Renaissance was worldwide.

In England there was an important change in religion and politics when King Henry VIII made himself the head of the Church of England, bringing church and state together (1529–39). He cut all contact with the Catholic Church and the Pope in Rome, part of a reaction against the Catholic Church in many parts of Europe. Protestantism became more and more important, and gave a whole new vision of man's relations with God. The king or queen became the human being on earth who was closest to God, at the head of the Great Chain of Being which led down to the rest of mankind, animals, insects and so on. The Dutch thinker, Erasmus, wrote of mankind as central to the world, and this humanist concern was the basis of most Renaissance thought.

Henry VIII's daughter, Queen Elizabeth, became the symbol of the Golden Age, the period of stability from 1558 to 1603. England's enemies, Spain in particular, were defeated, and the English controlled the seas of the world, exploring and bringing valuable goods from the New World.

As Elizabeth grew older, with no child to succeed her, a new concern grew with the passing of time and with the shortness of human life. This is closely linked with the Renaissance search for new ways of believing, new ways of seeing and understanding the universe.

The Renaissance was the beginning of the modern world in the areas of geography, science, politics, religion, society and art. London became not only the capital city of England, but also the main city of the known world. And English, in the hands of writers like Shakespeare, became the modern language we can recognize today. The invention of printing meant that all kinds of writing were open to anyone who could read. Many new forms of writing were developed. But the most important form of expression was the theatre. This was the age of Shakespeare, and the Golden Age of English Drama.

William Shakespeare (1564–1616)

The most famous line in all English literature is probably from *Hamlet* (1600): 'To be, or not to be, that is the question.' That one quotation expresses many of the issues and problems which Shakespeare put into his plays. Hamlet, the Prince of Denmark, is deciding whether to go on living, or to die. He has to face the fact that his father, the king, has been murdered by his own brother, Claudius, who is now the king; and Gertrude, Hamlet's mother, has married this new king. Hamlet's duty is to avenge his father's death. However, to kill a king is one of the great moral problems – if the king is next to God, how can it be right to kill him? Hamlet asks such questions of duty, honour and revenge in his role as prince. And as a man he also faces questions of love (with Ophelia), friendship, study (he is a student at the Protestant University of Wittenberg) and of family.

Hamlet has become the best known of all Shakespeare's plays. The main character faces a familiar series of problems: they are not simply the problems of a prince, but many of them are questions which every individual in the modern world will face at some time or another, as they learn to live in the world. The final problem Hamlet has to face is his own death and, in the new, non-Catholic [non = not] world, religion cannot offer the help it used to in the medieval world.

From the earliest times, writing on paper meant that single copies of texts were written by hand. In England, before the fifteenth century, books were usually written in monasteries because most people outside the church could not read or write. These books are called illuminated manuscripts. They reached only a few readers.

1428 Johann Gutenberg, a German, experimented with moveable type: separate letters of metal, placed in lines to make words. The process advanced rapidly by the middle of the century. This meant that books were produced very quickly, so many more people could read them.

1477 William Caxton printed the first book in England. Publishing became an industry. There were several different versions of the Bible, and the printed word became an important political, religious and social influence.

1533 Foreign books came under government control (at the time of King Henry VIII's argument with the Roman Catholic church). Many old and valuable books were destroyed in this decade, during the dissolution [closing] of the monasteries, and in 1538 the licensing of English books was introduced.

1540s There was a growth in the production of pamphlets – short printed texts, often on political themes – which continued through the reign of Queen Elizabeth I (1558–1603). These pamphlets reached many readers and the printed word had more and more social and political effect.

1611 The publication of the *Authorized Version* of the Bible, and of Shakespeare's plays (finally grouped together in the *First Folio* of 1623) had a huge influence on the language and culture of Britain, giving authority to the printed word.

1622 The first weekly newspaper was published. Journalism did not progress during the Commonwealth (1649–60) but grew quickly after the Restoration.

1709 First edition of *The Tatler*, the earliest successful magazine. In the same year, the first Copyright Act was introduced, to protect authors' rights. The most important addition to the Act was made in 1911.

1726 Allan Ramsay started, in Edinburgh, the first circulating library (one that moves from place to place), for borrowing rather than buying books. This system of reading remained very popular throughout the nineteenth century, but died out during the twentieth century.

1785 Britain's most famous newspaper, *The Times*, was started, originally with the title *The Daily Universal Register*.

1847 The first library paid for by public money, in Canterbury. The spread of public libraries gradually forced the circulating libraries out of business.

c.1840–1900 Most novels were published in parts in magazines and later republished in book form – often in three volumes, which were known as triple-decker novels. Readers borrowed them from libraries as they were still very expensive to buy.

1935 Paperback publishing had its first major success in Britain with the beginning of Penguin Books. This brought writing to a mass market, as the books were very cheap to buy.

1990s Developments in information technology caused a revolution as important as Gutenberg's: CD-ROM and other forms make many kinds of writing quickly available.

The actor Paul Scofield as Hamlet, Prince of Denmark.

Hamlet is a tragedy. At the end the hero dies, the harmony in the universe is overturned, and the audience has been deeply moved by the description of the struggles involved. Of Shakespeare's thirty-seven plays, many of the best known are tragedies. Each is, however, different from all the others. Shakespeare, in his long writing career, from his first plays, *Henry VI* and *The Comedy of Errors* in about 1590, to his last, *The Tempest* [storm] and *Henry VIII* in 1611 and 1613, was constantly experimenting with different styles, techniques and themes.

HISTORY PLAYS AND ROMAN PLAYS

Many of Shakespeare's plays are history plays. These usually have
as their title the name of an English king, such as *Henry IV* (which is
in two parts), *Henry V*, *Henry VI* (in three parts) and *Henry VIII*.
They study what it is to be a king. Shakespeare examines every king
as a human being first, and they are very human, strong or weak,
clever or not so clever, good or bad. Some of these history plays are
more than historical stories, and become tragedies, like *Hamlet*.
Richard II and *Richard III* are examples of Shakespeare developing
the range of his plays in this way.

The words of some of these plays show Shakespeare's concern
for his own nation, and for the human individual who 'plays the
king':

> This royal throne of kings, this scepter'd[1] isle,[2]
>
> [1]ruled by a king   [2]island

is a description of the island nation of Britain (from *Richard II*), and
the following is young King Henry's encouragement to his army at
the Battle of Agincourt in *Henry V*:

> Once more unto[1] the breach,[2] dear friends, once more,
> Or close the wall up with our English dead.
>
> [1]to   [2]break in the city wall

But not all kings are as heroic as Henry. Richard II, the most
tragically weak of Shakespeare's kings, shows his deepest feelings in
these words:

> For God's sake let us sit upon the ground
> And tell sad stories of the death of kings . . .
> For you have but mistook me all this while.
> I live with bread like you, feel want,
> Taste grief, need friends – subjected thus,[1]
> How can you say to me I am a king?
>
> [1]controlled in this way

This is one of the clearest expressions of the humanity of Shakespeare's kings: Richard is a real man, with real worries and concerns, no longer a distant Godlike figure. Shakespeare manages to create sympathy for his heroes, making them understandable, complex, recognizable characters.

In a similar way, Shakespeare describes the classical history of Ancient Rome in the Roman plays, which also combine the historical with the tragic: *Titus Andronicus*, *Julius Caesar*, *Antony and Cleopatra* and *Coriolanus* make up this group of plays. Like the history plays, they were all written at different times in Shakespeare's career (see the table of all Shakespeare's plays on p. 34). He liked to return to different historical periods at different times, and it is interesting to see that the same historical subjects return in his early period, his middle period and his late plays.

Very often the political questions examined in the history plays and the Roman plays have clear links with the political situation in England at the time Shakespeare was writing – but he is always careful not to offend the monarch, or the earls and lords who

William Shakespeare

financially supported his theatrical company. Many other writers at that time were not so careful (or clever) and were put in jail for criticizing their superiors.

SOLILOQUIES AND STRUCTURE

Of course, not all the heroes are good men. The opening words of *Richard III* present the evil Richard. He is the Shakespearian character most often described as Machiavellian, meaning someone who tricks and deceives others, after the Italian Renaissance political writer Machiavelli, whose works were always regarded with disapproval in England. Richard, as a wicked man, immediately shows his character to the audience by commenting on his enemy, his older brother, the Duke of York, who is now King Edward IV:

> Now is the winter of our discontent
> Made glorious summer by this son of York.

This is a soliloquy, like Hamlet's speech beginning 'To be, or not to be'. The actor, alone on stage, uses the soliloquy to give his thoughts to the audience, who are all around the 'thrust' stage (see illustration on p. 28). The first theatres in London, from The Theatre, built in 1576, to Shakespeare's own Globe in the 1590s, had a thrust stage, and many of the audience stood around the stage. They paid one penny to see the play. Others paid more to sit in the rows looking over the heads of the audience to the stage. All the audience was very near to the actors. So Shakespeare's words are shared between actor and audience: the audience can become closely involved with the characters and their problems.

Sometimes a character will make a big, public speech, like Mark Antony's:

> Friends, Romans, countrymen,[1] lend me your ears

[1] people from the same nation

from *Julius Caesar*. But usually the soliloquy is a private rather than a public speech. It is this kind of involvement with characters that

The Globe Theatre

makes Shakespeare's plays different from those of most other playwrights, especially in tragedy.

Shakespeare's plays were written to be performed; he did not intend them to be published. All the plays are now divided into five sections called acts and smaller sections called scenes. But this only happened about a century after the publication of the *First*

Folio (first edition) of his complete plays in 1623. Shakespeare wrote his plays for performance, so it was more important that the audience follow the progress of the plays on the stage than see the act and scene division on the page. *Hamlet* is built around seven soliloquies, which show Hamlet's progress from 'nothing' at the beginning, to king at the end of the play.

THE TRAGEDIES

Most of Shakespeare's great tragedies were written in the years between 1598 and 1607, sometimes called his 'black' period. Little is known about Shakespeare's own life, but it is known that he had a son, called Hamnet, who died at the age of ten in 1596. This may have influenced Shakespeare's black period, when many of his plays concern fathers and children.

Romeo and Juliet, the most famous tragedy of love in all literature, was one of Shakespeare's earliest tragedies, and it is less complex and philosophical than most of the later tragedies. As we have seen, some of the history plays and Roman plays are also tragedies.

The major tragedies are *Hamlet*, *Othello*, *King Lear* and *Macbeth*. They are tragedies of revenge, jealousy, family and ambition, but of course, as we have seen with *Hamlet*, they touch on many other subjects, too. They have in common the fact that mankind is constantly trying to go beyond its limits in order to achieve perfection and harmony in the world. But mankind itself is not perfect, and so must fail in these attempts. At the end of *Macbeth*, Macbeth, who has killed the king in order to become king himself, realizes that all his murders have been useless:

> Tomorrow, and tomorrow, and tomorrow,
> Creeps in this petty pace[1] from day to day
> To the last syllable of recorded time . . .
>   it is a tale
> Told by an idiot,[2] full of sound and fury,
> Signifying[3] nothing.

[1] slowly like this   [2] fool   [3] meaning

Many of the tragedies have pessimistic endings, where life has lost its meaning. But usually there is some hope for the future – a new king in *Hamlet* and *Macbeth* for instance.

Of all the tragedies, *King Lear* is the most pessimistic. As an old man, King Lear gives his land and power to two of his daughters, Goneril and Regan, but they treat him badly. His third daughter, Cordelia, who really loves him, is, however, misunderstood by her father. There is no real hope for the future at the end of the play, as Lear's words show. His daughter Cordelia lies dead in his arms:

> No, no, no life!
> Why should a dog, a horse, a rat have life,
> And thou[1] no breath at all? Thou'lt[2] come no more,
> Never, never, never, never, never!

[1] you   [2] you will

Only in his last plays, after the tragedy which shows a hatred for mankind, *Timon of Athens*, did Shakespeare begin to find hope again. And this hope is usually expressed in the younger generation, who represent the future of the world.

THE COMEDIES

The question of the future harmony of the universe is also important in Shakespeare's comedies. In the tragedies the harmony is lost, and, as Othello says, 'Chaos is come again' [chaos = confusion]; a tragedy always ends with the death of the hero. In the comedies, the world is threatened and shaken but a comedy always ends happily. But the subjects of the comedies are just as serious as some of the subjects of the tragedies: identity in *The Comedy of Errors*, *Twelfth Night* and *As You Like It*; the role of women in *The Taming of the Shrew* [shrew = wild woman]; love and jealousy in *Much Ado About Nothing* (very similar to *Othello* in some ways); love and power in *A Midsummer Night's Dream* [midsummer = middle of the summer]; the power of money and the attempt to deceive in *The Merchant of Venice*.

Shylock, the Jewish money-lender at the centre of this last play, uses words which are very similar to King Richard II's to show the audience (and the other characters in the play) that he is a man just like them:

> Hath[1] not a Jew eyes? Hath not a Jew hands, organs,[2] dimensions,[3] senses, affections,[4] passions,[5] fed with the same food, hurt with the same weapons, subject to the same diseases, healed by the same means, warmed and cooled by the same winter and summer, as a Christian is? If you prick[6] us do we not bleed?

[1] has [2] parts of the body [3] sizes [4] fond feelings
[5] strong feelings [6] break the skin with a sharp object

This concern of Shakespeare's with the shared humanity of mankind is found in all his works. In the tragedies, again and again the characters ask 'What is a man?' This was in many ways the main question of the age. In *The Merchant of Venice* the answer to the question is very complex. Antonio, a merchant, borrows money from Shylock, a Jewish money-lender, in order to help a friend, Bassanio, marry Portia. Shylock agrees, but says that if Antonio does not pay before a certain date, he can be repaid by cutting a piece off Antonio's body, 'a pound of flesh'. When Antonio is unable to pay, Shylock wants his 'pound of flesh' from Antonio but, in one of the many tricks in the play, he cannot have it if 'one drop of blood' is lost. All the characters try to win: in this play, man's (and woman's) nature is one of tricks and self-interest. Shylock is eventually defeated in court, but the court itself is tricked by Portia, who has dressed as a lawyer (a man) in order to save Antonio. The play seems to have a happy ending, but it is not what it seems, since it depends on the tricks of the characters, rather than on natural humanity.

For this reason *The Merchant of Venice* is often considered a serious comedy, one which raises very serious issues but does not really attempt to solve them. There is a group of these serious comedies, sometimes called problem plays. They include *Measure for Measure*, which handles major themes of sexual and social behaviour, and the strange love comedy *All's Well That Ends Well*. But most of Shakespeare's plays discuss problems in one way or another!

Shakespeare's comedies contain many of the things which still make people laugh today: mistaken identity, very funny jokes, characters like Falstaff in *The Merry Wives of Windsor* and Bottom in *A Midsummer Night's Dream*, sexual comedy in *Much Ado About Nothing* and *Measure for Measure*, and lots of activity, the kind of comic action we cannot see on the page, but which comes to life wonderfully on the stage.

THE FINAL PLAYS (1608–13)

Shakespeare's final plays are difficult to define – some of them are considered serious comedies or problem plays. Some critics prefer to call them pastoral comedies, since their settings often involve an escape to the countryside. Others call them fables. Whatever we call them, they are different in tone from all Shakespeare's earlier plays, although very close to them in the themes they handle. *The Tempest* is the most perfect of these plays. Like the others, it is about giving back harmony to the universe. Prospero has been on his island for sixteen years, sent there by his brother, who stole his kingdom. Prospero, who is a man of learning, uses his magic powers to bring together all the contrasting parts of society, in a final scene of peace and hope. He wins his kingdom again, and defeats the evil spirit of nature, Caliban. Prospero's daughter Miranda marries Ferdinand, and together they are the hope for the future. But at the end of the play Prospero reminds the audience that the whole play is unreal. He says that 'We are such stuff as dreams are made on' and the whole question of dream and reality is seen to be a metaphor for all theatrical images. Prospero's final speech, giving up his magic powers, is sometimes read as Shakespeare's farewell to his art, in the words:

Now my charms are all o'erthrown.[1]

[1] my magic power is all ended

On many occasions a character in Shakespeare uses the image of theatre as a kind of metaphor for human existence, and the passing of time. Macbeth speaks of man as:

> a poor player[1]
> That struts and frets[2] his hour upon the stage,
> And then is heard no more.

[1] actor   [2] walks and talks anxiously

Shakespeare was an actor himself, as well as a playwright and the director of his company, the King's Men, and he often uses this kind of theatrical metaphor. Indeed, it is one of the most important images of the age. The nature of human life was a new theme in literature, and shows the Renaissance concern with how to understand life and death in the modern world. Religion no longer gave the answers as it had done in earlier periods of literature. The literature itself questions and discusses and looks for answers. Shakespeare's plays are still performed all over the world. The questions he asked are still relevant, the characters he invented still living in the imagination of audiences and readers four hundred years after they were first created.

Christopher Marlowe (1564–93) and Ben Jonson (1572/3–1637)

The Golden Age of English Drama produced a great many plays and playwrights. Marlowe and Jonson are the two whose names are most closely connected with Shakespeare.

Christopher Marlowe died violently in a fight in a pub just as Shakespeare's dramatic career was beginning. But he was already, at the age of only twenty-nine, the most famous and successful playwright of his generation. He was one of the University Wits, the young generation of writers who were educated at the universities of Oxford and Cambridge. Shakespeare was almost the only great writer of this period who did not have a university education.

THE PLAYS OF SHAKESPEARE

Early plays from 1589 to 1593

1 Henry VI, Part One
2 Henry VI, Part Two
3 Henry VI, Part Three
4 Titus Andronicus

5 The Comedy of Errors
6 The Two Gentlemen of Verona
7 The Taming of the Shrew
8 Richard III

Plays from 1593 to 1598

9 Love's Labours Lost
10 A Midsummer Night's Dream
11 Richard II
12 Romeo and Juliet

13 King John
14 The Merchant of Venice
15 Henry IV, Part One
16 Henry IV, Part Two

17 The Merry Wives of Windsor

Plays from 1598, with likely dates of writing

18 Much Ado About Nothing (1598)
19 Henry V (1599)
20 Julius Caesar (1599)
21 As You Like It (1600)
22 Hamlet (1600)
23 Twelfth Night (1602)
24 Troilus and Cressida (1602)

25 All's Well That Ends Well (1603)
26 Measure for Measure (1604)
27 Othello (1604)
28 King Lear (1605)
29 Macbeth (1606)
30 Antony and Cleopatra (1607)
31 Timon of Athens (1607)

32 Coriolanus (1608)

'Late' plays

33 Pericles (1608)
34 Cymbeline (1610)

35 The Winter's Tale (1611)
36 The Tempest (1611)

37 Henry VIII (1613)

Marlowe's plays are quite different in style and content from Shakespeare's. They are tragedies with superhuman heroes who stretch the limits of human life in several ways. The language of Marlowe is more classically based than Shakespeare's: where Shakespeare's characters speak the same language as their audience, Marlowe's characters use a more poetic style, which was influenced by his university studies of Latin and Greek dramatic poetry.

Marlowe's best-known hero, Doctor Faustus, has sold his soul to the devil in exchange for all knowledge and power. The play, *Doctor Faustus*, is a series of scenes showing Faustus's ambitions, but in the end he has no more time and when the devil returns to claim the soul he has bought, Faustus in his final moments tries to keep death away:

> O soul, be changed into little water-drops,
> And fall into the ocean, ne'er[1] be found!
> Ugly hell, gape[2] not! come not, Lucifer!
> I'll burn my books!

[1]never   [2]open the mouth wide

Faustus does not speak to the audience; he speaks to his soul, to hell, and to the devil himself in this example of his poetic style.

Marlowe's other heroes include the first major homosexual character in a historical tragedy, the king in *Edward II*, and Barabas in *The Jew of Malta*, a Jew who is even greedier than Shakespeare's Shylock in *The Merchant of Venice*. Barabas has one of the first black servants in English drama, Ithamore, and the play also represents Machiavelli on the English stage for the first time.

Marlowe's theme was always power, in many of its forms: from the power of Tamburlaine, who conquers the whole world, to the classical figures of Dido and Aeneas, who represent love and power. Marlowe stretches drama further than before in subject matter and dramatic performance. Ben Jonson was also influenced by classical writers, but his tragedies were not so successful as his comedies and later masque entertainments.

Many of Ben Jonson's early plays caused controversy because of their political relevance, and he was put in jail more than once. Of his early plays two comedies *Every Man in his Humour* (1598) and *Every Man out of his Humour* (1599) are well known for the idea that a character can be ruled by a 'humour', meaning an emotion. In these plays characters are guided by, for example, jealousy, or moral concern, or false bravery. The belief that people can be ruled by a particular emotion in this way was soon abandoned but, using this idea, Jonson later wrote two of the best-known comedies in English, *Volpone* (1606) and *The Alchemist* [medieval chemist] (1610). Most of Jonson's best-known works come from the period after the death of Queen Elizabeth in 1603, during the reign of James VI of Scotland who became King James I of England. The plays written during his reign are called Jacobean. Where Marlowe was wholly an Elizabethan, Jonson's best work is mostly Jacobean.

At the court of King James I there was a fashion for entertainments, called masques, which were presented on special days. These were moral fables, with very expensive settings and costumes – and were usually presented only once. This was different from the public theatre, where a company like Shakespeare's King's Men would present a play many times, if it was a success, like *Hamlet* or *A Midsummer Night's Dream*. The masques were for a small audience, at court, and the actors were often members of the noble families of the court, rather than the professional actors of the Globe Theatre and other similar theatres.

Ben Jonson wrote the texts for many masques, including *The Masque of Queens* (1609) and *Pleasure Reconciled to Virtue* [pleasure having come to terms with good behaviour] (1618). The titles show the two aspects of nobility, and moral themes which were common in masques.

The most important feature of the masques was not the text, however, but the complex settings. Inigo Jones (1573–1652) was the greatest designer of these settings, and his work with Jonson on many masques took the form to its highest achievements. Jones introduced the proscenium arch to the English stage, and this influence from Italian architecture would later be the major theatre

A proscenium arch designed by Inigo Jones for The Temple of Love, *1634.*

structure in England for the next three centuries. The thrust stage of Shakespeare's theatre, which was for a large, popular audience, almost completely disappeared. After the introduction of the proscenium arch, there was a greater distance between the audience and the performers but greater theatrical effects were possible behind the proscenium.

Elizabethan and Jacobean Drama – Other Major Figures

There were many other playwrights who were part of the Golden Age of English Drama, and many of their plays are still successfully performed. Thomas Kyd wrote *The Spanish Tragedy* in 1592, and if he had written no more he would be remembered for this play. It was one of the most popular plays of its time, and gave rise to a whole series of revenge tragedies, the greatest of which was Shakespeare's *Hamlet*.

The 'tragedy of blood', influenced particularly by the Latin writer of poetic tragedies, Seneca, took many forms during Elizabeth's reign. They were called tragedies of blood because they usually ended in the violent death of most of the main characters. The first was *Gorboduc* by Thomas Sackville and Thomas Norton in 1561, and the greatest *Hamlet* in 1600. The form remained popular for many years, reaching its final expression in the tragedy of sexual love between brother and sister, *'Tis Pity She's a Whore* ['tis = it is, whore = prostitute] by John Ford, which was published in 1633, during the reign of James I's son, King Charles I. The reason for the popularity of these plays is that they were full of action and violence, passion, emotion and often madness. Revenge was such a major theme because it was part of the 'code of honour' of the age, and was particularly important where the family was involved. Most of these plays, like *The Spanish Tragedy* and *Hamlet* involve a family: the father, Hieronimo, avenging his son's death in the first, and the son avenging his father's death in the latter.

The plays of the Jacobean period become even more complex, even more passionate and violent than the plays of the Elizabethan age, as they go more deeply into problems of corruption and human weakness. The masterpieces of Jacobean tragedy include the plays of John Webster, especially *The White Devil* (published in 1612), and *The Duchess of Malfi* [duchess = noble lady], written about the same time. These plays contain two of the most memorable tragic heroines in English drama, Vittoria Corombona and the Duchess of Malfi herself; women who are the victims of male violence, and whose sufferings show many of the problems that Jacobean society was experiencing.

The plays of Thomas Middleton include both comedy and tragedy. His comedies are of a new kind which are called city comedies. They are set in London, and are filled with local characters, tradesmen and families, all mixed into very funny social comedy. *A Mad World, My Masters* and *A Trick to Catch the Old One*, both dating from about 1605–6, are among the best of these.

Middleton's tragedies are, like Webster's, dark, violent and complex. They explore themes of madness, politics and revenge, *c.*950 Hrotsvitha, a Saxon nun, wrote religious plays in Latin: these were not performed, but were the first European dramas. They represented Biblical scenes. Later, from about 1200, the acting out of Bible stories inside or outside churches and monasteries brought religion to ordinary people on holy days.

1300s Bible stories acted by groups of workers called guilds on moving carts, to mark religious holidays. Known as mystery or miracle plays, many texts remain from the late fourteenth and fifteenth centuries. Allegorical dramas, called morality plays, were popular in the fifteenth and early sixteenth centuries.

*c.*1500 The beginning of secular drama, at court and in the more popular 'interludes', often played publicly outside inns under aristocratic patronage.

*c.*1552/3 The first publicly performed comedy: *Ralph Roister Doister* at Eton College.

1576 London's first purpose-built theatre; when this was taken down, the wood was used for Shakespeare's Globe Theatre (1598).

1592–4 Theatres – including The Rose (opened 1587) – closed because of plague. The Swan Theatre opened in 1595.

*c.*1605 Masques, with their exciting effects, became fashionable at the court of King James.

1649 All public theatres closed by the Puritan parliament.

1656 Mrs Coleman was the first English woman to act (in a private performance of William Davenant's *The Siege of Rhodes*). Women's roles had traditionally been played by boys.

1662 Two London theatres given a Royal Patent [royal permission], by Charles II: Thomas Killigrew's Theatre Royal at Drury Lane and Davenant's theatre at Lincoln's Inn Fields (which later moved to Covent Garden). The patent applied only to spoken drama and did not include works which were principally musical.

1698 Playwrights of the Restoration attacked by Jeremy Collier for 'immorality and profaneness'.

1720s Burlesques were very popular; these were similar to modern musical comedies. Around 1750, burlettas, plays containing many songs, became fashionable, as they could be performed in unlicensed theatres.

1737 Stage Licensing Act introduced censorship, to avoid controversial political and moral themes. Approval of plays was required from the Lord Chamberlain, a royal official.

1843 Theatres Act took away the rights of Drury Lane and Covent Garden to put on plays without competition.

*c.*1865 Serious plays began to appear instead of melodrama, especially those written by Tom Robertson. Many new theatres built in the next thirty years. Development also of music hall – a kind of variety theatre – popular until the First World War.

1879 First annual Shakespeare festival at the town of his birth, Stratford-upon-Avon.

1898 Foundation of the Irish Literary Theatre.

1968 Censorship of plays was finally ended after more than 200 years.

1976 Opening of the National Theatre in London.

An advertisement for A Game at Chess, *by Thomas Middleton.*

going beyond Shakespeare's tragedies in their pessimistic view of life. The world they show is a world without settled values, a world without certainties, a world where all power is corrupt and all humanity weak. *The Revenger's Tragedy* (1607, sometimes said to be written by Cyril Tourneur), *The Changeling* [baby secretly put in the place of another] (written with William Rowley), *Women Beware Women* (both from about 1622) and the allegorical *A Game at Chess* [chess = board game] (1624) (some of them written together with other writers) are the classic Jacobean tragedies for which Middleton is known.

In the 1620s, the taste for violence, corruption and complex sexual feelings began to cause a reaction from extreme Protestants, the Puritans. The Golden Age of Elizabeth was long past, and new social, religious and political problems were facing the nation. The Puritans saw the theatre as a symbol of the bad features of the past, rather than as a major literary form.

This was the beginning of a time of criticism of the theatre and its morals which eventually led to the closure of the theatres by the Puritans in 1642. The theatre was never again so popular as a medium of entertainment, nor so effective in questioning and analysing the issues and concerns of an age. The Golden Age of English Drama ended in criticism, censorship and decline, very far from the achievements of Shakespeare and the other major dramatists of the time.

Poetry, from Renaissance to Metaphysical

After the popular, very English poetry of Skelton at the beginning of the sixteenth century, there was a great change. English poetry was read much more by the upper classes, and the native rhythms of Skelton gave way to formal, courtly verse, influenced by the Italian Renaissance.

The sonnet becomes a very important poetic form in Elizabethan writing. William Shakespeare's *Sonnets*, published in 1609, but written more than ten years before, are the most famous examples. The sonnet, a poem of fourteen ten-syllable lines, came from the Italian of Petrarch. The first examples in English were written by Sir Thomas Wyatt, and the form was then developed by Henry Howard, Earl of Surrey. Their sonnets, written in the 1530s and 1540s, were published in an anthology called *Tottel's Miscellany* [miscellany = selection] in 1557.

The rhyme scheme of most sonnets in English, including Shakespeare's, is generally *ababcdcdefefgg* – this is called the Elizabethan scheme, and is different from the original Petrarchan scheme. In the sonnet by Shakespeare below the Elizabethan scheme is used. The first rhyme word is *a*, the second *b*, the third *c* and so on. The words rhyme every other line, except in the final lines, called a couplet, where the rhyme words *g* are repeated together.

Shakespeare's 154 sonnets cover a wide range of subjects: they are poems of love and loss, of loneliness and change, and they contain the mysterious dark lady and fair man, who can be seen as male and female ideas of love. They also introduce the theme of the passing of time which Shakespeare was to develop in his plays, a central theme of much Renaissance writing in English. Here is an example:

Two loves I have, of comfort and despair,
Which like two spirits do suggest me still;[1]
The better angel is a man right fair,[2]
The worser spirit a woman colour'd ill.[3]
To win me soon to hell, my female evil
Tempteth my better angel from my side,
And would corrupt[4] my saint to be a devil
Wooing[5] his purity with her foul[6] pride.
And whether that my angel be turn'd fiend,[7]
Suspect I may, yet not directly[8] tell;
But being both from me, both to each friend
I guess one angel in another's hell.
    Yet this shall I ne'er know, but live in doubt,
    Till my bad angel fire[9] my good one out.

[1] continue to concern me   [2] very pale   [3] badly   [4] turn to evil
[5] attracting, so that something is shared   [6] horrible   [7] devil
[8] immediately   [9] burn

The first major poet of the Renaissance was Sir Philip Sidney. In many ways he was the ideal Renaissance figure: the perfect man; a soldier, a man of learning and a romantic lover. These are the three qualities which a dramatic hero like Hamlet has to have if he is to be perfect. Sir Philip Sidney died at the age of only thirty-two, after the Battle of Zutphen. His death, like the death of so many young poets, helped to create the romantic image of Sidney. His *Astrophel and Stella* is full of idealized love for Stella – but the poet can never have her, so love and loss are linked together. These lines contain much of Sidney's Renaissance philosophy:

Leave me, O Love, which reachest[1] but to dust;
And thou,[2] my mind, aspire to[3] higher things;
Grow rich in that which never taketh[4] rust;
Whatever fades, but fading pleasure brings.

[1] reaches   [2] you   [3] aim for   [4] takes

Edmund Spenser was known as the Prince of Poets in the Elizabethan age. He has always been a controversial figure, sometimes described as a great poet with new ideas, sometimes as only a writer who tried to flatter his superiors. He certainly wanted to take his place in the tradition of English poetry, following on from Chaucer. *The Faerie Queene* [faerie = fairy], published in the 1590s, is his great national epic to celebrate Queen Elizabeth. He used a new verse form, now called the Spenserian stanza, of nine lines rhyming *ababbcbcc*, the last line longer than the first eight. It

The Red Cross Knight, from Book I of The Faerie Queene, *by Edmund Spenser.*

is the most important poem in English since the time of Chaucer almost exactly two hundred years before, and celebrates Queen Elizabeth as Gloriana, the national heroine who brings peace and wealth to the nation. 'Sweet Thames! run softly, till I end my song,' from the wedding poem *Prothalamion* (1596) is one of Spenser's best-known lines.

Most of the playwrights of the Elizabethan and Jacobean age wrote poetry as well as plays. The poetry of Christopher Marlowe and Ben Jonson, for example, is among the greatest of the time. Poetry was, however, mostly a private form. Many of the poets of the late sixteenth and early seventeenth centuries did not publish their works, but showed them only to a small circle of friends and admirers. So the poets who are now regarded as the most important of the Jacobean age were not very well known as poets in their own lifetimes.

John Donne was one of the most famous churchmen of his time, and wrote poems from the 1590s, but his poems were not published until 1633, two years after his death. George Herbert, also a churchman, was less of a public figure than Donne. Most of his poems were first published also in 1633, shortly after his death at the age of thirty-nine. Donne and Herbert are known as metaphysical poets. The critic, Samuel Johnson, in the eighteenth century gave them this name, but he did not admire them because he found their poems too complex and difficult. But in the twentieth century, the poet and critic T. S. Eliot showed how important these poems were.

The metaphysical poets often wrote about religious themes, discussing their personal relations with God, often speaking directly to him, as in Donne's *Holy Sonnets*:

> Batter[1] my heart, three-personed God,
> . . . For I
> Except you enthrall[2] me, never shall be free,
> Nor ever chaste,[3] except you ravish[4] me.

[1]hit   [2]capture   [3]sexually innocent   [4]have violent sex with

In his themes, Donne moved easily from *Holy Sonnets* to very sensual love poems, from poems challenging death to poetry which states his personal religious faith, from a serious tone to a lighter spirit:

> Come live with me and be my love
> And we will some new pleasures prove.
>
> ('Song')

Donne and Herbert were university educated men, and interested in all the scientific and geographical exploration in the world around them. So their poetry is full of very modern ideas, original imagery, and the kind of inner conflict which we find in the soliloquies of Shakespeare's troubled heroes.

Herbert's fight with the difficulties of faith is well shown in these lines from 'The Collar':

> But as I raved[1] and grew more fierce and wild
>   At every word,
> Methoughts[2] I heard one call, 'Child!'
>   And I replied, 'My Lord.'

[1]shouted   [2]I thought

This poetry is different from the idealism of Elizabethan poetry. It reflects the experience of doubt and hopelessness, as well as the pleasure of life. It is sometimes considered difficult (that is why it was first called metaphysical) because of the richness and originality of its imagery, but it is also very modern in its attitudes.

The metaphysical poets were not afraid to use their poetry to face the intellectual, emotional and spiritual problems of the age. They experimented with language and verse forms, with great originality. Herbert even wrote one of his poems 'Easter Wings' in the shape of wings:

Easter Wings

Lord, who createdst[1] man in wealth and store,
Though foolishly he lost the same,
Decaying more and more,
Till he became
Most poor:
With thee[2]
O let me rise
As larks,[3] harmoniously,[4]
And sing this day thy[5] victories:
Then shall the fall further the flight in me.

My tender age in sorrow did begin:
And still with sicknesses and shame
Thou didst[6] so punish sin,
That I became
Most thin.
With thee
Let me combine,
And feel this day thy victory:
For, if I imp[7] my wing on thine,[8]
Affliction[9] shall advance the flight in me.

[1] created   [2] you   [3] songbirds   [4] musically

[5] your   [6] you did   [7] impress   [8] yours   [9] suffering

In the rest of the seventeenth century there were many poets who are grouped with Donne and Herbert as metaphysicals, but each of them is very different.

Henry Vaughan was a friend and follower of Herbert. He was Welsh and his poetry is often about the Welsh countryside. Vaughan is a poet of innocence, where Donne and Herbert are poets who describe experience. Thomas Traherne is the most joyful of all the metaphysicals, celebrating life and eternity. He asks fewer questions and presents fewer problems than previous poets did.

Andrew Marvell is probably the most important of the late metaphysical poets. He brings together religious and secular themes, the poetry of nature, and the old Elizabethan concern with time. He wrote the very famous lines 'To His Coy Mistress' [to his shy lover]:

> at my back I always hear
> Time's winged chariot[1] hurrying near.

[1] vehicle with wings

In the 1630s and 1640s the political problems of the nation grew, and the Puritans became more powerful. The Cavalier poets were a group who supported the king, Charles I, against the Puritans (the Roundheads). Their poems are simpler and more lyrical than the poetry of the metaphysicals. They can be concerned with love, and the passing of time, as in Robert Herrick's line:

> Gather ye [1] rosebuds [2] while ye may.
> ('Counsel [3] to Girls')

[1] you   [2] roses   [3] advice

But they can also write of more serious subjects, reflecting the troubled times they lived in, as in Richard Lovelace's lines about freedom:

> Stone walls do not a prison make,
> Nor iron bars a cage.
> ('To Althea, from Prison')

As the 1640s moved towards the overthrow of the monarchy and the execution of King Charles I in 1649, the Renaissance period of discovery, experimentation and of new intellectual worlds was coming to an end. From the middle of the century a new tone and new concerns entered English poetry.

Elizabethan and Jacobean Prose

Prose in the Renaissance may seem less important than drama and poetry. But, in fact, Renaissance prose is important in several ways: it helped to form the modern English language, and it gives the earliest examples of many forms of writing which later became very popular. Many forms of prose writing reached a wide audience through the new invention of printing. Travel writing, essays, guidebooks and political pamphlets all appeared.

While Shakespeare's plays took spoken English to a wide new audience, another great influence on the English language was the

Authorized Version of the Bible. The new king, James I, asked a group of translators to prepare it, and it was published in 1611. There had been many translations of the Bible into English (usually from Latin or Greek) since the first examples in the 1380s but the *Authorized Version* became the one standard version for use in all the churches in the nation. This meant that almost everyone, even if they could not read, heard the Bible in church on Sundays. The result was that the language of the *Authorized Version* became part of everyone's experience, indeed a major part of British culture. It has remained so until the present day, and the language of every writer in English since 1611 has been influenced by the Bible.

The simple language made the Bible's words memorable, as these examples show:

> Now we see through a glass, darkly; but then face to face.

> Now abideth[1] faith, hope and charity,[2] these three; but the greatest of these is charity.

> The wages of sin[3] is death.

[1] remain   [2] good deeds   [3] bad deeds

A different kind of prose, but a very popular kind, was found in low-life popular pamphlets, called Cony-catching Pamphlets, about the subculture of thieves, cheats and other similar characters. They show that there was a lot of crime, especially to do with money, as the new world of trade grew in the capital city of London. The tone of this writing is comic, and it gives us a view of Elizabethan and Jacobean city life we would not otherwise see.

Travel writing became popular as people wanted to read about the voyages of explorers to the new worlds of the Americas and the East. Richard Hakluyt collected and published the descriptions of many voyages, both famous and less well known; his work was continued by his assistant Samuel Purchas. Their publications were very influential in making people more aware of new worlds: voyages to America, to the West Indies and to the Arctic were

404 The *Vulgate* text, in Latin, produced in Rome by St Jerome.

c.700 Earliest Anglo-Saxon translations of parts of the Bible, usually from Greek; Bede's version of St John's Gospel; the Psalms.

c.1000 Aelfric translated the first seven Old Testament books (the Heptateuch) into Old English.

1382 John Wyclif translated the *Vulgate* text into Middle English; it caused argument, as Latin remained the language of the church, and English was 'not good enough' for the Bible.

1517 Rebellion of Martin Luther, in Germany, against Roman Catholic authority. (Luther produced a complete Bible, in German, in 1534.) From now on there were many versions of the Bible, reflecting the great argument and conflicts after the Reformation.

1525 William Tyndale's New Testament in modern English, translated from the original Greek, published in Germany. Tyndale also completed a translation of six Old Testament Books in the 1530s. He had to work abroad and was killed by burning as a result of his work. His aim was to bring the Bible to 'the boy that driveth the plough' (to anyone who could read).

1535 Miles Coverdale, working in Antwerp (Belgium) under the influence of Luther, published a complete modern English Bible, translated from German and Latin.

1539 The *Great Bible* printed in England, with the approval of King Henry VIII (after the Reformation of 1534) and Archbishop Thomas Cranmer; its production was guided by Coverdale.

1549 Cranmer's *Book of Common Prayer*.

1560 The *Geneva Bible*, in English, was published. This included notes which followed the ideas of the Protestant religious figure Jean Calvin. It is known as the *Breeches Bible*, [breeches = trousers] because Adam and Eve 'made themselves breeches'.

1568 The *Bishops' Bible*: this was mostly the work of Matthew Parker, Archbishop of Canterbury during the early reign of Queen Elizabeth I. This Bible tried to be acceptable to both Protestants and Catholics.

1582 New Testament of the *Douai Bible* published in English. This became the preferred text for Catholics. (The Old Testament followed in 1609–10).

1611 The *King James* or *Authorized Version* of the Bible published. The new king, in 1604, wanted a text in English which would be considered final. Many writers, using Tyndale's earlier versions as a base, produced what remains (nearly 400 years later) the most widely used and best-known text in English. It is also the number-one best-selling book, and probably the greatest single influence on the English language over the centuries.

1881 The *Revised Version* [revised = rewritten] of the New Testament published. This made an attempt to modernize the language of the *Authorized Version* for Victorian times. (The Old Testament followed in 1885.)

1961 The *New English Bible* (New Testament): another attempt at changing and updating the language, this time for twentieth-century readers. (Old Testament and apocryphal books, 1970).

described for the first time. The story of the voyages of Sir Francis Drake all round the world became an important part of the Elizabethans' pride in the successes of the nation. As he wrote:

> There must be a beginning of any great matter, but the continuing unto[1] the end until it be thoroughly finished yields the true glory.[2]

[1] to   [2] is a major achievement

This was the beginning of Britain's colonial glory. Many writers were influenced by these descriptions of travel – Shakespeare's *The Tempest* contains many of the new ideas of the growing colonial world, and already begins to question them.

The Italian traveller, Marco Polo, who had travelled as far as China in the late 1200s, and had written some rather fantastic stories about his travels, also became popular when his romance about his travels was translated into English in 1579. Imaginary voyages also appeared. They could bring together the flavour of the real voyage and add some fantasy – as Marco Polo probably did, to make his travels more exciting.

Utopia by Sir Thomas More brought a new word into the language. In Greek, utopia means no-place, and the book is about a journey to this imaginary country. It could be an ideal model for a society, or a satire on the society of its day: critics still discuss More's intentions. But his influence was great, and many novels of imaginary voyages have followed, right up to the science fiction writing of the present day.

Eldorado, the land of gold, might also be an imaginary place. But it is described in a real travel book, *Discovery of Guiana*, by one of the great figures of the age, Sir Walter Raleigh. Again a prose work of the sixteenth century has left a myth which has remained ever since. There was also a lot of romance in these books of voyages – and romance was also found in fiction. Sir Philip Sidney wrote *The Arcadia* [ideal pastoral place] in the 1580s and it became lastingly popular. In two versions, the Old and the New, it is a prose romance with many added verses and pastoral parts. Shakespeare based some of *King Lear* on a part of Sidney's work.

Travel writing was very popular. This is a page from a book about the new colony of Virginia in America, published in 1608.

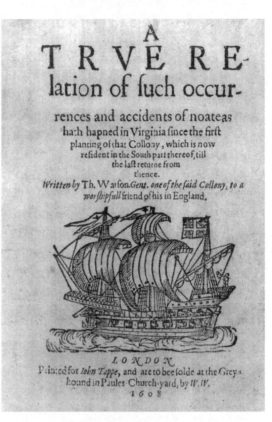

A
TRVE RE-
lation of fuch occur-
rences and accidents of noateas
hath hapned in Virginia fince the firft
planting of that Collony, which is now
refident in the South part thereof, till
the laft returne from
thence.
Written by Th. Watfon. *Gent. one of the faid Collony, to a worfhipfull* friend of his in England.

LONDON
Printed for *Iohn Tappe*, and are to bee folde at the Grey-
hound in Paules Church-yard, by W. W.
1608

Another prose romance which Shakespeare borrowed from was *Pandosto, the Triumph of Time* [triumph = victory] by Robert Greene. In *The Winter's Tale* [tale = story] the theme of the passing of time and the young generation's ability to cure the world's faults is mainly based on Greene's romance. Greene was the first writer to mention Shakespeare in his works: in his autobiography *Greene's Groatsworth of Wit* [groatsworth = tiny bit] (1592), Shakespeare is described as:

> an upstart crow[1] . . . [who] supposes he is as well able
> to bumbast out[2] a blank verse as the best of you.

[1] cheeky black bird   [2] produce (the image is of physical violence)

The first critical attack on the great writer!

The major figure in imaginative prose writing in the late sixteenth century was Thomas Nashe. He is sometimes called the inventor of modern narrative. *The Unfortunate Traveller* and *The Terrors of the Night*, both dating from 1594, introduce a clever mixture of genres, new kinds of fantasy, and both humour and social comment. In many ways Nashe's works are similar to the genre of the novel, which began to grow very popular about one hundred years later.

The essay form, in the hands of Sir Francis Bacon, brought much to the discussion of the issues of the time. These issues were represented in Shakespeare's plays, and found also in prose: Bacon's essays have titles like 'Of Truth' and 'Of Revenge' and his masterpiece *The Advancement of Learning* shows his concern with the new ways of thinking, the discovery of new ideas, and the increasing size of the world. '"What is truth?" said jesting Pilate and would not stay for an answer' [jesting = joking] is the famous beginning of Bacon's essay 'Of Truth'. In *The Advancement of Learning* he wrote, 'If a man begin with certainties, he shall end in doubts; but if he will be content to begin with doubts, he shall end in certainties.' This is a good example of the philosophical and religious thinking of the time.

Religious writing also became popular. The sermons of a churchman like John Donne were often published – in fact, they were better known in his own lifetime than the poems for which he is now famous. It was Donne who wrote, in *Devotions* [religious writings]: 'No man is an island, entire of itself: every man is a piece of the continent, a part of the main.' [main = sea]

One of the first classics of modern English prose is *Of the Laws of Ecclesiastical Politie* [church affairs] by Richard Hooker, published in the 1590s. This is a long essay on the church and intellectual freedom, and its style of academic argument influenced many later writers. One of his statements shows the intellectual climate of change and discussion which is found in Elizabethan and Jacobean prose: 'Change is not made without inconvenience, even from worse to better.'

Reading also gave instruction. For the first time, readers could find books which told them 'how to' – how to behave like a proper

Sir Francis Bacon

gentleman (*The Courtier*), how to be a proper politician (*The Book Named the Governor*) and even how to trick people (*The Gull's Hornbook*) [fool's guidebook].

Illustrated books, called emblem books, also became popular in the Renaissance. They usually contained pictures with verses to explain the symbolism of the pictures, on many subjects such as nature, history and morality. Later, some of these books also used prose writing to accompany the pictures.

All these forms of prose – fiction, essays, guidebooks, travel books and academic writing – were also well developed. They show the first great use of publishing to spread ideas, to cause discussion and to challenge the minds of readers. They are the beginning of a long tradition of the cultural importance of the printed word.

This picture of 1651 shows Oliver Cromwell and the English Revolution.

3 The Commonwealth and Restoration 1649–1713

Setting the Scene

After many years of difficult relations between the king and Parliament, in the 1640s the Puritans (Roundheads) and the king's followers (Cavaliers) went to war against each other.

The victory of the Roundheads led to the execution of King Charles I in 1649. After this, Oliver Cromwell became the leader of the Commonwealth, the Lord Protector. When he died in 1658, his son was named Lord Protector, but he was less successful than his father, and in 1660 Parliament invited Charles I's son to return from France. He was made king as Charles II.

Although the monarchy was restored, most of the power was held by Parliament; two parties, the Whigs and the Tories, and a prime minister governed the country. On the death of Charles II in 1685, his brother King James II became king, but after he became a Catholic his reign ended with the Glorious or Bloodless Revolution of 1688, and no Catholic monarch has reigned since then. The new king and queen were Mary, the sister of Charles and James, and her husband, William of Orange from Holland.

The main concern of the time was to avoid another revolution. The spirit of the Restoration was one of reason; society did not want to see again the kind of problems of the first half of the century. The new middle classes had more and more influence as their wealth grew and they wanted stability above all. This was also a time of great commercial growth, and of scientific advances. The Royal Society was begun in 1662–3 'for the improving of Natural Knowledge'. In 1694 another important institution, the Bank of England, was begun.

The main philosophical text behind the thinking of the second half of the century was *Leviathan* by Thomas Hobbes, written in exile in France in 1651. Hobbes's theory of society is presented in the medieval form of an allegory: the leviathan, a huge animal, is the commonwealth, and the individual man is totally controlled by the state. Self-interest is what mainly drives human beings, so a strong state is necessary, to keep the 'articles of peace' and to control the people of the nation. This very much reflects the society of Britain after the Restoration: a strong government to prevent the risk of another revolution, and self-interest as the driving force behind the individual and the new middle classes.

It was also a time of war in Europe, the War of the Spanish Succession lasting from 1701 until the Treaty of Utrecht in 1713. The United Kingdom was finally united when the Union of the Parliaments of England and Scotland took place in 1707. But Ireland was still a problem – the Battle of the Boyne in 1690 gave the Protestants victory, although the majority of the population was still Catholic.

Poetry, Politics and John Milton

The period between the execution of King Charles I in 1649 and the Restoration of the monarchy with his son Charles II in 1660 is called the Commonwealth. Oliver Cromwell, leader of the Roundheads, was named Lord Protector of the nation. One of the main texts of the Commonwealth is the poem by Andrew Marvell, 'An Horatian Ode upon Cromwell's Return from Ireland' (1650), which has been called 'the greatest political poem in English'. It celebrates Cromwell as the nation's hero:

> So restless Cromwell could not cease[1]
> In the inglorious[2] Arts of Peace.
> But through adventurous war
> Urged his active star . . .
> What field of all the Civil Wars
> Where his were not the deepest scars?

[1] stop   [2] not bringing good results

The theme of the poem is strength, and strong government. These were to become major concerns of the nation during and after Cromwell's rule. Marvell became the unofficial Poet Laureate to Cromwell, and wrote several of his major poems during the Commonwealth.

During this time poets contrasted the personal and the public life. In his poem 'To Lucasta, Going to the Wars', written in 1649, Richard Lovelace writes about having to leave his loved one in order to go to war:

> Tell me not (sweet) I am unkind
> That from the Nunnery [1]
> Of thy [2] chaste [3] breast, and quiet mind
> To War and Arms [4] I fly.

[1] religious house of nuns   [2] your   [3] sexually innocent
[4] things used by armies to cause injury

The political side of literature became important during the Commonwealth in a way it never was before. In the Renaissance, writers had been occupied with great, general philosophical problems. In *Hamlet* (1600), for example, Shakespeare had imagined the need to kill the king; in 1649 this event actually happened, and the shock was great. However, Marvell also contrasted the world of politics and city life with the quiet life in the country. Sometimes it seemed as if he found politics corrupt. In 'The Garden' he praises nature and the innocence of country life:

> Fair quiet, have I found thee [1] here,
> And innocence thy [2] sister dear!
> Mistaken long, I sought you then
> In busy companies [3] of men.
> . . .
> Society is all but rude,
> To this delicious solitude. [4]

[1] you   [2] your   [3] in the companionship of   [4] aloneness

In a world of constant change, Marvell searches for peace and quiet.

The new society of the Restoration gave much more importance than before to stable values, and much less importance to the search for new values, or the exploration of new worlds, as in the

Renaissance. So, the major figure who links the Renaissance and the Restoration, John Milton, can be seen as both a Renaissance and a post-Renaissance [post = after] man.

Milton lived from 1608 until 1674, and saw all of the greatest struggles of the century. In his early career he gave himself a role as a poet in the classical sense, influenced by Latin writers and traditions but with the clear ambition to make himself one of the great poets in English, in the line of Chaucer. His writing was also deeply Christian, as in 'On the Morning of Christ's Nativity' [nativity = birth]. Both classical and Christian influences run through all his work, particularly in *Lycidas* (1637), which is an elegy about the early death of his close friend Edward King. Its last lines are optimistic which was unusual in the 1630s:

> Tomorrow to fresh woods,[1] and pastures[2] new.

[1] small forests   [2] fields

But for the next twenty or so years Milton wrote little poetry. Instead he concentrated on writing prose pamphlets on many of the most controversial subjects of the time: he wrote about divorce, politics, education, freedom of the press and religion, and became Latin Secretary to Oliver Cromwell in the early years of the Commonwealth. After the Restoration, he went into hiding, and was later arrested, but he was able to return to his writing after some time. He was now blind, but his major work, *Paradise Lost*, was published in twelve books, in 1667.

Paradise Lost is the major epic poem in English. Milton had thought about using the English myth of King Arthur for his great epic poem, but finally decided to use the more general myth of the Creation, with the figures of God and Satan [the devil], Adam and Eve, and the Fall of Mankind as his subject. His aim, he said, was:

> To assert Eternal Providence[1]
> And Justify[2] the ways of God to men.

[1] to stress that God always looks after mankind   [2] explain

The Fall of Satan from Book VI of Paradise Lost, *by John Milton.*

This is a very ambitious aim, and the poem has always caused controversy as many readers and critics see Satan as the hero. The poem can be read as a religious text, supporting Christian ideals, or it can be read as the last great Renaissance text, stressing the freedom of choice of Adam and Eve as they choose the path of human knowledge and leave the Garden of Eden, Paradise. At the end of the poem, they follow the path towards the unknown future of all humanity:

> The world was all before them, where to choose
> Their place of rest, and Providence[1] their guide:
> They, hand in hand, with wandering steps and slow,
> Through Eden took their solitary[2] way.

[1]God's care   [2]lonely

Neither Adam nor Eve is blamed for the Fall, when Eve eats the Forbidden Fruit of the Tree of Knowledge and Adam loses the state of innocence. Satan, God and man are equally responsible.

Milton's poem is full of memorable descriptions. Here is a description of hell:

> A dungeon[1] horrible, on all sides round
> As one great furnace[2] flamed – yet from those flames
> No light but rather darkness visible . . .

[1] prison   [2] oven

The following lines show the beauty of Eve as she is compared to classical goddesses [female gods]:

> Soft she withdrew,[1] and like a wood nymph[2] light
> . . .
> Betook her to the groves,[3] but Delia's self
> In gait surpassed and goddess like deport.[4]

[1] moved away   [2] minor goddess   [3] went to the trees   [4] but was better than Delia, the goddess, in the way she walked and stood

He also expresses very wise ideas in single lines:

> . . . Long is the way
> And hard, that out of Hell leads up to light.

> So farewell[1] hope, and with hope farewell fear.

> Just[2] are the ways of God
> And justifiable[3] to men;
> Unless there be who think not God at all.
> (*Samson Agonistes*)

[1] goodbye   [2] correct   [3] able to be explained

In later works, the long poem *Paradise Regained* and *Samson Agonistes*, Milton goes beyond the humanity of Adam and Eve, writing about superhuman heroes. In *Paradise Regained*, Jesus Christ becomes an example of how to live by resisting temptation. He is a kind of hero for the Restoration age, almost a return to the kind of ideal figure of medieval religious texts.

John Bunyan

The best-known prose text of the second half of the seventeenth century was also a return to medieval rather than Renaissance forms. *The Pilgrim's Progress* by John Bunyan, published in 1678 (with a second part in 1684) is an allegory. It is also a dream-vision, like many medieval texts. The pilgrim, whose name is Christian, is described on his journey through this life towards the world 'which is to come'. He faces all sorts of difficulties from the Giant Despair and the Slough of Despond [depth of depression] to Vanity Fair – and all of these scenes question the false values of the world, stressing the values of the Christian faith.

These scenes in *The Pilgrim's Progress* are quite different from the exploration and questioning of the Renaissance. It is one of the

Christian and Hopeful escape from the Giant Despair, from The Pilgrim's Progress, *by John Bunyan.*

most important texts in English literature because it fixed the values of society as those of Christianity, faith and stability. These values were to be important to society for the next two hundred or more years. *The Pilgrim's Progress* is possibly the most widely read of all books in English literature, because it is the one text which is considered to be close to the Bible and almost a religious text in itself. Many of its images and phrases have entered the language, just as words from the *Authorized Version* of the Bible or *The Book of Common Prayer* (final version, 1662) are part of modern English. Some of Bunyan's words are still sung today in British churches.

> There's no discouragement[1]
> Shall make him once relent[2]
> His first avowed intent[3]
> To be a pilgrim.

> [1] lack of enthusiasm   [2] have a change of mind; abandon
> [3] promise and wish

Augustans and Satires

Set against this particularly religious kind of writing is the poetry of John Wilmot, Earl of Rochester. His life became a kind of symbol of the Restoration: he was a rake, a man who gave his life to pleasure, especially sex and alcohol. But just before he died Rochester became a Catholic (at least according to a priest). So his life shows both the good and bad sides of pleasure which illustrates a good moral. His poetry is often very witty and rude, celebrating the pleasures of life and satirizing all of society, from King Charles II ('a merry monarch, scandalous and poor') to mankind itself in 'A Satire against Mankind':

> I'd be a god, a monkey or a bear,[1]
> Or anything but that vain[2] animal,
> Who is so proud of being rational.

> [1] large, fierce animal   [2] having too good an opinion of oneself

*John Wilmot, Earl
of Rochester*

In some ways Rochester is the last of the metaphysical lyric poets, writing complex emotional poems about love and life, but in other ways he is the first of the new Augustan age.

The Augustans took their name from the classical Latin age of Augustus, who died in AD 14. They saw this period as the high point of Roman culture, and wanted their own period to be similarly important to English culture. Reason, and the very rational basis of thought which Rochester comments on, were very important to the Augustans: emotion takes second place to clear thought and reason.

Satire became an important kind of poetry: it looks wittily at the manners and behaviour of society, and very often uses real people and situations to make its humorous point. The long satirical poem *Hudibras* by Samuel Butler, published in three parts between 1663 and 1678, was one of the first of such poems. It became very popular. It is a mock romance, one of the first major English texts to be inspired by the Spanish text *Don Quixote*, and its satirical comments are aimed at every religious, academic and political subject of the age.

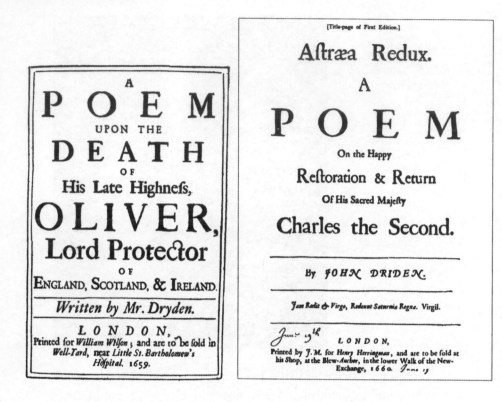

Two title-pages for poems by John Dryden.

John Dryden was a master of satire in poetry after the Restoration. He was a poet, playwright and essayist, and was at the centre of most of the important discussions and controversies of his time. One early poem, *Heroic Stanzas*, praised Cromwell on his death in 1658; another, *To His Sacred Majesty* [sacred = holy], welcomed the return of the king in 1660. Dryden became a Catholic in 1685, so when the new Catholic king, James II, was forced to leave in 1688, he was on the wrong side of the religious controversy, and lost his post as Poet Laureate at the court of the king.

Dryden's satirical poems of the early 1680s, in particular *Absalom and Achitophel* (1681) and *The Medal* [small piece of metal given as a reward] (1682) focus on the religious and political issues of the time, and show a different kind of satire from

Rochester's. Rochester comments in general on all mankind but Dryden satirizes particular people and situations. Here he shows something of the political atmosphere of the age:

> Plots, true or false, are necessary things,
> To raise up commonwealths and ruin kings.
> *(Absalom and Achitophel)*

Similarly, in *MacFlecknoe* (1682) he aims at his literary rivals, in particular the playwright Thomas Shadwell, whom Dryden represents as the master of dullness:

> The rest to some faint meaning make pretence,
> But Shadwell never deviates[1] into sense.

[1]moves

Dryden produced many works and was one of the first to make his career as a professional author. His essays on the nature of drama and representation, such as 'Of Dramatic Poesy' (1668), were the first of their kind in English, and late in his life, his translations from Latin and Greek greatly improved the Augustan age's knowledge of the classics which inspired them. He remains the major literary figure of the late seventeenth century, a writer of immense range, of wit and intellect, who was producing major poetry until the very end of his life. His final work, *The Secular Masque* (1700), provides a famous quotation to end an age:

> Thy[1] wars brought nothing about;[2]
> Thy lovers were all untrue
> 'Tis[3] well an old age is out,
> And time to begin a new.

[1]your   [2]achieved nothing   [3]it is

Important European writers have always influenced writers in English, and many well-known authors have translated foreign works into English. The classic texts from Greek and Latin, such as Homer's The Odyssey *and* The Iliad, *Virgil's* The Aeneid *and Ovid's* Metamorphoses *have been translated many times, and new versions appear regularly. These translations reflect how English has changed over the centuries. With poets like Dryden and Pope, these translations showed how English could be as rich and powerful as the original languages. Later translations were often written for readers who did not know the original Latin and Greek.*

HOMER (Greek, eighth century BC): *The Iliad* and *The Odyssey* by George Chapman (1598–1615); by Alexander Pope (1715–26).

PLUTARCH (Greek, AD 46–120): *Lives* by Thomas North (1579). Shakespeare used this as a source for many of his plays.

JUVENAL (Latin, AD 60–130): *Satires* by John Dryden and others (1693).

BOETHIUS (Middle Latin, AD 475–524): *Boece* by Geoffrey Chaucer (late fourteenth century); many of Chaucer's sources came from French and Italian, including Dante.

OMAR KHAYYÁM (Persian, c. 1050–1123): *The Rubáiyát* by Edward Fitzgerald (1859–79). A free adaptation rather than a proper translation, this became very popular.

DANTE ALIGHIERI (Italian, 1265–1321): *The Divine Comedy* definitively by Jonathan Richardson (1719); sections translated by Thomas Gray, in the 1740s, and by Dante Gabriel Rossetti. Dorothy L. Sayers also translated Dante.

PETRARCH, Francesco (Italian, 1304–74): various poems by the Earl of Surrey and by Thomas Wyatt in the sixteenth century; also, later, by George Chapman. These translations had a great influence on the sonnet in English.

RABELAIS, François (French, ?1494–1553): *Gargantua and Pantagruel* by Thomas Urquhart (books 1 and 2 in 1653, and book 3 in 1693) and by Peter Motteux (books 4 and 5 in 1693–4), who also translated Cervantes' *Don Quixote* (1703). The humorous language was a great influence on many comic novelists, from Smollett to Dickens and on to Alasdair Gray.

CERVANTES, Miguel de (Spanish, 1547–1616): *Don Quixote of La Mancha* by Thomas Shelton (1616); later, by Motteux.

GOETHE, Johann Wolfgang von (German, 1749–1832): Walter Scott was translating Goethe before 1800; the two parts of *Wilhelm Meister* by Thomas Carlyle (1824–7); *Italian Journey* by W. H. Auden (1962). Goethe was a great influence on later writers, especially of growing-up novels.

FEUERBACH, Ludwig (German, 1804–72): *The Essence of Christianity* by George Eliot (1854). The book was a great influence on the novelist's beliefs – she was Positivist rather than Christian.

DOSTOEVSKY, Fyodor (1821–81) and **TOLSTOY**, Leo (1828–1910): These two Russian novelists were translated into English from the 1870s but definitively by Constance Garnett, between 1910 and 1920. These are two of the most important world novelists.

IBSEN, Henrik (Norwegian, 1828–1906): most of his plays by William Archer, from 1880; many twentieth-century translators. Shaw and Joyce were among the first to be deeply influenced by Ibsen.

CHEKHOV, Anton (Russian, 1869–1904): plays and stories first in 1903; again Constance Garnett made the first major translations (1916–24), and many later twentieth-century versions followed.

GIDE, André (French, 1869–1951): all works by Dorothy Bussy, from 1924; she was the sister of James Strachey, who translated the *Collected Works of Sigmund Freud*, published between 1953 and 1973, and of Lytton Strachey, a leader of the Bloomsbury Group.

PROUST, Marcel (French, 1871–1922): *Remembrance of Things Past (A la recherche du temps perdu)* by C. K. Scott-Moncrieff (1922–31); Scott-Moncrieff's translation, considered a masterpiece in its own right, was reworked in the late 1980s by Terence Kilmartin and D. J. Enright.

KAFKA, Franz (Czech-German, 1883–1924): all works by Willa and Edwin Muir, from 1930. One of the great writers of the twentieth century, he asked that all his writings be burned after his death, but the Scottish poet Muir and his wife decided not to obey the request.

Restoration Drama

COMEDY

Dryden wrote more than twenty plays, from comedy to tragedy, and was especially successful in the new genre of tragicomedy, of which the best-known example is *Marriage-à-la-Mode* [fashionable marriage] (1672). His most famous tragedy is *All for Love* (1678), which returns to the characters of Antony and Cleopatra, the subject of a tragedy by Shakespeare earlier in the century.

After the Restoration, drama and the theatre were quite different from what they had been during the Renaissance. There were now only two public licensed theatres: the Theatre Royal, Drury Lane and the Lincoln's Inn Fields Theatre, which moved to Covent Garden in 1732. The audience was at first upper class or upper-middle class. The plays of the time reflect the manners and morals of the men and women who had returned with the king from France – so Restoration comedy is often called the Comedy of Manners. Dryden wrote several such comedies, but the most famous comedies were written by George Etherege, William Wycherley and William Congreve.

The main subject of these plays was love, but there were new concerns, developed from the earlier city comedy: older men or women looking for younger lovers, upper-class manners contrasting with middle-class values, and country life contrasting with city life. Sex was a major subject, and the plays became more and more obvious in their comic treatment of sexual themes.

George Etherege's *The Comical Revenge* (1664) was one of the first such comedies, and his two later comedies, *She Wou'd if She Cou'd* (1668) and *The Man of Mode* [mode = fashion] (1676), are among the most typical and successful of the genre. He satirizes the false fashions and selfish behaviour of the time in plots which become very complex and which remain very funny on stage. William Wycherley's *The Country Wife* (1675) was accused of immorality, and helped start a moral reaction against the kind of manners shown on the stage. The main character, Horner, pretends he is not able to have sex in order to attract more women, and the

The Theatre Royal, Drury Lane, in 1776.

whole plot very obviously explores sexual behaviour between men and women.

The main plot concerns Mr Pinchwife who is in London with his wife for the marriage of his sister. He warns his wife, Margery, many times about the loose morals of London society. She becomes curious, but thinks she is safe when approached by Horner who then makes love to her. Pinchwife's sister, Alithea, also takes a new lover.

Here Horner uses his reputation for not being able to have sex to attract Lady Fidget:

LADY FIDGET: I have so strong a faith in your honour,[1] dear, dear, noble sir, that I'd forfeit[2] mine for yours at any time, dear sir.

HORNER: No, madam, you should not need to forfeit it for me. I have given you security already to save you harmless, my late[3] reputation being so well known in the world, madam.

LADY FIDGET: But if upon any future falling out,[4] or upon a suspicion of my taking the trust out of your hands,[5] to employ some other, you yourself should betray your trust, dear sir? I mean, if you'll give me leave to speak obscenely,[6] you might tell, dear sir.

HORNER: If I did, nobody would believe me! The reputation of impotency[7] is as hardly recovered again[8] in the world as that of cowardice, dear madam.

LADY FIDGET: Nay[9] then, as one may say, you may do your worst, dear, dear, sir.

[1] good character   [2] abandon   [3] recent   [4] disagreement
[5] away from you   [6] bluntly   [7] inability to have sex   [8] more difficult to overcome   [9] no

As the century came to an end there were more and more objections to the kind of morals seen in Restoration comedy. These protests led to the publication of a pamphlet by Jeremy Collier called 'A Short View of the Profaneness and Immorality of the English Stage' in 1698. This recalls the Puritan complaints against the theatres in the 1630s and 1640s and was a major step in controlling the freedom of dramatists.

Collier attacked the plots of plays like Wycherley's *The Country Wife*. For example, the very name of Mr Pinchwife makes fun of the way in which wives can be stolen from their husbands. He also said much of the dialogue was not proper for the theatre. He also did not like plays which made people laugh at religious men. Large sections of the public agreed with Collier.

One of the playwrights whose work offended Collier was Sir John Vanbrugh, who was later also very famous as an architect. Vanbrugh's plays, such as *The Relapse* [the return to old behaviour] (1696) and *The Provok'd Wife* [provok'd = made angry] (1697), take the complex plots of Etherege and Wycherley even further, and make fun of the behaviour of high society. The names of his characters indicate some of the humorous possibilities of the plays: Sir Novelty Fashion, Sir John and Lady Brute, and Lady Fancyful, for example.

Many playwrights spoke against Collier, just as strongly as he criticized them. Among them was William Congreve, the major dramatist of the 1690s. He wrote only four comedies and one tragedy, but with these he proved to be one of the great dramatists in English. *The Way of the World* (1700), his final play, written when he was still under thirty years old, takes the comedy of manners to its highest level of achievement.

In *The Way of the World*, Mirabell is in love with Millamant, a niece of Lady Wishfort. Mirabell has pretended to make love to Lady Wishfort in order to hide his love for Millamant. But his plan is discovered and Lady Wishfort decides not to give Millamant money which she should have. Mirabell then persuades his servant to pretend to be an uncle of his and to pretend to marry Lady Wishfort so that he can force her to allow him to marry her niece Millamant. After many secret plans and tricks the play, which has a wide range of comic characters, comes to an end with the marriage of Millamant and Mirabell. Their love and real passion contrasts with the pretended love of the other characters for whom sexual pleasure and greed for money is more important. The play shows the London society of the time in all its limited interests.

The play also shows that Millamant has a mind of her own. She loves Mirabell but also lists her demands if she is to marry him:

> Let us be very strange[1] and well-bred:[2] Let us be as
> strange as if we had been married a great while; and as
> well-bred as if we were not married at all . . . These
> articles subscribed,[3] if I continue to endure[4] you a little
> longer, I may by degrees[5] dwindle into[6] a wife.

[1] distant; not close and loving   [2] show good manners   [3] agreed
[4] tolerate   [5] gradually   [6] become

This is the opposite of the usual romantic view of marriage, and stresses the woman's independence in a way which we might not expect. But, in fact, women had a strong voice in the Restoration period, and the discussion of male and female roles was an important part of much writing of the time.

After Congreve stopped writing, at the highest point of his success, the main writers of comedy were George Farquhar and Susannah Centlivre. Farquhar used places outside London and less wealthy characters to illustrate his male characters' ambitions to win rich women – *The Recruiting Officer* [recruiting = employing] (1706) and *The Beaux' Stratagem* [the dandies' plan] (1707) are fresh, original and socially conscious developments in drama. Farquhar died in 1707, aged less than thirty, and his death brought an early end to a promising career as a dramatist.

Susannah Centlivre was, with Aphra Behn and Mary de la Riviere Manley, one of the main female writers of the time. Behn wrote eighteen plays, such as *The Rover* [the wanderer] (in two parts, in 1677 and 1681) in which the main character may have been based on Rochester. One of her main themes was the result of arranged and unsuitable marriages. This kind of social problem and the false values involved is also found in Susannah Centlivre's plays, the best known of which is *A Bold Stroke for a Wife* (1718). The play shows the effects of different religious values on personal relationships when, in order to win permission to marry Anne Lovely, the main character, Colonel Fainall, pretends to be a

Aphra Behn

religious man. Her plays were among the most successful of the time, and continued to be played all through the eighteenth century.

In this scene Mrs Lovely discusses with her maid Betty the problems she has with the people who are looking after her, and her love for the Colonel:

MRS LOVELY: There are certain ingredients[1] to be mingled[2] with matrimony,[3] without which I may as well change for the worse as for the better. When the woman has fortune[4] enough to make the man happy, if he has either honour[5] or good manners, he'll make her easy.[6] Love makes but a slovenly[7] figure in that house where poverty keeps the door.

BETTY: And so you resolve[8] to die a maid,[9] do you, madam?

MRS LOVELY: Or have it in my power to make the man I
love master of my fortune.

BETTY: Then you don't like the Colonel so well as I
thought you did, madam, or you would not take such a
resolution.[10]

MRS LOVELY: It is because I do like him, Betty, that I take
such a resolution.

BETTY: Why, do you expect, madam, the Colonel can
work miracles? Is it possible for him to marry you
with the consent[11] of all your guardians?[12]

MRS LOVELY: Or he must not marry me at all, and so I told
him; and he did not seem displeased[13] with the news.
He promised to set me free, and I, on that condition,
promised to make him master of that freedom.

BETTY: Well, I have read of enchanted[14] castles, ladies
delivered from the chains of magic, giants killed, and
monsters overcome; so that I shall be the less
surprised if the Colonel should conjure[15] you out of
the power of your guardians. If he does, I am sure he
deserves your fortune.

[1] parts, as in cooking   [2] mixed   [3] marriage   [4] money
[5] good character   [6] comfortable   [7] dirty and lazy   [8] decide
[9] unmarried woman   [10] decision   [11] agreement   [12] protectors
[13] unhappy   [14] controlled by magic   [15] trick

TRAGEDY AND SERIOUS DRAMA

Both Dryden and his rival Shadwell wrote new versions of the plays
of Shakespeare. The new middle-class audiences could not accept
much of Shakespeare's violence and the tragic endings to some of
his plays. So *King Lear*, for example, was severely rewritten to give
it a happy ending, and Marlowe's *Doctor Faustus* was rewritten in
the 1690s as a farce. Dryden wrote a successful version of *The
Tempest* (1667) and another of *Troilus and Cressida* (1679). This
taste for quieter, problem-free Shakespearian drama continued for
about two centuries, and is an indication of the great changes in taste

An advertisement for The Beggar's Opera, *by John Gay.*

and in the role of the theatre between the beginning and the end of the seventeenth century.

The main tragic form of the Restoration was heroic tragedy. The best examples are the plays of Thomas Otway, another writer who died young, at the age of thirty-three. *Venice Preserv'd* (1682) shows, even in its title, the difference between this kind of tragedy and Jacobean tragedy, where death and disaster could destroy the whole of society. Here society is *preserved*, made safe, by the sacrifice of the hero Jaffeir. With the help of his friend Pierre, a foreign soldier, Jaffeir plots against the republic of Venice and a politician, Priuli, who has rejected his daughter because she has secretly married Jaffeir. Jaffeir is finally too guilty to hide his plot and, after killing Pierre, takes his own life. The moral is that it is wrong to be different and to threaten the stability of society.

At this time there were many theories about realism, how to show reality on stage, and the role of theatre. But pressure was growing to limit what theatre could say: it was not only a danger to public morals, but it also became too controversial politically. John Gay's play with music, *The Beggar's Opera* (1728), was one of the most popular works to satirize politicians and the false values of society. In 1737 the Stage Licensing Act was introduced to prevent playwrights making fun of politicians – of course religion and morals were part of the problem. But it was a play by Henry Fielding, a political comedy, *The Historical Register for The Year 1736* [register = record], which annoyed the prime minister, Robert Walpole, so much that he decided to censor all plays.

Henry Fielding moved on to become a novelist, but censorship of the theatre remained in force until the Theatres Act of 1968. Theatre and drama were not any longer the main forms of literary exploration – the novel was becoming the most important literary genre. Only in the 1770s, with the plays of Richard Brinsley Sheridan, does comedy reach the level of the Restoration again. His plays, such as *The Rivals* (1775), *The Critic* (1779) and the most famous, *The School for Scandal* (1777) were very successful, and are the greatest comedies after the comedies of Congreve. One of Sheridan's most famous characters is Mrs Malaprop in *The Rivals*, who keeps using words incorrectly. For example, she says someone is 'as headstrong as an allegory on the banks of the Nile' when she means alligator (the reptile). The word malapropism has entered the English language.

The actress Athene Seyler, as Mrs Malaprop, in The Rivals *by Richard Sheridan.*

The French Revolution in 1789 brought the spirit of Liberty, Equality and Fraternity.

4 Augustan to Gothic 1713–89

Setting the Scene

After the death of Queen Anne in 1714, the German House of Hanover took over the British throne. The monarchy was not popular, and there were two rebellions led by the Catholic son and grandson of James II in 1715 and 1745, but both were defeated. The power of Parliament and the prime minister continued to grow.

This was the time of the Industrial Revolution and the Agricultural Revolution. New inventions made manufacturing processes quicker, and British trade with the rest of the world grew enormously. The growing British Empire was a ready market for British produce. At the same time, new processes in agriculture forced many people to move from the country to the new cities to find work. It was also a time when many people, especially from Scotland and Ireland, went to live in the new colonies in America.

Towards the end of the century a new mood of freedom began to grow: the American Declaration of Independence in 1776 was the first sign of this, and later the French Revolution in 1789 brought the spirit of 'Liberty, Equality and Fraternity' to Europe. This was a great threat to the stability of British society, which did not want to see the revolution of 1649 repeated.

In literature the classical ideas of the Augustans changed. Later in the century the focus on the rational mind and on an ordered society changed to focus on the world of nature and natural feelings. Drama became less important, especially after the Stage Licensing Act of 1737, but the novel became more and more important, reaching a huge number of readers as the profession of writing became more important. Journalism and magazines formed and reflected the opinions of the new middle classes which gave the nation its strength and its political power.

The Rise of the Novel

The rise of the novel is usually said to begin from the early 1700s, but there are many earlier examples of fictional writing. To go back a century, there are the works of Thomas Nashe; after the Restoration of 1660, the figure of Aphra Behn (see chapter 3) is also important in the development of the novel.

In fact, women have always written a lot of fiction, and in the late seventeenth and early eighteenth century they were also the greatest part of the readership, the market for the new professional writers. Aphra Behn wrote about thirty novels, including *Love Letters between a Nobleman and his Sister* (1683), a novel in the form of letters, also called an epistolary novel. This became a very popular form about sixty years later, when the epistolary novel was at the top of literary fashion. Aphra Behn's most famous novel is *Oroonoko* (1688), sometimes called the first philosophical novel in English. It is inspired by a visit she made to Surinam in South America, and concerns the African royal prince Oroonoko who is captured and sent as a slave to the English colony of Surinam. It is a strong protest against the trade in slaves and against the power of colonialism, just at the time when such power was growing. Aphra Behn was not afraid of controversy, and, in fact, seemed to enjoy her role as a speaker for women's rights and sexual freedom. But she was an outsider in the society of the time, which was controlled by men, and her novels were not well considered by later critics.

Mary de la Riviere Manley was a similarly 'scandalous' woman, and although her novels were hugely popular in her own lifetime, they were completely ignored by the (mostly male) critics who followed. She brought the kind of political satire found in Dryden's great poems of the 1680s into the novel. She used false names for real characters, to tell scandalous stories about political and personal enemies. Mrs Manley was traditional and royalist in her politics, but very liberal in her views on the role of women in society. So her novels also show the struggle between the sexes: an innocent girl ruined by an older man is frequently a part of these stories. The novels are collections of stories rather than well-structured plots. *The Secret History of Queen Zarah* (1705), which was published in separate parts, had notes with every part to

Mary de la Riviere Manley

explain all the references to real-life characters. *The New Atalantis* (1709) was also political and handled many 'objectionable' themes such as rape, incest and homosexuality. When these themes were later handled in novels by men they were not considered quite so objectionable. The fathers of the novel, rather than the mothers of the genre, were seen as the writers who gave a strong moral position to the novel in the eighteenth century.

At first, and for more than a century, the novel was not well regarded by serious critics. Poetry was a higher form of literary art. But there was a growing market among the middle classes, especially among ladies, for novels, and this market grew during the eighteenth century until the novel reached a huge readership all over the world.

Daniel Defoe and Jonathan Swift, followed a little later by Samuel Richardson and Henry Fielding, are the most important male names in the story of the rise of the novel. Defoe produced a great many works and was a journalist for many years before publishing *Robinson Crusoe* in 1719. It was an immediate success, and has remained one of the most famous stories in the world. In it,

An illustration for Robinson Crusoe *by Daniel Defoe.*

Robinson Crusoe makes a kingdom of his island after a ship is wrecked, and remains there for over twenty-eight years, building a society of two men, with only his 'Man Friday' as his companion. The story can be read as a fable of survival in praise of the human spirit, or as an example of how the new society brought its values, religion and selfish behaviour to any place it colonized. Friday is considered inferior, his religion laughed at, and his ignorance 'cured'. Meanwhile, Robinson grows rich, and when he returns to society he has become a model of the new capitalist man of Europe. Property and the white man's power are more important than such things as love or marriage (Robinson's marriage occupies only a page of the story). The happy ending suggests the continuation of the way of life Crusoe has brought to the island, on the model of white European society.

Defoe's technique in most of his novels is to use a first-person narrator, an 'I' who tells the story as if it had really happened. (*Robinson Crusoe* was inspired by the story of Alexander Selkirk who had actually been on a desert island for many years.) *A Journal of the Plague Year* (1722) describes the plague in London in 1664–5 in a journalistic way, with documents and lists of the dead. *Moll Flanders* (also 1722) tells the story of a woman who has been a prostitute, a thief, committed incest, and been to prison. But when she tells the story, she has reformed and changed her life. The novel therefore makes a moral point about ways of living: the reader shares Moll's terrible experience in order to learn what life should be.

This reflects the age's concern with experience and how to live. Such a concern contrasts with the interest in the Renaissance in the exploration of new worlds and ideas. Hobbes, in *Leviathan*, had described life as 'solitary, poor, nasty, brutish and short'. Most of the novelists of the eighteenth century described the bad side of life, but with a happy ending to show that it was all worthwhile.

Jonathan Swift is perhaps the one writer who is different. His early satire *The Battle of the Books* (written 1697, published 1704) is one of the best descriptions of the differences between the Ancients (the classical writers) and the Moderns in the literary tastes of the Augustan period. Swift uses humour – his main question is will the Ancients make space for the newer Modern writers in the library? But it is the books which discuss this question almost as if they are people. Swift's satire becomes stronger in his later works. His *Gulliver's Travels* is a very angry use of satire against what he saw as being wrong with the world. But almost as soon as it was published in 1726, the novel was considered as a kind of children's story, a fable, rather than the strong social criticism which it really is.

The novel is in four parts. In the first part Gulliver travels to Lilliput, where he meets the very small inhabitants; in book two, on Brobdignag, the people are enormous. Religion and politics in particular are satirized, and the king of Brobdignag, after hearing Gulliver describe the society of England, decides that 'your natives' are:

> the most pernicious[1] race of little odious vermin[2] that
> nature ever suffered[3] to crawl upon the surface of the
> earth.

[1] nasty   [2] unpleasant rubbish   [3] allowed

But the satire gets even stronger: in the third book all the new learning of the Royal Society is the victim. The Royal Society was founded in 1662 and 1663 'for the Improving of Natural Knowledge'. It was a centre for science and culture, but, as Swift saw it, all the wisest men have no practical sense of how to live in the real world. And in the final book, Gulliver meets the cultured horses, the Houyhnhnms, and compares their ways with the nasty monkey-like Yahoos, who represent humanity. Swift's satire is particularly strong because Gulliver observes another world in which ordinary human actions are criticized when performed by extraordinary characters.

Swift's view of life was seen as pessimistic and against the mood of the times, and so his book was not taken seriously. But in fact a lot of Swift's writing was the most original satire of its day, and he is a writer of great range: a poet who could use everyday language in a way that now seems very modern, and a writer who commented on society but was not understood. His *A Modest Proposal* (1729) for example, suggested a way to solve the Irish

Gulliver in Brobdignag, an illustration for Gulliver's Travels, *by Jonathan Swift.*

problem of too many children – by selling the children to England to be eaten. Instead of seeing this as a satire on political solutions to the problem, Swift's readers took it seriously: exactly what they did not do with *Gulliver's Travels*! Swift's satire is characterized by shocking proposals which are treated as if they were normal and which are not commented on by the writer.

Samuel Richardson, however, met with enormous approval from his readers. He was a publisher, and thought of printing a guide to letter-writing for middle-class ladies. This idea became the novel *Pamela* (1740), and in it Richardson created the typical heroine of the times: Pamela is poor, but a good woman, and in her letters the readers can follow all her problems with Mr B who wants to marry her. She goes through uncertainties and crises, including an attempted rape, before agreeing to marry him, and becoming a model of the good wife. The novel has many themes: strong men and weak women; the power of sex; the social need for good behaviour. But some people thought that the ending was too artificial. Henry Fielding wrote his first novel *Shamela* as a parody of the moral tone of *Pamela*.

Many readers have found the moral tone of Richardson's novels difficult to accept, but in his own time he was very successful. *Clarissa* (1747–9) took the epistolary form a step further in a novel of eight volumes and over a million words. The novel is narrated through the letters of Clarissa Harlowe and Lovelace.

Lovelace is a handsome but not wealthy man who enjoys chasing women. When he turns his attention to Clarissa, her family say that he is not good enough for her and that she must marry the wealthy Solmes. Clarissa refuses and is locked up by her family. Lovelace persuades her to escape with him to London where she lives with prostitutes believing them to be respectable. Lovelace tries to make love to Clarissa but she refuses him and he becomes obsessed by her. Finally, he tries to rape her. He believes that she really does want to love him. He writes in one of his letters:

> Is not this the hour of her trial – And in her, of the trial
> of the virtue[1] of her whole sex, so long premeditated,[2]
> so long threatened? Whether her frost be frost indeed?
> Whether her virtue be principle?

[1] good moral character   [2] considered in the past

Then Lovelace drugs her and rapes her, after which she begins to go mad and Lovelace begins to lose interest in her. Clarissa finally dies and Lovelace is killed in a fight. Once again the woman is the victim of men – and Richardson's readers approved, as he took their advice and suggestions and changed his plot while the novel was being published in parts. In many ways the rules of moral behaviour in male/female relationships were fixed in the novels of Richardson, and it was not until the next century that female writers began to challenge them.

Henry Fielding stopped writing for the theatre in 1737, and turned to the novel. Richardson examined female ideas and circumstances, but Fielding examined male points of view. *Joseph Andrews* (1742) and *Tom Jones* (1749) are his best-known novels. Fielding called his novels 'comic epics in prose' and he follows his heroes through long, complicated epic journeys, stressing the experiences they go through and how they form their character. For example, in *Joseph Andrews,* we follow the life of Joseph in a novel which begins as a parody of Samuel Richardson's *Pamela*. Joseph goes to work for Sir Thomas Booby. Pamela, who he believes to be his sister, lives at the home of Squire Booby, who is a nephew of Sir Thomas. From the beginning Joseph is looked after by Parson Adams, a kind and gentle religious man who believes everybody to be innocent. While in London, Lady Booby tries to attract Joseph but he is in love with Fanny, one of the servants in Sir Thomas's home in Somerset. When he is made unemployed by Lady Booby, Joseph makes a long journey back to Somerset to look for Fanny. On the way he meets Parson Adams and Fanny. They have no money but are always helped by others. One person who helps them is Mr Wilson who later turns out to be Joseph's father; and Joseph later learns that Fanny is Pamela's sister. Joseph and Fanny are finally married and Adams becomes a successful churchman. During his mostly comic adventures Joseph comes to understand human nature better.

Fielding's purpose is, as he writes in his preface to this novel, 'to defend what is good by displaying the Ridiculous'. His plots show the strength and weaknesses of human nature, they show the innocent learning from experience and they show human goodness. In Fielding's novels there is a wide range of comic characters, and he helped to define the traditions of the English comic novel, focusing on the pleasures of life. Of course, the men always have rather more freedom than the women, and there is always a moral. Fielding's third-person narrator often puts in his own opinion for the benefit of the 'dear reader'.

Already the range of narrative styles and techniques in the novel was varied: from the journalistic first-person narrations of Defoe, through the letters and diaries used by Richardson, to the third-person all-knowing narrator of Fielding, we find the range of narrative voices which were used for the next two hundred years. And from narrative to political, from romantic to comic, from social to satirical, the novel already had a wide range of themes and styles by 1750.

The Novel after 1750

After Richardson and Fielding the novel had become a rich and varied genre. In the next fifty years it moved in several quite different new directions.

Again there were several women writers who led the way. Charlotte Lennox, who was born in the colony of New York in America, wrote *The Life of Harriot Stuart* in 1750 and *The Female Quixote* in 1752. She concentrates on female experience from a female point of view, as her titles imply. Arabelle, the heroine of *The Female Quixote*, expects all men to be her slaves, almost the opposite of the expectations of a Richardsonian heroine. Similarly, Eliza Haywood in her comic novel *Miss Betty Thoughtless* (1751) goes against the usual plot idea by making her heroine suffer in a bad marriage before all turns out well. Sarah Fielding, sister of Henry, called her most famous novel *David Simple* (1744, completed in 1753) which is the name of the innocent hero, who is looking for a 'real friend'. He is disappointed, and the novel is one of the earliest realistic works which avoids the traditional happy ending. Here the man rather than the woman is the victim.

The most unusual novel of the time was *Tristram Shandy* (1760–67) by Laurence Sterne. This is a long comic story which plays with time, plot and character, and even with the shape and design of the page. Traditionally, a plot had a beginning, a middle and an end, in that order. Sterne was the first to change this order. He wanted to show how foolish it is to force everything into the traditional plot. He shows his own plot-line in this famous illustration:

Sterne was the first writer to use what came to be known as the Stream of Consciousness technique, following the thoughts of characters as they come into their heads. In this he was influenced by the *Essay Concerning Human Understanding* (1690) by John Locke, and his theories about time, sensations and the relation of one idea to another.

Henry Mackenzie's novel *The Man of Feeling* (1771) also plays with time and plot. It seems to be a diary with pages and scenes missing. So the reader never gets the whole story, but can only feel part of the emotions of the new kind of hero: a man who cries, and who is easily moved by anything he sees or feels. This was a deliberate challenge to the idea of the strong masculine hero, and it had a great influence through all of Europe. The famous German novel *The Sorrows of Young Werther* (1774) by Goethe was directly influenced by Mackenzie's work. *The Man of Feeling* was the first Scottish novel to have a huge success, and its concentration on emotion changed the way readers felt and thought about emotion for many years.

Another Scot, Tobias Smollett, was the major comic novelist of the second half of the eighteenth century. His novels, such as *Roderick Random* (1748) and *Peregrine Pickle* (1751), are entertaining adventures, in which the heroes go travelling all over Europe. They are angry young men, who react against bad treatment and the ills of society with strong language and often violent behaviour. This is social observation, but it has a more comic tone than the satire of Swift a generation earlier. Many readers found Smollett's novels and their themes too strong. His final novel *Humphry Clinker* (1771) is an epistolary novel which describes how *dis*united the United Kingdom was nearly seventy years after the Union of the Parliaments in 1707. Above all,

Smollett uses rich and original language to suit his characters, and he brings a new tone of comic freedom to the novel after Fielding.

Towards the end of the eighteenth century the novel took a new direction. Horace Walpole's *The Castle of Otranto* (1764) started the fashion for the Gothic, and the horror novel was born. The story is set in medieval times, with castles and ghosts, appearances and disappearances, and a whole range of frightening effects, which are still popular in story and film. The Gothic novel developed the imaginative range of the genre, going beyond realism and moral instruction. It explored extremes of feeling and imagination.

William Beckford, author of the Gothic novel Vathek, *was one of the richest men in England. His home, Fonthill Abbey, was built in the Gothic style.*

As early as 1757, the philosopher Edmund Burke had analysed the pleasure of the mysterious and the frightening in his long essay *The Sublime and the Beautiful* [sublime = wonderful]. 'A sort of delightful horror' is the phrase Burke used to describe the kind of pleasure the Gothic novel would give. This analysis was a sign of an important break from the rational control of the Augustans, and was one of the first steps towards the focus on feeling found later in Henry Mackenzie and the early Romantic writers.

After Walpole, Clara Reeve with *The Old English Baron* [baron = noble] (1777) and Ann Radcliffe with *The Mysteries of Udolpho* (1794) had even greater success. *Vathek* (1786), by William Beckford, takes place in Arabia and contains all sorts of sexual and sensual exaggeration. Matthew Lewis's *The Monk* (1796), written when he was only twenty-one years old, is often considered the most completely Gothic of eighteenth-century horror stories, and was a great success at the time. The main character, Ambrosio, a monk, tries to capture a young girl who has come to the monastery for help. Ambrosio loves her but eventually kills her. He is caught and sentenced to death. The devil helps him to escape but then destroys him.

Augustan Poetry

When Dryden died in 1700, poetic satire was at its highest point, but no major poet followed him immediately. It was not until 1712 that the first two cantos of *The Rape of the Lock* [theft of the hair] were published, and Dryden's successor, Alexander Pope, arrived on the scene. The poem is a mock-heroic satire about a family quarrel over a bit of Belinda's hair which was cut off by a friend. It is quite different from Dryden's satire: Pope's world is much smaller, the issues exaggerated as if they were of major importance. Pope is mocking the stupid self-importance of the characters: this is why it is called mock-heroic.

Pope's *Dunciad* (1728, longer version 1743) is, like Dryden's *MacFlecknoe*, an attack on the dullness of his literary rivals. Much of Pope's writing is about other writers or figures from the upper-class society of the time. But his range of observation is not as limited as this might imply. His *Essay on Criticism* (1711) and *Essay on Man* (1733–4) contain a great deal of philosophical observation expressed wittily and wisely. And his *Imitations of Horace* (1733–8) are central texts for the Augustan age, following the Roman poet Horace, and creating a series of dialogues on many of the main issues of the day. Pope is the master of ironic observation, often angry in his tone. As a poet he made great use of the heroic couplet, and his many works have made the English language richer with a number of famous lines, such as these from *An Essay on Criticism*:

> A little learning is a dangerous thing.
> Drink deep, or taste not the Pierian spring.[1]
> True wit is nature to advantage dressed,
> What oft[2] was thought but ne'er[3] so well expressed.

[1] the power of imagination   [2] often   [3] never

Lady Mary Wortley Montagu is perhaps the best known of the many women poets of the time. She was a friend, and later an enemy of Pope. She was well known for her letters, from Turkey and from Europe, but her poetry is famous, too. It was she who told Pope that:

> Satire should like a polished razor keen[1]
> Wound with a touch that's scarcely felt or seen.

[1] sharp

Another woman poet, Mary Leapor, died at the age of only twenty-four, but left some remarkable poems which were influenced by Pope, and were published after her death with Richardson's encouragement. Here a man is making a proposal to a woman, in a distinctly unromantic way:

*Lady Mary Wortley
Montagu in Turkish
costume.*

Now, madam, as the chat goes round,
I hear you have ten thousand pound:
But that as I a trifle[1] hold,
Give me your person, dem[2] your gold;
Yet for your sake 'tis[3] secured,
I hope your houses too insured.
       ('A Modern Love Letter' 1746)

[1] small thing   [2] curse   [3] it is

This is irony like Pope's, pointing to their society's concern with money. It also explores ideas of women's role in society.

Most of the famous women writers of the century, from Susannah Centlivre to Clara Reeve, were also poets, but they are frequently not mentioned in histories of literature. The female poets, like Mary Leapor or Hetty Wright, are usually critical of male superiority in society – perhaps this is why male critics have ignored them. As Hetty Wright said to her husband, writing about an unhappy marriage:

I will not brook[1] contempt[2] from thee![3]

[1] tolerate   [2] lack of respect   [3] you

THE RETURN TO SIMPLER VALUES

In the 1740s the Graveyard School of poetry had a moment of success. Their concern with death and 'delightful gloom' came about twenty years before similar ideas in the Gothic novel. Edward Young's *Night Thoughts* (1742–5), 'on Life, Death, and Immortality' [immortality = living for ever] is a blank verse poem that created the taste throughout Europe for this kind of verse. It broke with the classical order and rationalism of Augustan poetry, and completely lacks the irony and wit of Pope and the other writers of his time. Robert Blair's *The Grave* (1745) is a celebration of death, and talks of being alone and of pain and madness.

An illustration for Elegy Written in a Country Churchyard, *by Thomas Gray.*

∞ ∞ POETS LAUREATE ∞ ∞

Ben Jonson, 1615, appointed by
   King James
Sir William Davenant, 1637
John Dryden, 1670
Thomas Shadwell, 1688
Nahum Tate, 1692
Nicholas Rowe, 1715
Laurence Eusden, 1718
Colley Cibber, 1730
William Whitehead, 1757
Thomas Warton, 1785

Henry James Pye, 1790
Robert Southey, 1813
William Wordsworth, 1844
Alfred Tennyson, 1850
Alfred Austin, 1896
Robert Bridges, 1913
John Masefield, 1930
C. Day-Lewis, 1968
John Betjeman, 1972
Ted Hughes, 1984
Andrew Motion, 1999

The most important single poem of the eighteenth century was probably Thomas Gray's *Elegy Written in a Country Churchyard* [churchyard = church ground], completed in 1750 and published in 1751. Despite the title, it has no real connection with the sad concerns of the Graveyard School – its aims are quite different. It celebrates the lives and deeds of the poor, ordinary people buried in the churchyard in the small village of Stoke Poges, talking of 'the short and simple annals of the poor' [annals = stories] rather than the gloomy enjoyment of the thought of death.

Gray's poem is a realistic pastoral in simple four-line verses, far from the social and intellectual world of the Augustans. 'Let not ambition mock their useful toil' [toil = work] he asks, and in doing this, he shows a return to simpler values which is the beginning of the Romantic movement's return (at the end of the century) to nature and to more natural language. His poem became one of the most popular and well known of all English poems, and made Gray famous – but he refused the offer to become Poet Laureate, following the theme of his poem even in his own life:

> Far from the madding[1] crowd's ignoble strife,[2]
> Their sober[3] wishes never learned to stray;[4]
> Along the cool sequestered[5] vale[6] of life
> They kept the noiseless tenor[7] of their way.

[1] rushing in a crazy way   [2] unpleasant argument   [3] modest
[4] go   [5] hidden, peaceful   [6] valley   [7] pattern

A little before Gray's time James Thomson wrote *The Seasons* (1726–30), a long blank verse nature poem. It can be seen as the first poem of its kind, and was very popular for well over a century.

Several poets followed Gray's return to village life and the values of the countryside which were being lost as the Industrial Revolution and the Agricultural Revolution forced many people to move from the country to the city. Oliver Goldsmith's poem *The Deserted Village* (1770) speaks of the loss of a village for the same reasons; William Cowper's *The Task* (1785) celebrates the working life of the countryside, and George Crabbe's narrative poems, *The Village* (1783) and *The Borough* [district] (1810), tell stories of the harder side of this kind of life. They stress the values of country life without making it seem simple or easy.

The *Odes* of William Collins, published in 1746, had a great influence on later poets. They were sad and lyrical, although not connected to the Graveyard School. This tone of sadness is also found in a major woman poet about forty years later: Charlotte Smith's *Elegiac Sonnets* were published in various editions between 1784 and 1797. They combine the note of sadness with a celebration of nature, and the Romantic poets Coleridge and Wordsworth admired them greatly. Mrs Smith was also a successful novelist. *The Old Manor House* [manor house = large house in the country] (1793) was one of the most popular novels of its time. She was an important figure in her own day, although she was always poor – it was not easy for a woman to earn her living as a writer. Here the mood of self-pity is well illustrated:

> Ah! then, how dear[1] the Muse's favours[2] cost,
> If those paint sorrow best – who feel it most!
> *(Elegiac Sonnets)*

[1] expensive   [2] good opinion of the Goddess, that is the female god, of artistic inspiration

Fanny Burney was more successful, at least as regards money and fame. Her first novel *Evelina* (1778) brought her immediate success, and she continued to write novels about young women in society for many years. She lived to be almost ninety years old, and her letters and diaries describe English (and French) society over a major period of historical change.

Some of these writers and their works are described as pre-Romantic [pre = before]. But this is only because they have been seen as coming before the Romantic poets at the end of the century: in fact their writing deserves its own place in history because it reacts against the rationalism and order of the Augustans and rediscovers the simple life and its values.

Robert Burns was the greatest Scottish poet, and many of his poems are written in Scots, a variety of English used in Scotland. His themes are nature and the humanity of nature. For example in 'To a Mouse' (1786) he shares the problems of the mouse whose home is lost when the farm worker destroys it by accident. The lines about this have become famous:

> The best-laid [1] schemes
> Of mice and men
> Gang aft agley. [2]

[1] most carefully considered   [2] often go wrong

Burns was himself a farm worker, in Ayrshire, and later a tax collector. He uses his own experience with humour and sympathy in poems describing the life of country people such as 'The Cotter's Saturday Night' [cotter's = farm worker's] (1786). His 'A Man's A Man for A' That' [A' = all] catches the mood of the times with its ideas of common humanity. Many of Burns's songs are still well known, and he was one of the poets most admired by the Romantic poets. In many ways Robert Burns is the first of the Romantics, but he is better thought of as a major figure writing in the Scots language as well as in English; the countryside poet whose work has worldwide appeal.

The Scottish writer James Macpherson caused a great controversy with his books of verse, *Fingal* in 1762 and *Temora* (1763). He had written these himself, but said they were old poems written by Ossian, an epic poet writing in the Gaelic language which Macpherson had translated. The poems of Ossian became very famous, and created a fashion for wild Scottish scenery and old stories. Even when the truth was finally reported in 1805 the influence of Ossian was great – he was one of the favourite writers of the German poet Goethe and the French emperor Napoleon.

Journalism and Criticism

With the growth of the new middle classes, there was an increasing demand for the printed word, and writing became a profession. Authors were now professional, full-time writers, not only of books or plays. Many famous newspapers and magazines were started at this time, and most of the great writers of the time were also journalists. Daniel Defoe, for example, worked for business magazines before he started writing his novels. Other writers became more famous for their journalism than their books or plays.

The journalism of the early eighteenth century took the opinions and fashions of the capital city, London, to the whole nation. This was an important change in ways of thinking, especially outside the capital. A parallel growth in the communication of information and ideas happened in Scotland, from its capital city Edinburgh. This was the time of the Scottish Enlightenment, and the intellectual currents of the two countries were quite different, despite the Union of the Crowns in 1603 and the Union of the Parliaments in 1707. Scotland in the eighteenth century was a centre of philosophical writings by, for example, David Hume, and the economist Adam Smith.

London, however, was more concerned with society and manners, and with the gossip of the coffee-houses, which were the centre of London's literary life in the first half of the century. *The Gentleman's Journal* was the first of these publications, from 1692 to 1694, and then *The Gentleman's Magazine* from 1731 to 1914. The most famous of the early magazines were *The Tatler* and *The Spectator* [observer]. The first, begun by Richard Steele, ran from April 1709 until January 1711. The second, started by Steele with Joseph Addison, ran from March 1711 until December 1712. Addison continued to run it by himself from March 1714. The idea of a magazine which represents the tastes of 'gentlemen' was

The title page of Volume I of The Tatler, *1709. The editor, Richard Steele, used the name Isaac Bickerstaff.*

THE

TATLER:

BY

Iſaac Bickerſtaff, *Eſq;*

VOL. I.

Quicquid agunt Homines noſtri Farrago Libelli.

The Actions of Mankind are the Subject of my Collections.

Tuesday, April 12, 1709.

THO' the other Papers, which are pub-
liſhed for the Uſe of the good People of
England, have certainly very whole-
ſome Effects, and are laudable in their
particular Kinds, they do not ſeem to
come up to the main Deſign of ſuch Narrations, which, I humbly preſume, ſhould be principally
intended for the Uſe of politic Perſons, who are ſo publick
ſpirited as to neglect their own Affairs to look into Tranſacti-
ons of State. Now theſe Gentlemen, for the moſt part, being
Perſons of ſtrong Zeal, and weak Intellects, it is both a
charitable and neceſſary Work to offer ſomething whereby
ſuch worthy and well affected Members of the Commonwealth may be inſtructed, after their Reading, what to
think ; which ſhall be the End and purpoſe of this my
Paper, wherein I ſhall from Time to Time report and
conſider all Matters of what Kind ſoever that ſhall occur

VOL. I.   B   10

The title page of
Volume I of The
Tatler, *1709. The*
editor, Richard
Steele, used the
name Isaac
Bickerstaff.

continued in these magazines. *The Spectator* was presented as the magazine of a fictional gentleman's club and its leader, Sir Roger de Coverley, gave his opinions on every subject. The magazines were therefore important in expressing ideas and a point of view, setting standards of taste and judgement, and influencing the values of the society they wrote for and about. The tone was not too intellectual or highbrow, and the term middlebrow later came to be used to describe this kind of journalism. It can be seen as comfortable and safe writing, and as a model of politeness and good taste. Addison wrote 'I live in the world rather as a spectator of mankind than as one of the species.' This gave the title to one of the magazines, and shows something of the attitude and tone which appealed to the new middle classes. Addison's prose was described by the critic Doctor Samuel Johnson as 'the model of the middle-style' and his essays proved to be very influential in the forming of eighteenth-century tastes.

Addison's sense of balanced argument can be seen in Sir Roger de Coverley's judgement between two sides:

> Sir Roger told them, with the air[1] of a man who would not give his judgement rashly,[2] that much might be said on both sides.
>
> (The Spectator)

[1] manner   [2] without thought

Richard Steele also started *The Guardian* and ran *The Englishman* (1713–14), *The Lover* and *The Theatre*. Steele was also a dramatist, and he attacked the excesses of Restoration comedy. His *The Conscious Lovers* (1722) was very successful for many years. It is a complete break from the spirit of Restoration drama, introducing the kind of feeling and polite behaviour which were to rule the theatre for the next century.

Essays of criticism were also becoming popular. Dryden had written several important critical pieces, and magazines often caused a lot of controversy when literary or political arguments were printed in their pages. Many writers and editors had to pay fines or were even sent to prison for expressing their opinions too strongly. Daniel Defoe was sent to prison for writing a pamphlet 'The Shortest Way with the Dissenters' [dissenters = protesters] (1702).

The major critic of the eighteenth century was Samuel Johnson. He started writing for magazines in 1737, and wrote a tragedy *Irene* (1737) and the novel *Rasselas* (1759) to help pay his debts. But he made his name with the publication of his *Dictionary of the English Language* published in 1755. After the success of the dictionary he wrote a preface to Shakespeare (1765). This was one of the first critical essays on Shakespeare, and the beginning of a major tradition. Johnson also wrote *The Lives of the English Poets*

(1779–81) which is important because it began a tradition of English literary criticism. Johnson, of course, made some wrong judgements, like any other critic. For example, he did not like Sterne's *Tristram Shandy* or any of Swift's writing. But he was the first of a long line of critics who discussed and judged writers and their place in the growing tradition of English writing. Dr Johnson wrote many witty and memorable lines. In his dictionary he directs humour at himself when he defines a lexicographer as 'a writer of dictionaries, a harmless drudge' [drudge = person doing a boring job].

Here is Johnson on Shakespeare:

> Shakespeare is above all writers, at least above all
> modern writers, the poet of nature; the poet that holds
> up to his readers a faithful mirror of manners and life.
> His characters are not modified[1] by the customs of
> particular places, unpractised[2] by the rest of the world;
> by the peculiarities of studies of professions, which can
> operate but upon small numbers; or by the accidents of
> transient[3] fashions or temporary opinions: they are the
> genuine progeny[4] of common humanity, such as the
> world will always supply, and observation will always
> find. His persons act and speak by the influence of
> those general passions and principles by which all
> minds are agitated,[5] and the whole system of life is
> continued in motion. In the writings of other poets a
> character is too often an individual; in those of
> Shakespeare it is commonly a species.[6]

[1] changed   [2] not followed   [3] passing
[4] children   [5] disturbed   [6] frequently a section of mankind

Doctor Johnson himself was lucky in his biographer, James Boswell, whose *Life of Samuel Johnson* is the first great biography in English. Boswell was a Scot, and he knew Johnson very well for over twenty years. He travelled with him in Scotland, and noted his conversations for many years. The biography was published in 1791, seven years after Johnson's death.

Oliver Goldsmith, well known as a novelist for *The Vicar of Wakefield* [vicar = churchman] (1766) and as a dramatist for *She Stoops to Conquer* [stoops = takes a lower social position] (1773), also ran a magazine, *The Bee*, in the late 1750s, and wrote for many other magazines. The novelist Tobias Smollett ran magazines such as *The Critical Review* (from 1756 to 1763) and *The British Magazine* in the 1760s, for which Goldsmith frequently wrote between 1760 and 1767.

One of the most important books of the second half of the eighteenth century was a history – Edward Gibbon's huge *The History of the Decline and Fall of the Roman Empire*, published between 1776 and 1788. It was a controversial book, looking at the greatness of Rome, but also at how that greatness ended. *The History* shows, in particular, how the Roman Empire declined after the age of Augustus, and this change was seen also in Gibbon's own time, as the Augustan age moved towards the new spirit of freedom and revolution in many parts of the world. It was published between the American Declaration of Independence and the French Revolution, and made Gibbon the most famous historian in the world.

All this professional writing shows a wide market for opinions and discussions of all kinds of subjects. Almost all the writers of the time could not be professional, full-time authors, and many of them worked very hard at their journalism: they wrote for money, and journalism gave them a more or less regular income. In a society where money was so important, authorship was a profession just like many others.

Letters and Diaries

Other kinds of writing which began to grow in importance in the eighteenth century include diaries and letters. Lady Mary Wortley Montagu's letters in the first part of the century were famous. Later, Lord Chesterfield's *Letters* to his son, published in 1774 after both of them were dead, became very popular as a book of good manners. But many people, including Doctor Johnson, did not like the kind of manners the letters described. The diaries of Samuel Pepys, describing the period between 1660 and 1669, and of John Evelyn,

The Capitol in Rome. It was here, in 1764, that Edward Gibbon first had the idea to write his book The History of the Decline and Fall of the Roman Empire.

concerning the second half of the seventeenth century, were not published until the nineteenth century. But they give details of daily life at the time of the Restoration which novels and plays cannot give.

The Wanderer, *by Caspar David Friedrich (1818), shows the spirit of the Romantic Age.*

5 The Romantic Age 1789–1832

Setting the Scene

The Romantic period lasts about forty years, from the French Revolution in 1789 to the Reform Act of 1832. It is sometimes called the Age of Revolutions: the American Revolution of 1776, and the spirit of 'Liberty, Equality and Fraternity' of the French Revolution made it a time of hope and change.

William Wordsworth in *The Prelude* [introduction] wrote 'bliss was it in that dawn to be alive'. This shows the hope for the future when French politics changed, and many writers like Wordsworth hoped the same would happen in Britain. But the Reign of Terror began in 1793, the period of Napoleon followed rapidly, and by the early 1800s most of Europe was at war against France.

So the poetry of the Romantics, from Wordsworth and Coleridge's *Lyrical Ballads* (1798), is in many ways poetry of war. Society was changing, becoming industrial rather than agricultural as towns and cities developed; the government encouraged free trade; the new middle class became powerful, and there were moves towards voting reform and greater democracy. But change was slow, and there was a lot of suffering, especially among the poor: they had to move from the country to the city; the soldiers who returned after Napoleon's final defeat at Waterloo in 1815 found themselves unemployed; there were many social and political problems, the worst example of which was the Peterloo massacre of 1819, when government soldiers attacked a large group of protestors, killing eleven people and injuring about four hundred. (The name Peterloo (after Waterloo) was given by supporters of free speech.) War abroad was followed by war between social classes at home.

In literature, Romantic writing is mostly poetry: Wordsworth and Coleridge wanted a revolution too, in poetic language and in themes which contrasted with the earlier Augustan age. Then the head controlled the heart; now the heart controlled the head. For Augustans, feelings and imagination were dangerous; for Romantics, reason and the intellect were dangerous. The individual spirit rather than an ordered society became important. The government did not like this spirit – many of the writers went abroad because their spirit was too dangerous, and many were not recognized in their own lifetimes. In fact the name Romantic was only given to the period later, when its spirit of freedom and hope could be recognized as different, as an important moment of change. In Europe, Romanticism was different: music and art, politics and philosophy were all stirred by the Romantic spirit. In Britain it was limited to a few poets, but they changed the face of English literature for ever.

Blake

William Blake had a very individual view of the world, and his poetic style and ideas contrast with the order and control of the Augustan world. Blake's best-known collection of poetry *Songs of Innocence and Experience* was published in 1794. His poems are simple but symbolic – the lamb is the symbol of innocence, the tiger the symbol of mystery:

> Little lamb, who made thee?[1]
> Dost thou[2] know who made thee?
> ('The Lamb')

[1] you [2] do you

> Tyger! Tyger! burning bright
> In the forests of the night,
> What immortal[1] hand or eye
> Could frame[2] thy[3] fearful symmetry?[4]
> ('The Tyger')

[1] godlike [2] arrange; invent [3] your
[4] frightening balance or perfection

Blake's later poems are very complex symbolic texts, but his voice in the early 1790s is the conscience of the Romantic age. He shows a contrast between a world of nature and childhood innocence and a world of social control. Blake saw the dangers of an industrial society in which individuals were lost, and in his famous poem 'London' he calls the systems of society 'mind-forged manacles'. For Blake, London is a city in which the mind of everyone is in chains and all individuals are imprisoned. Even the River Thames has been given a royal charter [chartered = given rights] so that it can be used for business and trade:

> I wander thro'[1] each charter'd street
> Near where the charter'd Thames does flow,
> And mark[2] in every face I meet
> Marks of weakness, marks of woe.[3]

An illustration by William Blake for his Songs of Innocence.

In every cry of every Man,
In every Infant's[4] cry of fear,
In every voice, in every ban[5]
The mind-forg'd manacles[6] I hear.

('London')

[1] through   [2] notice   [3] sadness   [4] very small child's
[5] law to stop something   [6] chains around the hands, which are made
in the brain

'London' contrasts with Wordsworth's 'Sonnet composed upon Westminster Bridge' [composed = written] (1802, published 1807): 'Earth has not anything to show more fair' – Wordsworth wanted always to see the positive side, where Blake's vision is more social and political.

Wordsworth

William Wordsworth's poetry looks inward rather than outward, and in *The Prelude*, his long autobiographical poem, we read how an individual's thoughts and feelings are formed. Wordsworth is the main character in most of his poems. He wants 'to see into the heart of things', as he says in 'Lines Written Above Tintern Abbey'. He considers in 'Daffodils' [daffodil = kind of flower], for instance, how the past relates to the present, and *The Prelude* takes that as its main theme. He continued to write *The Prelude* for many years. It is a psychological poem in which the individual searches for personal understanding, in a manner which has become a main theme of modern literature.

When Wordsworth wrote that the 'child is father of the Man' he means that adults can learn from children. However, the Augustans believed that children should be controlled as soon as possible. Augustan writers believed that an ordered society was important, whereas Romantic writers believed that the life of the individual spirit was important. These different ideas resulted in different styles of writing and different uses of language. For example, Augustan poets often use a special poetic language and a special poetic pattern of heroic couplets (see p. 252).

Romantic writers loved the wild nature of the Lake District in the north of England. William Wordsworth lived there for many years.

Here is a section from the Preface to *Lyrical Ballads* in which Wordsworth states that he wanted to write in a clear and simple way about everyday life and people:

> The principal object[1] . . . in these poems was to choose
> incidents[2] and situations from common life, and to
> relate or describe them throughout, as far as it was
> possible, in a selection of language really used by men.

[1] aim   [2] events

Sometimes Wordsworth does indeed write in simple direct language which is close to the spoken language of ordinary people. For example:

>   A slumber[1] did my spirit seal;[2]
>   I had no human fears;
>   She seemed a thing that would not feel
>   The touch of earthly years.
>   ('A Slumber Did My Spirit Seal')

[1] sleep   [2] close tightly

However, sometimes he uses more difficult grammar and vocabulary, and seems a long way from his poetic ideals.

Wordsworth writes frequently about nature and about ordinary people such as 'The Old Cumberland Beggar' and 'The Leech Gatherer' [leech = blood-sucking worm] who live against the background of the world of nature. Later in his life he stated that he wanted his poetry to show that men and women 'who do not wear fine clothes can feel deeply,' and to praise those who live close to nature. Above all, Wordsworth wanted to show the importance of the human memory, because it is the memory which continues to give life to our major experiences. The memory allows us to keep our understanding of the world fresh and alive, although there is despair in Wordsworth's later poetry when the imagination fails and memory no longer works. In this section from 'Lines Written Above Tintern Abbey' Wordsworth praises the power of his memory and the pictures which his memory can recreate:

>   But oft[1] in lonely rooms and 'mid the din[2]
>   Of towns and cities, I have owed to them
>   In hours of weariness,[3] sensations sweet,
>   Felt in the blood and felt along the heart.

[1] often   [2] among the noise   [3] tiredness

These lines also stress the importance of the feelings and show the power of nature, rather than 'towns and cities', to lift the imagination.

Coleridge

Wordsworth worked closely with the poet Samuel Taylor Coleridge. They were both responsible for *Lyrical Ballads* and for the influential Prefaces to the second edition (1800), but they are very different poets. Wordsworth's poetry is more about the day-to-day, ordinary world; Coleridge's poetry is more about the extraordinary and supernatural world.

There are only four poems by Samuel Taylor Coleridge in *Lyrical Ballads*, but one of them is his best-known poem, *The Rime of the Ancient Mariner* [rhyme of the old sailor]. In the poem an old mariner tells of how he shot an albatross. When his ship can no longer sail, and he has terrible dreams, he understands that he must suffer for what he has done. He learns from his suffering and learns that he cannot drink until his soul is refreshed:

> Day after day, day after day
> We stuck,[1] nor breath nor motion;
> As idle as a painted ship
> Upon a painted ocean.
>
> Water, water, everywhere
> And all the boards did shrink;
> Water, water, everywhere,
> Nor any drop to drink.

[1] did not move

The Wedding Guest, who listens to the story, learns he must love all creatures and becomes a 'sadder and a wiser man'. The journey symbolizes a Christian journey from innocence to experience.

> He prayeth[1] well, who loveth[2] well
> Both man and bird and beast.[3]
> He prayeth best, who loveth best
> All things both great and small.

[1] prays [2] loves [3] animal

An illustration for The Rime of the Ancient Mariner, *by Samuel Taylor Coleridge.*

In *Christabel* and *Kubla Khan*, both written in 1797 but not published until 1816, Coleridge also creates symbolic landscapes. *Kubla Khan* is a poem about the creative imagination which is, for Coleridge, the most powerful of all the human senses. The poem is not complete and has a subtitle: 'A Fragment'. We can conclude that the vision is complete but is so powerful that it can only be stated in parts and fragments. *Christabel* is another poem about a journey which is not completed, but in which there is a search for fuller meaning and understanding. Both *Christabel* and *The Rime of the Ancient Mariner* use medieval verse forms and styles, capture an atmosphere of the distant past and look for meanings in a contrast between past and present. Like Coleridge's poem 'Dejection: An Ode' [dejection = sadness] (another fragment), *Christabel* shows that lasting truths can be found even if complete understanding is not possible.

Coleridge is also well known for his conversation poems. Although Coleridge's poetry is different in many ways from Wordsworth's, his conversation poems are similar to Wordsworth's, and poems such as 'Dejection' and 'Frost at Midnight' and 'This Lime-Tree Bower My Prison' [bower = sheltered place] have everyday observations about an ordinary environment, and are written in a clear and simple conversational style. Here are some lines from 'Dejection: An Ode':

> I may not hope from outward[1] forms to win
> The passion and the life, whose fountains are within.

[1]external

Both Coleridge and Wordsworth believed that poetry should be a 'language really used by men', and in some poems they write in a style which, at the end of the eighteenth century, was new and different and which influenced many poets who followed them.

Both Coleridge and Wordsworth were also influential as writers about literature. In the Prefaces to the 1800 edition of *Lyrical Ballads*, in letters and in Coleridge's *Biographia Literaria* (1817) they started a movement in which modern writers both write about literature and become much more conscious about themselves as writers and about literature as an art.

Keats

Wordsworth and Coleridge are the first generation of Romantic poets. Most of the second generation were not even born at the time of the French Revolution, but their poetic concerns are shared with Wordsworth and Coleridge. John Keats was born in 1795, three years before *Lyrical Ballads* was published, but Keats also wrote about the nature of literature, the imagination and poetry, and his *Letters* are important critical works. Many of Keats's poems are incomplete fragments, but they make a lasting pattern, and by the time of his death, at the very young age of twenty-five, Keats was one of the most important Romantic poets. Although his best-known poetry was written almost twenty years after the publication of *Lyrical Ballads*, Wordsworth and Coleridge were important influences on his poetry and on his ideas.

In a period of two years (1818–20) Keats wrote much of his poetry, both long narrative poems and the famous odes. The narratives (from these years) *Isabella*, *Lamia*, *The Eve of Saint Agnes* [eve = night before] and *La Belle Dame Sans Merci* [the beautiful lady with no pity] have mythic, classical or medieval backgrounds. Like Coleridge, Keats was interested in the irrational, mysterious and supernatural world of the distant past. The main themes of the poems are the search for lasting beauty and happiness and for permanent meanings in a world where everything fades and dies.

These themes are central to the odes. In 'Ode to a Nightingale' [nightingale = songbird] and 'Ode on a Grecian Urn' [urn = vase] the song of the nightingale and the artistic images on the urn show that art and artistic creation can make things permanent, and that poetry can keep human feelings and ideas alive for ever in the words of the poem. In these lines from 'Ode on a Grecian Urn' Keats, speaking directly to the urn, describes how the artist has created a permanent object of art in which the figures continue to live:

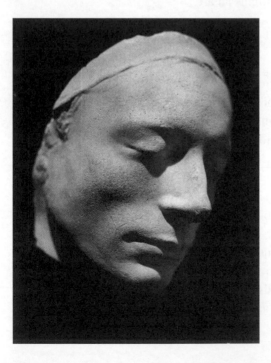

John Keats, a life mask. Keats, one of the most important of the Romantic poets, died at the age of 25.

When old age shall this generation waste
Thou shalt[1] remain, in midst of other woe[2]
Than ours, a friend to man, to whom thou sayest,[3]
'Beauty is truth, truth beauty' – that is all
Ye[4] know on earth, and all ye need to know.

[1]you shall   [2]with other sorrow   [3]you say   [4]you

In 'To Autumn' Keats paints a picture of a world of nature which is dying at the end of the year, but ends the poem by stressing the beauty and fullness of autumn which cannot die. The death of Keats at the age of twenty-five made him a symbol for the Romantic movement: of the contrast between life and death, between completeness and incompleteness, and between permanence and impermanence.

Shelley

Percy Bysshe Shelley felt the death of Keats particularly deeply, and wrote about it in his poem *Adonais* (1821). Shelley's poetry is similar to Keats's poetry in some ways; they both wanted to capture deep personal experiences. But Shelley's writing is, like Blake's, more political. In the poem *Queen Mab* (1813) he attacks the religion and morals of the age, and in an essay 'The Necessity of Atheism' (1811) he states that we cannot prove that God exists. In the long poem *The Mask of Anarchy* (written in 1819 but published in 1832) he writes about the future revolution of the working classes as he responds to the Peterloo massacre of 1819, when government soldiers attacked a group of workers in Manchester who were meeting to ask for social and political reforms. Shelley wanted greater freedom, and in his best-known lyric poem 'Ode to the West Wind' (1819) he makes the wind a symbol of the power of change as the wind blows away the old life and spreads the seeds which will create a new life of greater freedom for all. Some of Shelley's poems are self-pitying and his own feelings are sometimes too directly at the centre of a poem. For example:

Percy Bysshe Shelley

> I fall upon the thorns[1] of life! I bleed!
> ('Ode to the West Wind')

[1] sharp bits of plants, such as roses

Other short lyric poems such as 'The Widow Bird' communicate deep feelings through descriptions of the world of nature:

> A widow bird sat mourning[1] for her love
> Upon a wintry bough;[2]
> The frozen wind crept on above,
> The freezing stream below.
>
> There was no leaf upon the forest bare,
> No flower upon the ground,
> And little motion in the air
> Except the mill[3] wheel's sound.

[1] feeling sad about death   [2] branch   [3] place where corn is made into flour

The cold, the bare trees, the emptiness of the land and the lack of motion communicate inner feelings of waste because a love has died.

Shelley was both optimistic and pessimistic. In 'Julian and Maddalo' (written in 1818, published 1824) he sees the modern world as a wasteland which shows that all individuals are isolated from one another, but which also shows that everything is possible for the human soul. Like other Romantic poets, Shelley also wrote about poetry. He wrote in particular about the poet as a hero who can show the way to a better society. In his essay *The Defence of Poetry* (written in 1821 but not published until 1840), he states that poetry can reform the world. In *The Defence of Poetry* Shelley also writes: 'The rich have become richer, and the poor have become poorer.' This is one of the clearest statements of the division which happened in English society during the Romantic period. Only five years after *The Defence of Poetry* was published, the novelist and politician Benjamin Disraeli described this effect as 'The Two Nations', in the subtitle of his novel *Sybil*. The other famous quotation from Shelley's *Defence* is that 'Poets are the unacknowledged legislators of the world.' These lines mean that poets are able to write the laws of the world by which we live our lives (they are legislators) and that in this role they are unacknowledged, that is, no one recognizes that they do this. Idealism and social observation go together in Shelley.

Byron

Lord Byron was one of the most influential and, for many, is one of the most typical Romantic poets. He was a great influence across Europe in the nineteenth century. His picture of the romantic hero, an isolated individual who attacks social conventions and challenges the authorities of the age and who searches for, but never finds, peace and happiness, was particularly influential. His hero, Childe Harold, in the long poem *Childe Harold's Pilgrimage*, made Byron famous, the first popular best-selling poet, in 1812, when he was twenty-four.

Manfred, in Byron's poem *Manfred* (1817), and Childe Harold are both heroes with passionate feelings who rebel against society,

In English poetry, metre and rhyme are important. Both depend on the number of syllables in a line. In this stanza from Gray's *Elegy* (see p. 93) each line has ten syllables:

> Far from the madding crowd's ignoble strife,
> Their sober wishes never learned to stray;
> Along the cool sequestered vale of life
> They kept the noiseless tenor of their way.

Metre is the pattern of stressed (/) / unstressed (U) syllables in verse.

The first line reads: $/\ U\ U\ /\ U\ /\ U\ /\ U\ /$

or, more regularly: $U\ /\ U\ /\ U\ /\ U\ /\ U\ /$

The stresses depend on how the poem is read and they can vary. The other three lines are regular: $U\ /\ U\ /\ U\ /\ U\ /\ U\ /$

There are five **feet** of two syllables, unstressed and stressed. This is called **iambic pentameter** [pentameter = Greek for five measures] and is the most common metre in English poetry. Tetrameter has four feet; hexameter has six.

In English verse the following metres are the commonest:

iambic $U\ /$ anapaestic $U\ U\ /$ spondaic $/\ /$

trochaic $/\ U$ dactylic $/\ U\ U$

Coleridge's poem, *Metrical Feet*, helps to illustrate these feet, using the noun forms for the names:

$/\ U\ /\ \ U\ \ /\ U\ /$
Trochee trips[1] from long to short.   [1] walks lightly

$U\ /\ U\ /\ \ U\ /\ U\ /$
From long to long in solemn[2] sort   [2] serious

$/\ \ /\ /\ /\ \ \ /\ \ \ /\ \ /\ /\ U$
Slow spondee stalks;[3] strong foot yet ill[4] able   [3] strides [4] not

$/\ U\ U\ /\ \ U\ U\ \ U\ /\ U\ U\ /\ U\ U$
Ever to come up with[5] the dactyl trisyllable.[6]   [5] produce [6] three syllables

$U\ /\ U\ \ /\ \ \ U\ \ /\ U\ /$
Iambics march from short to long.

$U\ U\ /\ U\ U\ /\ \ \ U\ U\ \ /\ U\ U\ \ \ /$
With a leap and a bound[7] the swift[8] anapaests throng.[9]   [7] big jump [8] quick

[9] form a crowd

(The above is based on *A Dictionary of Literary Terms* by J. A. Cuddon, Penguin, 1977/82.)

Rhyme is the echo of sounds at the end of lines of verse. It helps both the music of the verse and the structure of the poem. The **rhyme scheme** holds the poems together. It is very common in English poetry. **Free verse** has no regular metre or line length and depends upon natural rhythms of speech. **Blank verse** is often used in drama, especially by Shakespeare. It uses regular lines with five stresses and, usually, no rhyme. Milton's *Paradise Lost*, and many of Wordsworth's and Coleridge's poems use blank verse.

who want to experience what is forbidden, and who seem to be beyond good and evil. Manfred, in particular, is more an anti-hero than a hero, but he is an attractive figure to all readers of the poem. In *Don Juan* (1819–24) Byron is more satirical. He invites his readers to be involved in the poem, to laugh with him at his hero, and to question their own values and the values of their society. These lines from *Don Juan* illustrate Byron's use of irony:

> He pored upon[1] the leaves, and on the flowers,
> And heard a voice in all the winds; and then
> He thought of wood-nymphs[2] and immortal bowers[3]
>
> And when he looked upon his watch again
> He found how much old Time has been a winner –
> He also found that he had lost his dinner.

[1] studied closely   [2] minor female gods   [3] hiding places for the gods

The sudden changes in style and context (from immortal nature to losing his dinner) are common in Byron's poetry. Here the style helps Byron comically to show that love of nature can have its problems.

In *Don Juan* the narrator writes at the beginning that 'I need a hero.' He needs to have a hero who struggles to find meaning and who fights for justice. Byron might have been writing about himself for he died, at the age of thirty-six, as he fought on the side of the Greeks in a war of independence against Turkey. Byron lived a dangerous life. He shocked many people by his beliefs and actions. He was a poetic hero of his age, bringing together many of the concerns of Romanticism since Blake, as in:

> I live not in myself, but I become
> Portion of that around me; and to me
> High mountains are a feeling, but the hurt
> Of human cities torture.[1]
>   (*Childe Harold's Pilgrimage* Canto III)

[1] great pain

An illustration for Don Juan, *by Byron.*

Other Romantic Writers

Nature is a major concern of poets from Robert Burns, through all
the Romantics and on to John Clare. Clare is the least known of the
Romantics, and in many ways the most unusual. He watched and
described the decline of the agricultural countryside, and himself
suffered a mental decline, ending his life in a mental hospital. His

descriptions of nature are also descriptions of an individual personality who is anxious and uncertain:

> The crows sit on the willow[1] tree
> The lake is full below
> But still the dullest thing I see
> Is self that wanders slow.
>
> ('Song')

[1] a tree which is often said to be weeping

Clare wrote until his death in 1864, and Wordsworth, the first of the Romantics, lived and wrote until 1850. The style and vision of both poets are essentially Romantic. The Romantics were poets of change. They found constants in nature and in art, but they could also see the new dangers of the modern world, and in many of their writings the security of the individual is threatened; Shelley's 'Julian and Maddalo' and 'Ozymandias' show a similar decline to that seen on a psychological level in the poetry of John Clare. With John Clare, Romantic poetry reaches its most personal expression.

The Romantic period was a time in which prose writing developed rapidly. Writers such as Thomas de Quincey, Charles Lamb and William Hazlitt changed the styles and topics of the eighteenth-century essay and also created new forms in which their personal impressions and the subjects of everyday life were central. Thomas Love Peacock, whose work was written in both the Romantic and Victorian periods, satirizes some of the main Romantic ideas and lifestyles in novels such as *Nightmare Abbey* [nightmare = frightening dream] (1818), in which the main characters are based on Coleridge, Byron and Shelley, and *Gryll Grange* (1860–1).

The most important novelists of the time were Jane Austen and Walter Scott. At this time a number of novelists were women; the most famous of them was Fanny Burney who wrote novels such as *Evelina* (1778) and *Camilla* (1796) about young women's experiences of the society of their day. Maria Edgeworth, an Irish novelist, wrote about the details of everyday provincial life, and both Ann Radcliffe and Clara Reeve (see p. 89) wrote Gothic novels which were popular for their exciting plots.

A later Gothic novel, *Frankenstein* by Mary Shelley (1818), the wife of Percy Bysshe Shelley, shows an extraordinary world in which a living being is made by a Genevan student from the bones of the dead, but becomes a monster which nobody can control. The monster murders Frankenstein's brother and his wife and finally Frankenstein himself. The novel shows the interest of the Romantics in the supernatural and in the attempts of man to be as powerful as God. *Frankenstein* can be seen as one of the first modern science fiction novels.

Jane Austen is different from other writers of her time, because her main interest is in the moral, social and psychological behaviour of her characters. She writes mainly about young heroines as they grow up and search for personal happiness. Jane Austen's pictures are detailed, often ironic, and always about a

Frankenstein, *by Mary Shelley, is one of the first science fiction novels. Boris Karloff played the monster in the film,* Frankenstein, *1931.*

Jane Austen

small number of people. She wrote in one of her letters that 'Three or four families in a country village is the very Thing to work on.' She does not write about the Napoleonic Wars or the social and political issues and crises of her age, but her observations of people apply to human nature in general. She gives her main characters choices and then shows how and why they make the choices. In *Sense and Sensibility* (1811) she contrasts two sisters: Elinor who is rational and self-controlled (sense), and Marianne who is more emotional (sensibility), in a novel which is also a contrast between the Romantic and Augustan ages. In *Northanger Abbey* (her first novel to be written but not published until 1818, the same year as Mary Shelley's *Frankenstein*) Jane Austen satirizes the plots of the Gothic novel; in *Pride and Prejudice* (1813), *Emma* (1816) and

Mansfield Park (1814), she shows that it is important to know oneself in order to make the right choices in love and marriage. Although her endings are generally happy, her novels make readers feel that they have been made to think about themselves and their moral lives. For example, in *Pride and Prejudice*, Elizabeth Bennet, the central character, dislikes Mr Darcy, the wealthy man 'in want of a wife' [in want of = needing]; she is prejudice, while he is pride. But during the novel the characters learn about themselves and, in reaching self-awareness, they realize what they want from life, and the novel reaches its happy ending with their marriage.

Sir Walter Scott writes about revolution, history and social change, and about characters from all levels of society. Most of his early novels from *Waverley* (1814) to *The Bride of Lammermoor* (1819) are set in the past, but comment on the present because they show characters who are trying to understand changes in their world. Scott uses historical facts and characters, such as the rebellion in 1745, led by Bonnie Prince Charlie, against the English king in *Waverley* to recreate the issues of power, politics and change from a historical period and make them relevant to the great issues of his own time.

Scott made the novel the most popular of literary forms in the nineteenth and twentieth centuries. He created Scotland as a historical setting and gave the nineteenth-century world, especially nineteenth-century Great Britain, historical identity. He was universally read because, like Shakespeare, he explored values in a world of rapid changes, and created exciting plots and characters who live in the memory because they are both of their time and beyond their time. Sir Walter Scott was a very popular author and an influential writer across Europe. He was one of the first international best-selling authors. The popularity of Scott also encouraged other regional Scottish novelists, such as John Galt and James Hogg, and Edinburgh became a major publishing centre. James Hogg's psychological study *The Private Memoirs and Confessions of a Justified Sinner* [memoirs = written memories, justified = shown to be correct] (1824) continues a Romantic interest in the deeper mysteries of the human personality.

An illustration for Rob Roy *(1817), by Walter Scott.*

Although the Romantic period is best known for the work of the major Romantic poets, the period also saw the rapid growth of the novel. In a period of rapid social and political change the novel became more and more important as a detailed record and exploration of change. The growth of the novel in this period prepared the way for the even larger growth of the novel in the Victorian period.

The opening of the Great Exhibition at Crystal Palace in 1851.

6 The Victorian Period 1832–1900

Setting the Scene

Queen Victoria reigned from 1837 until 1901, but the Victorian Age is sometimes said to begin with the defeat of Napoleon in 1815. In literature the period starts with the death of Sir Walter Scott in 1832, and sometimes goes up to 1914.

When Victoria became queen the monarchy was not very popular. There were many social problems: members of the working class were severely punished if they wanted to join together in trade unions; the Corn Laws kept the price of bread high; the Chartist movement wanted votes for all and social reforms. During Victoria's reign the population grew from 2 million to 6.5 million and the cities grew bigger. Britain became the richest manufacturing country in the world. The Great Exhibition at Crystal Palace (built specially for the occasion) in London in 1851 became the high point of this worldwide success; the colonies and Empire were a huge market for Britain's products.

But in the 1850s several events began to end this success. The Crimean War (1854–6), Britain's first war for forty years, was not a success and it was the first war to be reported daily in the newspapers. In India, the Indian Mutiny of 1857 showed that all was not well in the colonies. In 1859 the beliefs of the age were questioned in the book *On the Origin of Species* by Charles Darwin, which showed that man was descended from apes.

Queen Victoria's husband, Prince Albert, died in 1861, and the queen was a widow for forty years. The prime minister for most of the second half of the century was either William Gladstone or Benjamin Disraeli. There were many protests against the monarchy, and a strong republican movement grew in the 1870s. Disraeli challenged this by building up the image of the queen and she became Empress of India. As the problems of Victorian society increased, she became more and more a symbol of Britain, just as Queen Elizabeth was in the late sixteenth century.

The move towards democracy, giving the vote to all men over twenty-one, continued after the first Reform Act of 1832 with another act in 1867 – but the slow process was not completed until women got the vote in 1928.

This was an age of extremes: the working classes were poor, and lived and worked in terrible circumstances; the middle classes grew rich and comfortable. There were double standards in this society. Many writers used their works to show that although on the surface this was a successful society, below the surface there were many problems.

Victorian Novels

In the Romantic period, poetry was the most important literary form. In the Victorian period, the novel became the most popular and important form; in Britain and all over the world.

This was partly because of the success of the novels of Sir Walter Scott. His great series of Waverley Novels, published between 1814 and 1832, became best-sellers all over the world. They created a fashion for the series novel, published in monthly parts. This fashion went on for most of the rest of the century. When the novels were later published in novel form, usually in three volumes, sometimes called triple-decker novels, readers borrowed them from libraries. Private commercial libraries became a very important influence on the reading public. They sometimes refused to lend a book, especially later in the century, because they did not like the subject matter. However, in the early years of the century the novels did not cause offence. They were often historical, in the tradition of Scott. Then, with the novels of Charles Dickens, a social concern with the problems of the society of the time enters the novel.

Charles Dickens wrote thirteen novels between *Sketches by Boz* (1836) and *The Mystery of Edwin Drood*, published in the year of his death, 1870. His first great success was *The Pickwick Papers* (1836–7). This follows the activities of a gentleman's club, very similar to the activities of Sir Roger de Coverley in Addison and Steele's writings for *The Spectator* a century before. But Dickens soon moves forward from this old-fashioned view of England. In *Oliver Twist* (1837–8) and *Nicholas Nickleby* (1838–9) he writes of the social problems of young boys like Oliver and Nicholas: Oliver's bad treatment in an institution for the poor and working for criminals; Nicholas's life in a Yorkshire school where he suffers terribly. The sufferings of children were a main theme of Dickens's writing. He wanted education for all children, and shows his readers the kind of problems children had in the cities, where poor people had no chance to share in the success of the nation. Dickens's novels often tell the stories of victims, and he made his readers aware of many of the problems of Victorian society.

Dickens went on to write novels which criticized society in a more general way. *David Copperfield* (1849–50) is his most positive novel about growing up. The hero, David, becomes the kind of success which the Victorians admired – he is rich, he marries, and a general sense of a happy ending is given. This novel was based in part on Dickens's own childhood and his success. But when he came to write another partly autobiographical story, *Great Expectations* (1860–1), there is a sense that the ending will not be so happy: there is a feeling of disappointment, that hopes will not be met, and that the earlier ideals have been false. Even the title is ironic – the expectations or hopes of Philip are certainly not great in the way they were for David in the earlier novel.

This irony marks a change of tone in all Dickens's writing during the 1850s. *Hard Times* (1854) is described as a novel 'for these times' and is a 'state of the nation' novel. It shows the worst sides of the new industrial society of the Midlands of England, with contrasts between the terrible education system of Mr Gradgrind, who wants only 'Facts. Teach these boys and girls nothing but facts' and the circus of Mr Sleary, which represents the imagination. Industry is contrasted with the freedom of the individual and the whole novel presents a very pessimistic picture of the nation. *Sybil* (1845), a novel by Benjamin Disraeli, later the prime minister, had described the country as two nations, the rich and the poor. *Hard Times* is the novel by Dickens which most clearly shows how the poor lived.

Charles Dickens

Many of Dickens's later novels continue this theme: *Little Dorrit* (1855–7) and *Our Mutual Friend* [friend in common] (1864–5) in particular show the author's dislike for London society and the people in it, and are very different from the light comedy of *The Pickwick Papers*. Dickens is also known for his historical novels like *A Tale of Two Cities* [tale = story] (1859), about the French Revolution, and for his Christmas stories, like *A Christmas Carol* [carol = song] (1843). These stories give the traditional picture of Victorian family values, and helped to create the image of Christmas as the most important family festival. They show the range of Dickens's writing: from comedy to social criticism, and from history to journalism. Dickens edited several very successful magazines, and published many of his novels and stories in them. He also performed scenes from his novels all over the world, turning the novel into a kind of theatre. His career is in many ways a mirror of the Victorian change from feeling optimistic, at the beginning of the queen's reign in 1837, to uncertainty and sadness thirty years later.

Dickens was a famous writer when he was alive and he is now one of the best-known and most widely read of English writers. People know his name as they know the name of Shakespeare. Like Shakespeare, the names of his characters have entered the English language. For example, Mr Micawber in *David Copperfield*, who always believed something would turn up (meaning something good would happen) has given us the word 'micawberish'.

The philosophy of the time was led by the writings of the Scotsman Thomas Carlyle. He wrote *On Heroes* (1841), *Past and Present* (1843) and *The French Revolution* (1837). Carlyle criticized, in particular, the 'laissez-faire' economy because it encouraged a situation in which payments of cash became the 'sole nexus between man and man' [sole nexus = only connection]. He believed that this situation could cause revolutions. He writes with sympathy about the industrial poor and the need for greater democracy, although in his later life that sympathy became weaker. The utilitarian philosophy of John Stuart Mill, aiming for 'the greatest good of the greatest number' was also very influential. But it was this philosophy that Dickens criticized most strongly in *Hard Times*.

The writings of Friedrich Engels and Karl Marx were also very important. Engels studied the life of the workers in Manchester and published the result in *The Condition of the Working Class in England* (1845). Marx's *Das Kapital*, published in 1867–95, was one of the most important texts of political theory of the century, criticizing the whole capitalist system. Marx lived and worked in Britain and believed that a worker's revolution would begin in Britain.

One of the most important authors encouraged by Dickens was Elizabeth Gaskell. She lived in Manchester, and had close knowledge of the lives of the working people there – the same lives as Engels had studied. Her novels are possibly the closest to the reality of the times: *Mary Barton* (1848) and *North and South* (1855) are particularly clear in their social concerns. Mrs Gaskell was also the biographer of Charlotte Brontë, one of the three sisters who all wrote novels.

Jane Eyre (1847) by Charlotte Brontë was immediately successful, and it is still one of the most famous novels about a woman. Jane starts as a poor child with no parents and goes through many sufferings until she meets Mr Rochester, who has locked his wife in a room because she is mad. The novel examines many sides of the circumstances of women, and Jane's words at the end, 'Reader, I married him' show a new move towards freedom and equality. Jane controls her own life and, through all her difficulties and problems, becomes more independent. This is a great difference from the role given to women such as Pamela or Clarissa in the novels of Samuel Richardson a century before.

Wuthering Heights (1847) by Emily Brontë is quite different – it is a novel of passion, an early psychological novel. The central characters, Cathy and Heathcliff, live out their passion in the windy, rough countryside of Yorkshire, and the landscape is as wild as their relationship. The novel is very original in the way it is written, moving backward and forward in time, and in and out of the minds of the characters. Again it presents a new view of women and their emotions. Here Cathy is telling her housekeeper Nellie Dean of her feelings for Heathcliff compared to her feelings for Edgar Linton whom she marries:

> My love for Linton is like the foliage[1] in the woods.[2]
> Time will change it, I'm well aware, as winter changes
> the trees. My love for Heathcliff resembles[3] the eternal
> rocks beneath – a source of little visible delight, but
> necessary. Nellie, I **am** Heathcliff – he's always, always
> in my mind . . . as my own being . . .

[1]leaves [2]small forest [3]is like

The youngest Brontë sister, Anne, wrote *The Tenant of Wildfell Hall* [tenant = occupier] (1848) also with an unusual central female character and involving complex relationships and problems. All three Brontë sisters faced these kinds of problems in the novel with unusual courage and directness, and together they changed the way the novel could present women characters: after the Brontës, female characters were more realistic, less idealized, and their struggles became the subject of a great many novels later in the nineteenth century.

Ever since Aphra Behn in the late seventeenth century there had been many women novelists. Possibly the greatest of them all was one who used a man's name – George Eliot. She was born Mary Ann Evans, and worked as a translator for many years before her companion, George Henry Lewes, encouraged her to write fiction. *Scenes of Clerical Life* [clerical life = church life] (1857–8) was a collection of three stories; this was followed by her first novel, *Adam Bede* in 1859. George Eliot was already writing about controversial women's themes, such as having a drunk husband, and being an unmarried mother. In her later novels she writes about the whole of society, especially in *Middlemarch* (1871–2), which

George Eliot

many people consider to be the greatest novel in the English language.

It is set in 1832, around the time of the first Reform Act, in the town of Middlemarch, a fictional town in the centre of England. Its themes are immense: from the changes in the voting system to medicine; from the coming of rail transport to the roles of women. It considers the importance of the 'dead hand' of the past, which comes into many complex novel plots in the nineteenth century, and it ends with the heroine Dorothea finding her own independence and happiness. She is not, however, a traditional heroine:

> The effect of her being on those around her was incalculably diffusive:[1] for the growing good of the world is partly dependent on unhistoric acts;[2] and that things are not so ill[3] with you and me as they might have been, is half owing to the number who lived faithfully a hidden life, and rest in unvisited tombs.[4]

[1] wide-ranging in so many ways that it was impossible to calculate
[2] ordinary deeds which will not be remembered [3] bad [4] graves

George Eliot's writing included poems and essays, as well as her novels. Her philosophy of life is sometimes called Positivism, as she saw humanity as continuing to move forward, although progress was always very slow. In her positive views, George Eliot went against some of the pessimistic moods which came into English writing in the later part of the Victorian age.

William Makepeace Thackeray and Anthony Trollope are two other important names in the history of the Victorian novel. They are quite different, however. Thackeray was born in India, the first major writer to be born in the colonies. Like Dickens he wrote for magazines, and was known as a comic writer, before he began writing his more serious novels. *Vanity Fair* (1847–8) is one of the best-known novels of its time. It is a view of all of society around the time of the Battle of Waterloo in 1815. So it is a historical novel, but also a comedy, describing the society of upper-class London with great irony and wit. The heroine, Becky Sharp, has no money, but still manages to make a great impression on high society. It questions many of the values of Victorian society, and this is something Thackeray continued to do in several other novels. He used a historical setting in *Henry Esmond* (1852) and a colonial setting in the novel which continues the story, *The Virginians* (1857–9); he followed the career of Arthur Pendennis in *Pendennis* (1848–50) and *The Newcomes* (1853–5).

The last lines of *Vanity Fair* are as follows:

> Ah! Vanitas Vanitatum![1] Which of us is happy in this world? Which of us has his desire? or, having it, is satisfied? – Come, children, let us shut up the box and the puppets,[2] for our play is played out.[3]

[1] (Latin) the most worthless thing   [2] things looking like people, which children play with   [3] finished

Thackeray here speaks to the reader directly, seeing the novelist as someone who decides what will happen to his characters but who knows he can never bring real happiness to them. Trollope used the idea of linked novels to an even greater extent: his two series of novels are known as The Barsetshire Chronicles (six novels, 1855–67) and the Palliser Novels (six novels, 1864–80). In the first series Trollope creates an entire town, Barchester, extending Jane Austen's idea of 'three or four families in a village'. There is a wide range of characters and opinions, giving a complete picture of the society and its concerns, especially its religious concerns, at a time when religious belief across the nation was in crisis. The Palliser Novels are set in the world of politics, and again create a complete society, in which many of the problems and questions of the time are discussed. Trollope wrote more than fifty novels, writing about Ireland and the kind of corruption and evil which Dickens also showed in his later novels. *Orley Farm* (1862) and *The Way We Live Now* (1875) are among the best known of Trollope's novels.

The detective story was another genre of the novel which became popular. At first they were called Novels of Sensation. They take the old-fashioned Gothic novel on to a new level of mystery – and a solution is almost always found. The first such novel was *The Woman in White* by Wilkie Collins, published in 1860. *The*

The Palliser Novels by Anthony Trollope are set in the world of politics and aristocratic society.

Moonstone (1868), also by Collins, is the first real classic of the genre, with a complex plot about a stolen diamond. The most famous fictional detective is, of course, Sherlock Holmes. He was the main character in a long series of stories by Arthur Conan Doyle, starting with *A Study in Scarlet* [scarlet = red] in 1887.

As the century proceeded, there were many problems, in society, religion and politics. The publication of Charles Darwin's *On the Origin of Species* in 1859 caused a great crisis of faith. This was reflected in many writings of the time. Perhaps Thomas Hardy is the novelist who best reflects the problems of the last years of the nineteenth century. Many of his novels caused offence, and they were even burned in public, and not bought by the private libraries.

The tone of Hardy's novels is tragic. His novels show a part of the movement of the century: from the light comic tone of early Dickens, through the sadness and anger of his later novels; through the social concerns of Gaskell, Eliot and Trollope; to the tragic vision of Hardy's own writings. Most of Hardy's writing is set in the fictional area of Wessex, in the south-west of England. He shows the older truths of the country and the conflict between the traditional and the modern in the move from country to city. His characters are often victims of destiny, who cannot save themselves from their tragic end. *Far from the Madding Crowd* [madding = rushing in a crazy way] (1874) uses for its title a line from Gray's *Elegy Written in a Country Churchyard*, and shares with it the concern with ordinary people's lives and struggles. Hardy's major novels include: *The Return of the Native* (1878), *The Mayor of Casterbridge* (1886), *Tess of the D'Urbervilles* (1891) and *Jude the Obscure* (1895).

Hardy's novels are all concerned with characters who try to go beyond their own limits: Henchard, the mayor of Casterbridge, rises and falls, becoming a tragic figure as he loses all his success; Tess, 'a pure woman' according to the subtitle of the novel, is punished by society after her baby dies. The father of the child, Alec, leaves her, and her new husband, Angel Clare, also leaves her when he hears about her past. Eventually she kills Alec, and is punished for her crime. Hardy describes this ironically by referring to a Greek tragedy:

> 'Justice' was done, and the President of the Immortals
> in Aeschylean phrase [1] had ended his sport with Tess.

[1] King of the Gods, as described by (the Greek dramatist) Aeschylus

Jude's crime, in the novel *Jude the Obscure*, is to have the ambition to go to study at Christminster, the university town he can see in the distance from his village and which is Hardy's name for Oxford. But his complex relationships with Sue Bridehead, and their children, as well as his working-class background, prevent him. Love, sexual attraction, the institution of marriage (Jude marries Arabella Donn, but not Sue) and the struggle between ambition and human weakness, make this Hardy's most deep and disturbing novel. All these novels are tragedies. They are about a successful society which keeps out the outsiders, like women, ambitious working-class men and others who do not belong.

After the suicide of their children, Sue and Jude talk of destiny, and he remembers a similar scene in a Greek tragedy:

> Again Sue looked at the hanging little frock,[1] and at the socks and shoes; and her figure quivered[2] like a string. 'I am a pitiable[3] creature,' she said, good neither for earth nor heaven any more! I am driven out of my mind[4] by things! What ought to be done?' She stared at Jude, and tightly held his hand.
>
> 'Nothing to be done,' he replied. 'Things are as they are, and will be brought to their desired issue.'
>
> She paused. 'Yes! Who said that?' she asked heavily.
>
> 'It comes in the chorus of the *Agamemnon*.[5] It has been in my mind continually.'
>
> 'My poor Jude – how you've missed everything! – you more than I, for I did get[6] you! To think you should know that by your unassisted[7] reading, and yet be in poverty and despair!'

[1] dress   [2] shook; moved backward and forward   [3] deserving pity
[4] made crazy   [5] a Greek drama   [6] win (as a husband)
[7] without help

Victorian Poetry

The last of the Romantic poets was also one of the first – William Wordsworth, who lived on until 1850. By the time he died, a new tone had entered English poetry. The major figures in Victorian poetry had made their reputations some time before the death of the last Romantic poet.

Alfred Tennyson, later Lord Tennyson, began his career in 1830, with the publication of *Poems, Chiefly Lyrical*. It is interesting that the title uses the word lyrical, which was also used by Wordsworth and Coleridge in their *Lyrical Ballads* of 1798. But, despite this close connection, the tone of Tennyson's poetry was quite different from the poetry of the Romantics. For Tennyson nature is not simply the object of beauty:

> Nature red in tooth and claw[1]

[1] sharp nail on the foot of an animal

shows a more realistic vision of nature, stressing its cruelty more than its effect on the senses and the memory. Tennyson is best known for *In Memoriam A.H.H.*, an elegy to a friend, Arthur Hallam, who died young. Written between 1833 and 1850, its tone of regret and loss reached a very wide audience in the second half of the century. When Queen Victoria became a widow on the death of her husband, Albert, in 1861 *In Memoriam* became her favourite text, and Tennyson became the nation's favourite poet. He is usually considered to be a poet of sadness and loss, but his poetry shows a wide range of subject matter and not all his poems have a tone of unhappiness. In the 1830s he wrote a lot in the dramatic monologue form. This form uses a speaking voice which shows his or her thoughts, and a full idea of the character comes out from the words. Tennyson's speakers in his dramatic monologues include Ulysses, the hero of Homer's *Odyssey*, who speaks in old age about the need to go on and find new ambitions:

> 'Tis[1] not too late to seek a newer world
> ('Ulysses')

[1] It is

Tennyson became the national poet and when something historic, like the Crimean War, happened it was Tennyson who wrote about it, in for example 'The Charge of the Light Brigade' [brigade = a group of soldiers] (published in 1855). This became famous for its praise of the heroes, as well as for its acceptance of the role of the soldiers who died:

> Theirs not to reason why
> Theirs but to do or die.

In his later years, Tennyson's poetry continued its lyrical sadness, and he wrote many poems on the legends of King Arthur and the Knights of the Round Table, known as *The Idylls of the King* [idylls = poems]. He had begun working on these poems in the 1830s, and returned to the subject in the 1850s, going on to publish several parts, until the twelve poems were published together in 1891. The parts published in 1859 and 1869 were the best-selling books of their day, one of them selling 10,000 copies in six weeks. The poems combine history, dramatic effect and the kind of sadness which Tennyson was famous for. They use Arthur as a symbol of the nation, just at the time when people were questioning all their values, and all belief was in doubt:

> For now I see the true old times are dead,
> When every morning brought a noble chance
> And every chance brought out a noble knight.

Times had changed, and Tennyson is the poet who followed that change through the Victorian age.

The master of the dramatic monologue form in the Victorian age was the other major poet of the period, Robert Browning. 'My Last Duchess' [duchess = noble lady] is one of the most famous of all such poems. It appeared in 1842, in a volume called *Dramatic Lyrics* – repeating the use of the word lyric again. Many of Browning's dramatic monologues contain moments of violence, of hidden emotions under the surface. They show many of the sides of Victorian society and behaviour which were normally not seen. In 'Porphyria's Lover' a man speaks about the woman he loves, who is sitting on his knee – he has just killed her. In 'Bishop Blougram's Apology' a man of the church shows many of the secret desires and actions of his life, just before he dies. In 'Andrea del Sarto' a Renaissance Italian painter speaks about his art, and his ambitions:

> Ah, but a man's reach should exceed his grasp,
> Or what's a heaven for?

The Charge of the Light Brigade, 1854.

Another painter, Fra Lippo Lippi, in his dramatic monologue, says:

> If you get a simple beauty and nought[1] else,
> You get about the best thing God invents.

[1] nothing

Browning became famous when he ran off with Elizabeth Barrett, who was also a poet. They went to live in Italy for many years. Elizabeth Barrett Browning was the best-known female poet of the century. Her *Sonnets from the Portuguese* (1850) are love poems to her husband, and her *Aurora Leigh* (1857) is a long poem on women's themes, sometimes considered a Victorian feminist text. Here is an example from *Sonnets from the Portuguese, No. 14*:

> If thou[1] must love me, let it be for nought[2]
> Except for love's sake only. Do not say
> 'I love her for her smile – her look – her way
> Of speaking gently, –'

[1]you   [2]nothing

Many of Robert Browning's poems are set in Italy, which he loved, including his long poem in twelve books, *The Ring and the Book* (1868–9). It tells a murder story from different points of view in a collection of dramatic monologues. *Dramatis Personae* (1864) is probably his best-known collection. In Britain, Browning's reputation was never as high as Tennyson's, perhaps because he lived in Italy. He wrote, in *The Ring and the Book*, about this:

> Well British public, ye[1] who like me not.

[1]you

But his poetry has always been enjoyed for its clever use of different voices to tell its stories, its constant love themes and its technical skill.

Matthew Arnold wrote 'Dover Beach' (1867) – a short poem (thirty-seven lines) about the crisis of belief of his times. He had written many other poems, including the epic 'Balder Dead' (1855), about the death of a Viking God, and 'The Scholar-Gipsy' [student traveller] (1853), a pastoral poem about the old University City of Oxford. But with 'Dover Beach' he caught the mood of the period in a way that has made it for many critics the most important single poem of the age. The poet looks over the English Channel from Dover, seeing the calm sea, but then thinking how the calm hides the struggles and changes which affect everyone. By the end he calls to his love:

> Ah, love, let us be true
> To one another! for the world . . .
> Hath[1] really neither joy, nor love, nor light,
> Nor certitude,[2] nor peace, nor help for pain.

[1]has   [2]certainty

'Dover Beach' is a vision of how pessimistic later Victorian writing (and indeed twentieth-century writing) became.

The poetry of Arthur Hugh Clough also reflects some of the feelings of doubt of the time. 'The Latest Decalogue' [decalogue = ten commandments] and 'There is no God' are witty reflections on the crisis of faith. His other works show Clough as a poet who experimented with form and language in many ways: 'Dipsychus' (1865) is perhaps his most important work.

One very popular poem of the middle of the century was *The Rubáiyát of Omar Khayyám* [rubáiyát = verses] by Edward Fitzgerald, published in 1859. It is a free translation from a Persian poem, and its popularity was due to its escapist note of pleasure and freedom, with a touch of sadness:

> Ah Love! could thou[1] and I with Fate[2] conspire[3]
> To grasp this sorry Scheme of Things entire
> Would not we shatter[4] it to bits – and then
> Re-mould it[5] nearer to the Heart's Desire.

[1]you [2]destiny [3]agree [4]break [5]form it again

The problems of the working people were expressed in some of the poetry of the Victorian age. Ebenezer Elliott was called the Corn Law Rhymer after the Corn Laws which kept the price of bread high, so that poor people could not eat. His famous line 'Poor men pay for all' comes from one of the popular ballads in *Corn Law Rhymes* of 1830. Thomas Hood's 'The Song of the Shirt' (1843) became very popular. It is a protest by a woman who works all day sewing shirts:

> It is not linen[1] you're wearing out
> But human creatures'[2] lives.

[1]kind of strong cloth [2]men's (or women's)

The voice of protest was not so much found in poetry as in the novels of Elizabeth Gaskell, Charles Dickens and others. But James Thomson's 'The City of Dreadful Night' [dreadful = fearful] (1874) is a later vision of 'dead Faith, dead Love, dead Hope', which shows

An illustration for The Rubáiyát of Omar Khayyám.

how much the Victorian mood moved to one of despair. It is a strong protest against the effects the city had upon people, as well as being a very personal vision of suffering.

Edward Lear's poetry was also popular but it was not serious in the same way. Lear became famous for his nonsense poems, often in a rhyming form called a limerick. *A Book of Nonsense* (1845)

A limerick and illustration by Edward Lear.

There was an Old Man of Port Grigor,
Whose actions were noted for vigour;
    He stood on his head,
    Till his waistcoat turned red,
That eclectic Old Man of Port Grigor.

was followed by many books of travel writings, then by three more volumes of nonsense in the 1870s. Lear's poems are still read and enjoyed by many readers.

The Pre-Raphaelite group of writers and artists used the idea of beauty to challenge the pessimistic mood of the times. Their paintings were full of beauty (sometimes they are called fleshly because so much of the human body was shown). But their enjoyment of the senses was important. Dante Gabriel Rossetti's sonnets were published in magazines such as *The Germ* [original idea] and *The Fortnightly Review* over many years, until he put together the volume *Poems* in 1870. His sister Christina falls into the mood of sadness, rather than enjoying the senses, but her wide range of poems, from love poems to texts for children, brought her work a wide audience. After Elizabeth Barrett Browning she is the most technically successful and popular woman poet of the Victorian age.

The poetry of Algernon Charles Swinburne follows Dante Gabriel Rossetti in some of its themes. He is a sensual poet: the balance between intellect and sensuality had been important in poetry since Keats. Towards the end of the nineteenth century the senses became more important and Swinburne is perhaps the poet who took sensuality in poetry to its highest levels. His *Poems and Ballads* was published in 1866, a second series in 1878 and a third in 1889. He, like Tennyson, wrote about the Arthurian legend, in *Tristram of Lyonesse* (1882). Also like Tennyson, his poetry is very musical, but Swinburne uses alliteration for his main effects, where Tennyson's music has a wider range of effect:

> Maiden,[1] and mistress[2] of the months and stars
> Now folded in the flowerless fields of heaven.
> (Atalanta in Calydon)

[1]young woman [2]lady

In the 1890s, the poet who perhaps best expresses the passing nature of all things is Ernest Dowson: 'They are not long, the weeping and the laughter' expresses the general feeling of the sadness of the age, as the century was ending.

Victorian Essays

Most writers of the Victorian period wrote for newspapers and magazines. Dickens, Thackeray and others also edited some of these magazines. Dickens encouraged authors like Elizabeth Gaskell to write for his magazines, and her writings were published in *Household Words* [familiar words] and *All the Year Round* in the 1850s. The tradition continues today as writers and journalists write in newspapers and magazines about the issues of the present.

The best-known essayist of the 1820s was Charles Lamb. His *Essays of Elia* were written for the *London Magazine* and published in book form in 1823. Another series was published in 1833. Lamb's essays gave him a very high reputation, but he was more a social observer than a critic, carrying on the tradition of Addison and Steele, rather than the critical tradition of Doctor Johnson in the previous century. William Hazlitt and Leigh Hunt are more serious critics of literature and society. Hazlitt's *Spirit of*

GOBLIN MARKET
and other poems
by Chriſtina Roſſetti

"Golden head by golden head"

London and Cambridge
Macmillan and Co. 1862

The title-page for Goblin Market, *by Christina Rossetti. The illustration is
by her brother, Dante Gabriel Rossetti.*

the Age (1825) was an important book, and his essays on writers,
such as *English Comic Writers*, and his *Political Essays* (both
1819) had many readers. Hazlitt was a critic who described rather
than analysed his subjects, but he was an important figure in the
literature of his time.

Leigh Hunt helped Keats, Tennyson and Charles Lamb to have their early work published, and in his essays wanted to support writers and their work. He wrote for many magazines, from 1808 until the 1850s. The most important of his essays were published in the magazines *The Companion* and *The Tatler* between 1828 and 1832. The best-known collection is *Men, Women and Books*, which appeared in 1847. With Lamb and Hazlitt, Leigh Hunt opened the way for much Victorian critical writing. Literature was, for all these critics, a positive force for the good of society. This was criticism for pleasure rather than the more serious criticism which later came from writers like Thomas Carlyle (see p. 129) and Matthew Arnold.

Matthew Arnold was both a poet and a critic. For many years his criticism was considered more important than his poetry, but now perhaps they are equally highly regarded. *Culture and Anarchy* (1869) and the two volumes of *Essays in Criticism* (1865 and 1888) are important because they helped to form the taste of generations of readers. For Arnold, culture was 'sweetness and light' and was an important defence against anarchy or the breakdown of society: he believed that culture is all that is best in civilization, and this idea remained an important one for many years. Here are his definitions of criticism and culture:

> Criticism: a disinterested endeavour[1] to learn and propagate[2] the best that is known and thought in the world.
> Culture: the acquainting ourselves with[3] the best that has been known and said in the world, and thus[4] with the history of the human spirit.

[1]attempt without prejudice [2]spread [3]learning [4]therefore

The artistic criticism of John Ruskin and the writings of Walter Pater had a great influence on the aesthetic movement of the final years of the century. Ruskin was the first real art critic in Britain, and his *Modern Painters* (five volumes, 1843, 1846, 1856, 1856 and 1860) changed the way the Victorians saw and understood art. *The Stones of Venice* (1851–3) helped people to rediscover the art and architecture of the Italian Renaissance. *Unto this Last* [unto = to]

An illustration from The Stones of Venice, *by John Ruskin.*

(1860) attacked the scientific and selfish spirit of the times. In his many books, written over a period of more than fifty years, Ruskin helped the Victorians better to appreciate art – 'art for art's sake' became the phrase for the age.

Walter Pater has been called the father of aestheticism. His *Studies in the History of the Renaissance* (1873) continued Ruskin's work of art history and criticism. He was a writer of memorable lines and his *Studies* include a famous essay on Leonardo da Vinci's picture *Mona Lisa* where he described her as one 'who has learned the secrets of the grave'. His novel *Marius the Epicurean* (1885) and his essays were read by his students at Oxford where he was a teacher. Many writers, from Rossetti and Swinburne to Oscar Wilde, were influenced by Pater, and his belief in beauty became a central part of the aesthetic movement of the 1880s. However, this movement expressed itself more in terms of fashions and tastes than in writing – only one or two novels by Oscar Wilde and George Moore can be considered part of the movement.

There is a growing social sense in the essays of major writers as the Victorian age moves towards its close. The playwright and novelist Oscar Wilde wrote, for example, *The Soul of Man under*

Socialism in 1891. Even the title shows a very clear move away from the essays of literary appreciation which were popular in the 1820s and 1830s. The world was changing, and there was a much more serious tone in most of the essays and novels of the final years of the century than there had been before the Victorian age began.

The Irishman George Bernard Shaw was a theatre critic before he began writing plays himself in the 1890s – some of his essays were very important in introducing the plays of the Norwegian dramatist Henrik Ibsen to Britain, and in spreading new political ideas. *Fabian Essays in Socialism* (1889) was one of the most important of the books he edited and wrote essays for. Social issues could now be discussed, and Shaw used essays, journalism and plays to bring these issues to a wide audience.

1890s

Oscar Wilde is the most important writer in the final years of the nineteenth century. He became a figure of fashion, a dandy, in the 1880s, long before he became famous as a writer of stories and plays. His first stories, from 1885, include 'Lord Arthur Savile's Crime' and 'The Canterville Ghost'. He also wrote fables for children that show a concern with appearance and reality which is central to all his writings. *The Happy Prince and Other Stories* (1888) was followed by Wilde's only novel, *The Picture of Dorian Gray* (1891). The theme of appearance/reality here reaches its highest point. Dorian Gray's picture grows older while he remains as young as ever, whatever he does. The novel leaves Dorian's bad actions to the reader's imagination, but the book still caused a great scandal. Its preface contains many of the paradoxes and deliberately controversial statements for which Wilde was famous:

> There is no such thing as a moral or immoral book.
> Books are well written or badly written, that is all.
> All art is quite useless.

Wilde's great period of success began with the first of four comic plays, *Lady Windermere's Fan* in 1892. Again appearance and reality

late 1300s	**The Alliterative Revival** Texts such as *Piers Plowman*, *Sir Gawain and the Green Knight* and *Winner and Waster* copied the alliteration features in Old and Middle English works from the years 600 to 1200 (see PP/GG/WW in the titles).	
c. 1500	**The Scottish Chaucerians** Scottish poets who showed the influence of Chaucer.	Henryson • Dunbar
late 1500s	**The University Wits** The plays and pamphlets of this group showed their education; the name was given in the nineteenth century in contrast to Shakespeare, who had not been to university.	Greene • Nashe Lyly • Marlowe
1600–50	**The Metaphysical Poets** These poets' works were criticized for difficulty and for lack of feeling. Johnson, in 1777, used the word metaphysical to describe their complex poems. T. S. Eliot's 1921 essay 'The Metaphysical Poets' helped return their works to favour.	Donne Herbert Marvell
late 1600s –*c.* 1750	**The Augustans** These authors hoped to write in the formal and classical style of the best writers in Latin, who produced their works when Caesar Augustus ruled Rome (27 BC–AD 14).	Dryden Pope
1764– *c.* 1810	**The Gothic Novel** The name comes from the decorated style of medieval buildings and ruins; Walpole used the subtitle 'A Gothic Story' for his novel *The Castle of Otranto* (1764). His followers used similar features of sensation and horror.	Walpole Lewis Radcliffe
1780s– 1830s	**The Romantic Movement** Romantic poets wrote – often with regret – about disappearing nature and changing social conditions, rejecting earlier Augustan ideas. The title Romantic was given by late-Victorian critics, although the movement in Britain was not the same as German or French Romanticism.	Blake • Wordsworth Coleridge • Keats Shelley • Byron
1830s– *c.* 1900	**The Social Novel** Social novels also concentrated on changes in society; examining, in particular, relationships and issues of class.	Dickens • Gaskell Gissing • Eliot
1848–60s	**The Pre-Raphaelite Brotherhood** Writers and artists who wanted to represent nature with the simplicity of pre-Renaissance times. (Raphael was an Italian artist active at the beginning of the sixteenth century.)	D. G. Rossetti
1880s–90s	**The Aesthetic Movement** The critics Ruskin and Pater formed a bridge from the Pre-Raphaelites to Aestheticism; the movement claimed that Art brought Truth and Beauty into dull daily life.	Ruskin • Pater Wilde • Dowson
1930s	**The Thirties Poets** These poets are often grouped together because of their focus on realism. Like the Georgians and the Imagists of the period between 1910 and 1922, they often had little in common with each other.	Auden • Spender Day-Lewis
1946–57	**The Movement** A group of writers seen as sharing anti-romantic lower-middle-class values, in both poetry and the novel.	Larkin • K. Amis
1956-65	**The Angry Young Men** Playwrights and novelists introduced a feeling of bitterness and political discontent. Another movement at the same time was kitchen-sink drama where realistic plays were set in lower-class homes rather than in the drawing rooms of rich people.	Osborne • Wesker C. Wilson
1990s	**The New Generation Poets** Young poets who have achieved success, and whose works have been promoted as a movement.	Armitage • Maxwell Duffy

are questioned, as the past of the main female character is discovered, although the whole play is highly comic. In 1895 Wilde's masterpiece *The Importance of Being Earnest* [earnest = serious] was performed. It remains the high point of English comedy after the Restoration. It is a complex story of social behaviour, and appearances: the main character, Jack (whose real name is Ernest – the title of the play also refers to him), turns out to have been lost as a child, and then found in a handbag. All ends happily, of course, but the prejudices and manners of Victorian society are shown to be very strongly fixed. One of the characters speaks in the play of 'the shallow mask of manners'. This is one of Wilde's main interests; in an essay entitled *The Truth of Masks* (1891) he again looks at this theme of real and hidden identity, something which he experienced in his own life. While *The Importance of Being Earnest* was being performed in London, Wilde was arrested and later charged with homosexual offences. Although he had the chance to escape he stayed in England and was sent to prison for two years. His later poem about this experience, *The Ballad of Reading Gaol* [gaol = jail], published in 1898, comments on his suffering.

A homosexual novel, *Teleny*, published privately in 1893, has often been linked with Wilde's name. Although it was published anonymously, it remains very important, as it is the first gay novel to show a positive sense of homosexual love; a love one could die for if necessary. Wilde's conviction two years later meant that any such themes were kept out of English writing for years.

Another important decadent novel was *Mike Fletcher* (1889) by George Moore. (The word decadent here means that the novel explores feelings and ideas which were considered improper by society as a whole.) The hero, described as Bohemian, is an artist – he is almost the only character who actually lives the idea of 'art for art's sake'. Moore's most famous novel was *Esther Waters* (1894). It is a realistic novel about a servant girl, quite similar in some ways to Hardy's *Tess of the D'Urbervilles*. It was equally controversial because of its 'scandalous' heroine. The novels of George Gissing were also very naturalistic, but were not well regarded. *The Nether World* [nether = lower] (1889) looks at the life of the poor in the city, and *New Grub Street* (1891), his most famous work, tells the story of a writer who is trying hard to be

BASIL HALLWARD
G '86

Dorian Gray's picture grows older while he remains as young as ever. This picture appeared at the end of the 1945 film of Oscar Wilde's novel The Picture of Dorian Gray.

successful and to rise out of the poverty in which he lives. Gissing's realism was, however, too extreme for many late Victorian readers.

The Scottish novelist Robert Louis Stevenson is remembered for his novels of adventure, such as *Treasure Island* [island of riches] (1883), with the figure of the pirate [robber of ships] Long John Silver, and *Kidnapped* (1886). These books have become classic children's stories, are popular today and have been made into films. But he also wrote many other kinds of work, including the travel books *Travels with a Donkey in the Cevennes* [donkey = animal similar to a horse] (1879), set in France, and *The Amateur Emigrant* (1892–5), about journeys in America. Stevenson's best-known work is probably *The Strange History of Doctor Jekyll and Mister Hyde* (1886). In this story the respectable Doctor Jekyll becomes his opposite, the evil Mr Hyde – showing the double nature of man: good and evil. It is a horror story and a psychological novel at the same time. For many critics it is one of the best expressions of the Victorian compromise between appearance and reality. The same double-sided nature can be seen in Wilde's *The Picture of Dorian Gray*, and in an important earlier novel by the Scottish writer James Hogg, *The Private Memoirs and Confessions of a Justified Sinner*, published in 1824 (see p. 122).

Rudyard Kipling was the most important writer to come from the colony of India. His *Plain Tales from the Hills* (1888) and *The Jungle Book* (1894) made him famous. *The Jungle Book* and *The Second Jungle Book* (1895) tell how the child Mowgli was brought up in the jungle by animals and was taught that the jungle has its own rules and laws. The books are very popular today, especially with children, and have been made into a very popular film. But Kipling was mostly known as the poet of Empire. On the celebration of the sixtieth year of Queen Victoria's reign in 1897 he wrote a poem, 'Recessional' [going back], which came to be seen as one of the most imperialist and Victorian texts of all: its values were passing out of favour and it shows the last great moment of Victorianism, when Great Britain was perhaps still great. The times were changing, and the new century brought many further changes. Kipling became the first English writer to win the Nobel Prize for Literature (in 1907) but his nationalistic feelings became less and

Robert Louis Stevenson (seated, centre) lived with his family on the Pacific Island of Samoa until he died in 1894.

less popular, and his reputation declined for many years. He is now recognized as a very important short story writer, and one who was in fact sympathetic to the problems of the colonies. It was Kipling who wrote:

> Oh, East is East, and West is West, and never the twain [1]
>   shall meet.

[1] two

The British Empire had tried to make them meet and make them become part of one whole. But in the new century a new process started, as things began to fall to pieces.

Other Fiction

In the Victorian age, many writers wrote books for young readers. Ever since *Robinson Crusoe* and *Gulliver's Travels* in the eighteenth century, some books had been considered children's books, although they were originally written for adult readers. But now, as more young people, especially in the middle classes, could read, novels were written for them. Often these novels had a tone of instruction, and a moral, but sometimes they were simply enjoyable stories.

The Water Babies by Charles Kingsley (1863) is one of the most famous moral stories of the time. It was a favourite of Queen Victoria's and she read it to her grandchildren. It is about a chimney-sweep who falls into the bedroom of a little girl, Ellie. He runs away, falls into a river, and becomes, after a series of adventures, a clean, good child, ready to return to the clean middle-class life Ellie represents. (Kingsley also wrote one of the more important industrial novels, *Alton Locke* (1850).) Among the most famous 'school' novels is *Tom Brown's Schooldays* (1857) by Thomas Hughes. It is set in Rugby School, one of the best-known public schools. It made a great impression, and the public school way of behaving and thinking became a part of the English way of life for many years. *Coral Island* by R. M. Ballantyne (also published 1857) is an adventure story, about children on a desert island. Ballantyne went on to write more than eighty popular novels. For girl readers Anna Sewell's *Black Beauty* (1877) is a classic children's novel about a horse.

One of the books which has been popular with both children and adults is Lewis Carroll's *Alice's Adventures in Wonderland* (1865). Carroll, whose real name was Charles Lutwidge Dodgson, taught mathematics at Oxford University. He wrote the book for the daughter of a friend, the original Alice. *Through the Looking Glass* [looking glass = mirror] (1871) continues the strange story of Alice's adventures. Carroll plays with reality, language and logic in ways that are both comic and frightening. He is sometimes seen as one of the first modern writers, for example in this moment when Alice is told to keep running in order to stay in the same place:

Now, here, you see, it takes all the running you can do,
to stay in the same place. If you want to get somewhere
else, you must run at least twice as fast as that!

This kind of writing was sometimes called fantasy. Many other
kinds of fantasy writing are now popular, but in the nineteenth
century what is now known as science fiction was just beginning.
H. G. Wells wrote *The Time Machine* in 1895, and in the next few
years followed it with such novels as *The Invisible Man* [invisible
= cannot be seen] (1897), *The War of the Worlds* (1898) and *The
First Men in the Moon* (1901). Wells continued writing far into the
twentieth century.

Another kind of fantasy is found in *Erewhon* by Samuel Butler,
published in 1872. The book is more a satire, like *Gulliver's
Travels*. The title is almost the word 'nowhere' backwards, and the
characters also have backwards names, like Yram (Mary) and Mr
Nosnibor (Robinson). The novel is based on work the author had
done on Charles Darwin, and is one of the most unusual

An illustration for Alice's
Adventures in Wonderland,
by Lewis Carroll.

observations of what was wrong with Victorian society. *Erewhon Revisited* (1901) continues the story, and the satire.

News from Nowhere by William Morris (1891) is about another kind of nowhere. This is a utopia, or perfect place, where society is as perfect as it can be. Morris was a socialist, and all his writings have a political intention, even when they are fantasies. In his ideal world many of the main features of the Victorian age no longer exist: money, industrialism and central government among them.

Drama

In the early years of the Victorian period, drama was not considered part of serious literature. Melodramas and farces were the main types of play produced until, in the 1850s, Tom Robertson began to write 'cup and saucer' dramas. These, as the name suggests, brought some realism into the presentation, the acting and the themes of the drama. Robertson's plays have titles like *Society*, *Caste* [caste = class], *Play* and *School*, all performed between 1865 and 1870.

More realism came into drama with the plays of George Bernard Shaw in the 1890s. He was a strong admirer of the plays of Ibsen, and in his own plays discussed themes which were politically and socially controversial. *Widowers' Houses* (produced 1892) was about greedy landlords, *Arms and the Man* [arms = weapons] (1894) about war and heroism, and *Mrs Warren's Profession* (published 1898) about prostitution. Shaw always wrote a preface to the published version of his plays, making them into documents for discussion and argument. He continued to write all through the first half of the twentieth century.

Although Oscar Wilde was the most successful playwright of the 1890s, the plays of Sir Arthur Wing Pinero were also very popular. He wrote comedies like *The Magistrate* (1885), but it was *The Second Mrs Tanqueray* (1893) which showed his social concern. Like the novels of Hardy and George Moore, and like Wilde's *Lady Windermere's Fan*, this play examines the double standards of the time, especially in relation to a woman's past and her possibly scandalous behaviour.

The end of the century looked back at the Victorian age, and did not particularly like what it saw: compromise, double standards, the bad treatment of the poor, very slow progress towards democracy, problems in the colonies. The past did not look happy – but the future was not particularly promising either.

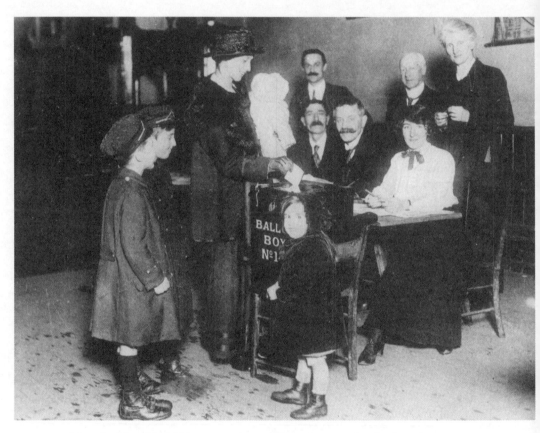

After the First World War women were allowed to vote for the first time.

7 The Twentieth Century to 1939

Setting the Scene

In 1900 the economy of Britain had become mostly industrial and in 1911 nearly 70 per cent of the 25 million people in the country lived in cities. A village way of life had almost disappeared.

In 1900 the British Empire had grown to include many parts of the world. However, the Boer War in South Africa was not a successful war for the British. Colonies throughout the world began to rebel and British control of other countries began to disappear.

These were years of change. The First World War (1914–18) changed for many people their view of the world. Millions of men, including very young soldiers, were killed. The loss of so many lives was a horror the country had not experienced before, and for many people there seemed to be no purpose to the war. Basic religious and political beliefs were questioned by more people. Communism grew in Russia, and fascism grew, especially in Germany and Italy. The rise of fascism in Germany happened at the same time as Germany became a very powerful nation and fascist beliefs were a main cause of the Second World War (1939–45). Also, workers in large industries became more interested in socialism and joined trades unions. The British Labour party grew; women were allowed to vote for the first time in 1928.

In the arts, one clear change was that artists felt they had to express their ideas very differently in new forms, which were difficult for everyone to understand. On the other hand, some artists felt a duty to communicate simply and in popular forms to a wider and better educated audience.

The Novel 1900–39

The novel of the Victorian period had social themes. The novel of the twentieth century has more personal, individual themes. But at the same time as the novel examines the problems of the individual, it also becomes an examination of the whole world. England is no longer the main scene – many writers use the wider world, outside England, as their setting. Often England is seen in contrast with the other countries described.

Writers began to use different points of view, rather than seeing the world through only one character's eyes. The many points of view, the range of settings and quick moves from scene to scene all became part of modern writing. So too did a psychological approach. This approach meant going deeply into the thoughts of the characters. The stream of consciousness technique, named by the American psychologist William James, became an important part of novelists' techniques in the early twentieth century.

William James's brother Henry James, though born in America, became a British citizen later in his life. His novels move from America to Europe in a search for fixed cultural and social values. From his early novels in the 1870s and 1880s, such as *Roderick Hudson* and *Washington Square*, James moved on to write three of his masterpieces in England in the early years of the new century. These were *The Wings of the Dove* [dove = bird of peace] (1902), *The Ambassadors* (1903) and *The Golden Bowl* (1904). All three are international in their themes, contrasting the American culture and character with the European. Like most of James's writing, the language and the plot are very complex and very subtle. In James there is always a move from innocence to experience or awareness, and the heroine of *The Golden Bowl*, Maggie Verver, is a good example of this. At the end of the novel she marries an Italian whose name is Amerigo: the American girl and the European whose name means America create a new harmony. However, Maggie has doubts about Amerigo and his relationship with an old friend of hers, Charlotte Stant. The bowl of the title is not really solid gold. It is also cracked inside, under the gold surface. It is symbolic of the perfection which can never be completely perfect.

Joseph Conrad, like James, was not born in England, but in the Ukraine, of Polish parents. He became a British subject in 1886. He travelled the world as a sailor, and this gave him ideas for many of his works. *Lord Jim* (1900) and *Nostromo* (1904) are two of his most typical novels. They are both novels of the sea, and they explore the dangers, the questions of honour and the moral conflicts of man's struggles at sea. *Nostromo* is about weakness and corruption, in which the characters go through a voyage of self-discovery. The novel is set in an imaginary country in South America, during a revolution, and its main character, Nostromo, becomes obsessed by silver. This eventually destroys his relationships with others and makes him lose his moral responsibilities. In *Lord Jim*, the hero dies at the end, but he has reached honour, even after making the terrible mistake of leaving his ship because of fear.

Joseph Conrad

One of Conrad's most famous works is the short novel *Heart of Darkness* (1902), which goes deep into Africa to explore the mysteries of human behaviour. A central character is Mister Kurtz, a successful colonial trader in Africa who has a mysterious power over the local people. Kurtz lives and works in the very centre of Africa and the journey to find him is 'like travelling back to the earliest beginnings of the world'. The words of Mister Kurtz, at the moment of his death, have become a kind of refrain for the twentieth century, especially after T. S Eliot used them to preface his poem *The Hollow Men* in 1925. His words may be words of fear, of wisdom or of simple understanding, but they also echo through the years: 'The horror! The horror!' Conrad's later novels, such as *Under Western Eyes* (1911), became more political in their themes. It was not until *Chance* (1913) that he had a popular success.

Both Henry James and Joseph Conrad were named as part of the Great Tradition by the critic F. R. Leavis in 1948, along with such earlier writers as Jane Austen and George Eliot. This judgement has been widely discussed as, for Leavis, one of the most important features of a novelist's work is moral authority. James and Conrad were certainly trying to define the moral codes of the new century.

E. M. Forster, although an Englishman of the middle class, was also an outsider: as a homosexual his view of society could show some of the conflicts, especially class conflicts, which were part of England at the turn of the century. *Howards End* (1910) shows the tensions between classes and values in an England which was soon to change; in *A Room with a View* (1908) Forster had already shown these tensions in the setting of English tourists in Italy. 'Only connect,' Forster had said in *Howards End*, and this need to communicate, to make connections, is in many ways also the theme of his final novel, *A Passage to India* (1924). Here the tensions are between the culture of East and West – the British colonial way of life and the local culture of India. The story of *A Passage to India* is centred on an Englishwoman, Adela, who has gone to India to marry a colonial official but who quickly makes friends with local Indian people. She believes she is sexually attacked by one of the Indian men in the Marabar Caves. She later changes her mind and no longer accuses the man but her action shows differences in beliefs and attitudes between the two cultures. Forster's homosexual novel *Maurice*, written in 1913, was not published until 1971, after the author's death. Although not at the level of his best work, this is again a novel which explores the conflicts within a society which cannot accept behaviour outside the accepted codes and manners.

D. H. Lawrence was the first important writer to come from the working class after the Education Act of 1870 brought education to all. His early works are about his own background: a mining family in the East Midlands, with a strong mother and a father he hardly knew. *Sons and Lovers* (1913) is an autobiographical novel as well as the best-known of his works with this setting, and is one of the most successful psychological novels of the century. Lawrence was always an outsider, first because of class, then later at the time of the First World War, because he was married to a German woman. After 1919 he spent most of his life outside England, travelling all

Victoria Street in Eastwood, the mining village where D. H. Lawrence was born in 1885.

over the world, and writing about many of the countries he visited, including Australia and Mexico.

His novels *The Rainbow* (1915) and *Women in Love* (1920) caused some scandal as their subjects were men's and women's roles in sexual relationships. For many years, Lawrence's reputation was as a writer on sexual themes, especially after *Lady Chatterley's Lover* (1928), which was banned in Britain until 1960. However, his themes are much wider than that. He examines all aspects of human relationships, as well as the relationship between man and nature, and between the spirit of man and the spirit of industrialism which can deny the true nature of humanity.

In these lines from *Women in Love*, Gerald, who wants to control everyone, including the miners in the coal mine he owns and the women with whom he has a relationship, is riding a horse. Gudrun Brangwen is both attracted to him and disgusted by him and his mechanical spirit:

> A sharpened look came on Gerald's face. He bit himself down on the mare[1] like a keen[2] edge biting home . . .
> She roared and as she breathed, her nostrils[3] were two wide, hot holes . . . Both man and horse were searing[4] with violence. Yet he seemed calm as a ray[5] of cold sunshine.
>   Meanwhile the eternal trucks were rumbling[6] on, very slowly, heading one after the other, one after the other, like a disgusting dream that has no end.

[1] female horse   [2] sharp   [3] the end of the nose
[4] burning   [5] a line of light   [6] moving easily

Lawrence produced a great many works: he wrote poetry, essays, plays, many short stories, travel writings and criticism. His interests include psychology, primitive religions and the nature of spiritual existence. Among his more important writings are *Psychoanalysis and the Unconscious* [psychoanalysis = method of analysing someone's mind] (1921), the plays *David* (1926) and *The Widowing of Mrs Holroyd* (1914), the novels *The Plumed Serpent* [feathered snake] (1926) and *Kangaroo* [Australian animal] (1923) and the volumes of poetry *Birds, Beasts and Flowers* [beasts = animals] (1923), *Pansies* [brightly coloured flowers] (1929) and *Look! We Have Come Through* (1917).

Lawrence was interested in the journey of the human soul to truth and knowledge through nature and through contact with the deepest forces of spirituality. For James Joyce and Virginia Woolf the journey was through the mind of their characters. The term stream of consciousness is connected with both these writers, but should not limit them. Both Joyce and Woolf are writers of great range; the technique of following a character's thoughts in a very free way is only one of many ways in which both writers go inside their characters' minds and feelings, to find the deeper inner truths.

James Joyce's first published work was a volume of poems called *Chamber Music* [music played with a small group of instruments] (1907). Like Lawrence he wrote in many genres, including drama. His play *Exiles* was staged and published in 1918. *Dubliners* (1914) is a collection of stories set in Dublin. It has become one of the best-known books of its time. Joyce analyses Dublin as a city which cannot change, and whose people are dying – the last story in the volume is called 'The Dead'. The same theme is found in *A Portrait of the Artist as a Young Man* [portrait = picture], published in 1914/1915. This is almost an autobiography, although the hero is called Stephen Dedalus. He wants to become a writer, like Joyce himself, and finally has to leave Ireland to find his true voice as an artist. He says, near the end of the novel:

> I will not serve that in which I no longer believe,
> whether it call itself my home, my fatherland or my
> church: and I will try to express myself in some mode[1]
> of life or art as freely as I can and as wholly as I can,
> using for my defence the only arms[2] I allow myself to
> use, silence, exile,[3] and cunning.[4]

[1]style   [2]weapons   [3]departure from your own country
[4]cleverness; intelligence

In 1922, the same year as T. S. Eliot's *The Waste Land*, James Joyce's *Ulysses* was published. It was published in Paris, and immediately caused great controversy – some people saw it as the most important novel of the century, but for others, including the British authorities, it was obscene, and was banned until 1936. The novel is about one day (16 June 1904) in Dublin, and one of the main characters is Stephen Dedalus again. Leopold and Molly Bloom are the other main figures in the novel, which follows the two men through a day, and ends with a stream of consciousness monologue by Molly, alone in her bed:

> What shall I wear shall I wear a white rose those cakes
> in Liptons I love the smell of a big rich shop at 7 1/2d a
> pound or the other ones with cherries in them of course
> a nice plant for the middle of the table I love flowers
> I'd love to have the whole place swimming in roses.

Molly's thoughts and feelings here flow in a stream of consciousness. There is no punctuation as thoughts and feelings move into one another.

Joyce also uses a wide range of references (as Eliot does in *The Waste Land*) as well as using the styles of many works of literature from the *Odyssey* of Homer, on which the structure of *Ulysses* is based, through Chaucer to the moderns. Joyce wanted to write the novel that was the climax of the traditions of English literature. And after *Ulysses* he went further. With *Finnegans Wake*, which was finally published in 1939, Joyce took language and the novel to new limits. It is a highly experimental novel and very surprising to read. The main theme is the Fall and Resurrection, told around Dublin settings. The novel uses dreams, play on words, invented words and jokes to make a unique text.

FURTHER DEVELOPMENTS

Virginia Woolf came from a literary family, and her home in Bloomsbury became the centre of literary interest among the intellectuals and artists of her time – the Bloomsbury Group was to last for many years from its beginnings in 1905–6, and was at its highest point in the 1920s.

Virginia Woolf's first novel was *The Voyage Out* (1915). It was followed by *Night and Day* (1919). Then, in the great literary year 1922, she published *Jacob's Room*. It was set during the First World War, and tells a story very close to the death of the author's own brother Thoby. It was the first of her novels to use the impressionistic techniques which were to make her famous. She wanted to leave realism, and move into a new kind of expression which would allow a more internal exploration of the events and emotions described. She continued this in her next novels, *Mrs Dalloway* (1925) and *To the Lighthouse* [building to guide ships] (1927). In *The Waves* (1931), which is her most experimental novel, Woolf shows six different characters, all at different points

Virginia Woolf (centre right) in 1908; sitting on her left is the poet, Rupert Brooke.

in their lives, and explores how they are each affected by the death of someone well known to all of them. *Orlando* (1928) is a very literary fantasy which takes its main character from the Elizabethan age to modern times, and through a change of sex, as he/she meets all sorts of literary and historic figures. It is in *Orlando* that Woolf uses the phrase 'time on the clock and time in the mind', which shows the concern of the early twentieth-century novelists with time, and the nature of memory, emotion and action.

Virginia Woolf uses stream of consciousness techniques, but she is also original in many other ways. She spoke out for women, particularly in *A Room of One's Own* (1929). She also published a lot of criticism, such as *The Common Reader* (two series, 1925 and 1932). Her final works *The Years* (1937) and *Between the Acts* (1941) continue her experiments, and prove her to be one of the most important and original novelists of the twentieth century. Virginia Woolf committed suicide in 1941.

Among the more traditional writers of the early part of the twentieth century, many had already begun writing towards the end of Queen Victoria's reign. Both Arnold Bennett and John Galsworthy published their first novels in 1898, and went on to write many more. Bennett wrote novels of provincial life, many of them set in Staffordshire in the Midlands where he was born. *Anna of the Five Towns* (1902) was the first of these novels, and it began a series of realistic novels including *The Old Wives' Tale* (1908) and *Clayhanger* (1910). Bennett then set *Riceyman Steps* (1923) in London, again describing the life of ordinary and obscure characters in very realistic detail. *Riceyman Steps* is the story of a second-hand bookseller who is very mean. Money, or lack of money, is often at the centre of Bennett's works. He wrote a great many works, including comic novels, and was the most popular and highest-paid journalist of his time. Virginia Woolf, in one of her essays, 'Mr Bennett and Mrs Brown' (1923), attacked Arnold Bennett's realism, and spoke for the kind of impressionist fiction she herself was writing.

John Galsworthy's novels describe a higher social class than most of Bennett's. His series of novels known as *The Forsyte Saga* (completed 1922) is similar to Trollope's novels in some ways. It follows the lives of a successful upper-middle-class family, the

Forsytes. Galsworthy intended the saga to be ironic, examining the greed of the family. There are three novels in the series, plus some short stories, beginning with *The Man of Property* (1906). Several more novels continuing the family's story were written later in the 1920s, but are not part of the saga. His other novels, and several plays, looked at the subject of poverty, the social problems of the lower classes, most notably in *The Island Pharisees* [pharisee = person with traditional views] (1904) and *Fraternity* (1909), which is an attack on the ways of city society. Galsworthy also wrote several plays on social themes, but it is the upper-middle-class family of the Forsytes for which he is remembered, rather than his more socially concerned works.

*

In Scotland several writers presented a strongly realistic picture of small town life. George Douglas Brown in *The House with the Green Shutters* [shutters = window covers] (1901) is similar to Thomas Hardy in his telling of his hero's tragedy. John Macdougall Hay's *Gillespie* (1914) is similarly concerned with evil and tragic destiny. Scottish writers often use the subject of destiny and moral awareness in their works. This reflects the different religious background, for Scottish Calvinism insists on a clear distinction between right and wrong, and Scottish writers use this in different ways; from the humanity of the poet Robert Burns to the psychological examination of character in the novels of Robert Louis Stevenson and the writers who came after him. Many of the themes of Scottish writing come together in the trilogy by Lewis Grassic Gibbon, *A Scots Quair* [book], published between 1932 and 1934. These novels follow the heroine, Chris Guthrie, through a hard life: three marriages, the death of one husband in the war and the depression of the 1920s, and give a very full picture of a part of Britain that is usually forgotten in fiction, the Mearns, in north-east Scotland.

The Northern Irish novelist Forrest Reid was the author of many novels, most of which look at childhood and the loss of innocence. He used classical Greek references in his search for a perfect world. His trilogy about Tom Barber goes backward, looking at the hero at the age of fifteen, then thirteen, then eleven. They are *Uncle*

Stephen (1931), *The Retreat* [the going back] (1936) and *Young Tom* (1944).

H. G. Wells was in no way a traditionalist. He had already become famous for his science fiction fantasies in the 1890s, and in the new century his range grew. He wrote several novels about working-class characters trying to improve their lives: *Love and Mr Lewisham* (1900) is about a teacher, *Kipps* (1905) is about a shop assistant, and *The History of Mr Polly* (1910) is about a shopkeeper who runs away from his responsibilities. *Ann Veronica* (1909) is a novel with feminist themes, but *Tono-Bungay* (also 1909) is perhaps the most interesting of Wells's early twentieth-century novels. It is a state of the nation novel, examining English society and its problems, in a different way and a different tone from E. M. Forster, and with a clearly political intention. Wells continued to write many more novels – he lived until 1946 – and was a very popular writer all his life, much more popular than Lawrence, Joyce and Woolf.

Popularity and intellectual success did not go together. The separation between intellectual, experimental writing and popular writing had never happened in the nineteenth century: Charles Dickens and George Eliot reached very wide audiences with most of their books. But after the First World War, critical fashions, set by the Bloomsbury Group among others, made a greater and greater distinction between high and low culture, and between serious and popular literature.

Popular literature could also be serious in some cases, such as the novels of Aldous Huxley and Evelyn Waugh in the 1920s and 1930s. Both wrote comic novels, about the young people of the Jazz Age and their attitudes to life. Their works show a new kind of satirical, upper-class humour, again probably a reaction to the shock of the First World War, and they deliberately challenge the serious intellectual attitudes of some of their readers. Huxley's *Crome Yellow* [crome = bright] (1921) was his first success, and *Antic Hay* [wild dance] (1923) continued this. Huxley is best remembered for his novel *Brave New World* (1932), with its vision of a society controlled by scientific progress.

Evelyn Waugh's first novel was also a great success. It was *Decline and Fall* (1928) and both it and *Vile Bodies* [vile = wicked]

(1930) described the social life of the 'bright young things' of London society. Waugh took on a more serious tone in *A Handful of Dust* (1934) – the title is taken from Eliot's *The Waste Land*. During and after the Second World War, Waugh became one of the more serious novelists of the time.

William Somerset Maugham was one of the most popular writers of his time. Well known for his short stories, and hugely successful as a playwright, he also wrote several novels. His first novel *Liza of Lambeth* was published in 1897. It is a realistic novel of London life, but Maugham's later novels have a wide range of settings. *Of Human Bondage* [bondage = lack of freedom] (1915) is almost autobiographical, like Lawrence's *Sons and Lovers* and Joyce's *A Portrait of the Artist as a Young Man* – a kind of novel that was very popular in this period. The novel describes the life of Philip Carey, beginning with his lonely boyhood in a seaside town in Kent, in southern England. Philip has a deformed foot and suffers in society as a result, perhaps in a similar way to Somerset Maugham who had a speech defect. *The Moon and Sixpence* (1919) is set in Tahiti; *Cakes and Ale* [ale = beer] (1930) is a comedy, and *The Razor's Edge* (1944) is set in India.

The novels of P. G. Wodehouse made comedy out of the relationship between Bertie Wooster and his butler, Jeeves, in a famous series of books starting with *The Man with Two Left Feet* (1917). Wooster is a vague, forgetful, very friendly and wealthy young man who enjoys the social life. Jeeves works for Wooster but really looks after him and helps him solve all kinds of problems. In lots of ways they depend on each other. In all, Wodehouse wrote over 120 books, between 1902 and his death in 1975.

The short stories of Saki (H. H. Munro), who was killed in the First World War, are also noted for their humour, but it is a cruel ironic humour, and his works have remained very popular, perhaps because of their new attitude to such things as family and good behaviour. His novel *The Unbearable Bassington* (1912) is almost a parody of Joseph Conrad in its ironic look at the British and their colonial ambitions.

A new technique came into the novel in the 1930s, when Christopher Isherwood used this distanced, objective, photographic

Bertie Wooster and his butler Jeeves, the famous comic characters created by P. G. Wodehouse.

kind of narration in his two novels about Berlin, *Mr Norris Changes Trains* (1935) and *Goodbye to Berlin* (1939). These novels give impressions of the Germany of the 1930s, during the rise of fascism. Isherwood, a close friend of the poet Auden, left Europe with Auden in 1939, and spent the rest of his life in America.

There were many kinds of popular novel: in the nineteenth century the adventure novel had become very successful. Writers like H. Rider Haggard and Anthony Hope took their readers to imaginary lands, either in the colonies, as in Haggard's *King Solomon's Mines* (1886) and *She* (1887), or in the invented country of Ruritania, as in Hope's *The Prisoner of Zenda* (1894). This fashion for adventure continued in the new century with the novels of John Buchan. *The Thirty-nine Steps* (1915) is his best-known work; *Prester John* (1910) follows Haggard in using an African setting. Buchan's novels of action were among the first examples of the spy novel, which became popular later in the century.

Graham Greene is one of the most important novelists of the century. Like Buchan he wrote 'shockers', adventure and spy stories, such as *Stamboul Train* (1932) and *The Confidential Agent* [agent with secrets] (1939). But he also wrote serious novels, often with a background of Catholic doubt. *Brighton Rock* (1938) is the best known of these; its hero, Pinkie, is a modern tragic hero, whose violence causes the novel's tragedy. *Brighton Rock* is set in Brighton, a town on the south coast of England. Pinkie, aged seventeen, wants to run a gang of criminals which will be the most powerful in the town. In order to have this ambition, Pinkie murders a journalist called Hale but then has to marry a sixteen-year-old girl, Rose, in order to stop her from telling everything in court. Both Pinkie and Rose are Roman Catholics. He is corrupt and she is innocent and the novel compares their states of mind. Pinkie continues to commit crime but is forced to his death by Ida, a friend of Hale.

*

There were several important women writers apart from Virginia Woolf. Katherine Mansfield was born in New Zealand but educated in London. She became well known after her three collections of short stories were published during her lifetime: *In a German Pension* [pension = small hotel] (1911), *Bliss and Other Stories* (1920) and *The Garden Party and Other Stories* (1922). Two more collections were published soon after her death in 1923. Her stories show she was an original and experimental writer; she wrote some very short, clear descriptions of character or place, as well as longer, more impressionistic stories of family life.

Dorothy Richardson used the stream of consciousness technique in her long series of novels called *Pilgrimage*, published between 1915 and 1938. Virginia Woolf said that Richardson invented 'the psychological sentence of the feminine gender' [gender = sex]; that is that she found a style which expressed the feelings and thoughts of women. May Sinclair was also very involved in women's issues. Her books include *The Three Sisters* (1914) and the stream of consciousness novel *Mary Olivier: a life* (1919). Rebecca West, for a long time the lover of H. G. Wells, wrote several novels which share some of the themes of Virginia Woolf's writing. *The Return of the Soldier* (1918), for example, tells of a soldier coming back from the war. *The Strange Necessity* (1928) and *The Thinking Reed* [reed = strong plant] (1936) continued the work of this early feminist. Rosamond Lehmann wrote several novels with sexual themes, including *Dusty Answer* (1927) and *A Note in Music* [note = musical tone] (1930). She handles female and male sexuality, including homosexuality, in clear and sympathetic ways, and was not afraid to write about difficult subjects such as abortion, as in *The Weather in the Streets* (1936).

Ivy Compton-Burnett wrote many novels all through the century, most of them with titles like *Brothers and Sisters* (1929), *A House and its Head* (1935) and *A Family and a Fortune* [fortune = large amount of money] (1939). Her subject was usually a family and its problems, and she uses dialogue in a particularly clear way to show the pain and suffering which lie under the usual ways of behaving. In this example of Compton-Burnett's dialogue, the tensions in the family become clear around the fire:

Sarah seemed not to hear.

'Are you deaf, Sarah? Oh, you evidently[1] are,' said Horace, speaking with contempt[2] for this infirmity.[3]

'What are you laughing at, Jasper?'

'If you call people deaf, you can't expect them to hear, and then you can't blame them for it.'

'Oh! That is a simple thing to be amused at. Do not stand in the centre of the fire, Tamasin. You are keeping the heat from other people.'

'If the fire is too large, that does not matter,' said Marcus.

Horace gave him a look and nodded to himself, as though confirmed[4] in his ideas.

'It's a nice fire now,' said Avery, 'but it need not be so big, if we all stay near it.'

'Perhaps there will be a rule that no one is to move away from it,' said Tamasin. 'It might save more in the end.'

'If you are not ashamed of what you have to say, Tamasin, say it so that we can hear.'

'I said it might be cheaper to have a smaller fire, and keep near to it, Father.'

Horace made no answer, as his heart had said the same thing.

'Coal would not cost very much,' said Jasper. 'Miners are not men who would earn a great deal.'[5]

'How much does it cost, Father?' said Tamasin.

Horace seemed not to hear.

'You have the most extraordinary ideas about money,' he said, 'I cannot think how you come by [6] them.'

(*Manservant and Maidservant* [male and female servant] 1947)

[1] clearly [2] lack of respect [3] weakness
[4] having received agreement [5] a lot [6] get

Novels about the First World War, apart from those by Rebecca West and Virginia Woolf, took their authors a long time to write. Richard Aldington's *Death of a Hero*, for example, was not published until 1929, more than ten years after the end of the war. Other writers used the experience to write autobiographical works. Robert Graves, the poet, published *Goodbye To All That* in 1929, and Siegfried Sassoon, also well known as a poet, told his story in a partly autobiographical trilogy between 1928 and 1936. The trilogy was published together in 1937 as *The Complete Memoirs of George Sherston* [memoirs = written memories]. All these works speak of life in the trenches during the war, and how the experience of war changed the characters, and the whole world they lived in.

Theatre and Drama

The Irishman George Bernard Shaw was the leading figure in English drama from the 1890s until his death in 1950. He was well known for his use of the theatre to discuss issues, from pacifism to Ireland, and from prostitution to language itself. His first popular success was a play about Ireland, *John Bull's Other Island* (1904). This was followed by many others, including *Man and Superman* [superman = new heroic man] (1905), *Major Barbara* (1905) and the famous works *Pygmalion* (1913) and *Saint Joan* (1923). Each of Shaw's plays were published with a preface, which added to the discussion of the issues in the play. He used the theatre for discussion, not only for entertainment. Shaw's *Pygmalion* is particularly well known because a film and a musical play, *My Fair Lady*, have been based on the original story. The play tells the story of Professor Henry Higgins who, for a bet, takes Eliza Doolittle, a flower-seller, and makes her into a lady. In particular, he helps her to change her accent so that she learns to speak properly and to use standard English. Eliza and Henry are contrasted in the play. Higgins wins his bet but is shown to be cold and heartless in his attitude to people and narrow-minded in his views of social improvement. Eliza behaves better than Higgins and is shown to be a real lady because she is warm-hearted and generous in her relations with people.

Although he was Irish, Shaw had little to do with the revival of Irish theatre in the early years of the century. This was led by the poet W. B. Yeats and Lady Augusta Gregory, and the Abbey Theatre in Dublin was the centre of the action. John Millington Synge and Sean O'Casey were the main playwrights of the moment, and they used Irish regional language and settings in their plays. Synge's *Riders to the Sea* (1904) is a one-act tragedy of a family which loses all its men at sea. *The Playboy of the Western World* [playboy = pleasure-seeker] (1907) is a comedy about a young man's arrival in a peasant village. O'Casey's plays are set in Dublin, and have a strong political content. *The Shadow of a Gunman* (1923) is about a terrorist and the personal relationships he has. *Juno and the Paycock* (1924) is about a Dublin family and the violence of the troubles Ireland was living through at the time. O'Casey's plays are tragicomedies, showing the Irish character

George Bernard Shaw with Sybil Thorndike, the first actress to play Saint Joan.

with sympathy and humour in a time of trouble, but his plays caused great offence, and he left Ireland in 1926 to spend the rest of his life in England.

   In addition to successful novels, Somerset Maugham was one of the most successful playwrights of his time – at one point he had four plays on in London at the same time. His plays, however, have not lasted well. They are social comedies, like *The Circle* (1921) and *The Constant Wife* (1926). The plays of Noël Coward have lasted better, perhaps because their themes are more relevant and their wit sharper. *The Vortex* [dangerous waters] (1924) is about a mother-son relationship and a drug problem. *Private Lives* (1930) is a comedy about marriage and divorce.

   Coward's comedies have a challenging attitude to the problems they discuss. This short dialogue from *Private Lives* shows the divorced couple when they meet in the same hotel with new partners:

AMANDA: What's happened to yours?

ELYOT: Didn't you hear her screaming? She's downstairs in the dining-room I think . . .

AMANDA: Have you known her long?

ELYOT: About four months, we met in a house party in Norfolk.

AMANDA: Very flat, Norfolk.

ELYOT: How old is dear Victor?

AMANDA: Thirty-four, or five; and Sibyl?

ELYOT: I blush[1] to tell you, only twenty-three.

[1] I am embarrassed

Where Maugham and Coward used the theatre mostly to amuse and entertain the audience, other writers, including George Bernard Shaw, used the theatre to explore ideas.

In the 1930s J. B. Priestley, well known as a novelist, wrote several plays on the theme of time. These are *Dangerous Corner* (1932), *I Have Been Here Before* (1937) and *Time and the Conways* (1937). These plays experiment with past, present and future in very adventurous ways, going backward and forward in time and examining the characters' actions from different points of view. His play *An Inspector Calls* [inspector = police officer], written in 1945, is a psychological study of a family's guilt and has remained Priestley's most popular play. It examines truth and reality, moral awareness and responsibility, using an inspector of police, who might not be real.

Poetry 1895–1918

Poets at the end of the Victorian age reflect the crisis of values of the time. Gerard Manley Hopkins and Thomas Hardy are the two best examples. Both can be seen as Victorians in some ways, and as modern poets in other ways. Hopkins died in 1889, but most of his poetry was not published until 1918. Hardy, well known as a novelist until the middle of the 1890s, stopped writing novels and spent the rest of his career writing poetry – for more than thirty years. He died in 1928.

Hopkins and Hardy are poets of changing times. Their poems celebrate nature, but also show the great sadness and anxiety of society after Darwin and *On the Origin of Species*. In his nature poetry, Hopkins looks at birds, trees and flowers in very close detail and uses his observations in praise of God. Some of these poems are very modern in their themes:

> What would the world be, once bereft[1]
> Of wet and of wildness? Let them be left,
> O let them be left, wildness and wet;
> Long live the weeds[2] and wilderness[3] yet.
>
> ('Inversnaid')

[1] lacking; without   [2] plants which grow in wild areas   [3] wild areas

Hopkins was a religious man, and became a priest. His best-known single poem is a long and complex examination of the death of five nuns (among others) in a disaster at sea in December 1875, called *The Wreck of the Deutschland*. Like many of his works it questions man's relationship with God, and tries hard to find faith and belief in the modern world. Most of Hopkins's poetry was private, however, and his 'terrible sonnets' are among the most painful examinations of mental suffering in English:

> O the mind, mind has mountains; cliffs of fall
> Frightful, sheer, no-man fathomed.[1] Hold them cheap
> May who ne'er[2] hung there.

[1] natural drops in the land which are frightening, vertical and not understood by man   [2] never

Hopkins wrote about the techniques of poetry, and his ideas became very important in the twentieth century, after his poems were published by his friend, the poet Robert Bridges, in 1918. Hopkins used what he called 'sprung rhythm' to create the 'inscape' of a poem. Inscape is 'the individual or essential quality of the thing'; sprung rhythm is a return to the rhythms of speech and the freedoms of earlier Anglo-Saxon verse forms.

Hardy's novels gave a pessimistic view of late Victorian life. His poetry is not all so pessimistic. Hardy's *Wessex Poems* (1898) use the same country area for their setting as he had used in his novels. The poems had been written over some thirty years before they were published. Like Hopkins, he celebrates nature in many of his works. One of the best known of these was written at the end of the nineteenth century, and published in December 1900. It is called 'The Darkling Thrush' and uses the image of a bird singing, in a way similar to Keats. But the tone is more pessimistic:

> I could think there trembled through
> His happy good-night air[1]
> Some blessed[2] Hope, whereof[3] he knew
> And I was unaware.

> [1]song   [2]approved by God   [3]of which

Many of Hardy's poems show the irony which he used also in his short stories like *Life's Little Ironies* (1894). 'The Convergence of the Twin' [coming together of the two] tells the story of the sinking of the Titanic, the ship which nobody thought could sink, in 1912. He imagines that while it was being built, a destroying power called 'the Immanent Will' was building an iceberg to sink it:

> . . . they were bent
> By paths coincident[1]
> On being anon[2] twin halves of one august[3] event,

> Till the Spinner of the Years
> Said 'Now!' And each one hears,
> And consummation[4] comes, and jars[5] two
>   hemispheres.[6]

> [1]moving together   [2]soon   [3]memorable; major
> [4]end   [5]shakes   [6]two halves of the Earth

Hardy's poems are of all kinds, from short love lyrics to the huge three-act drama in verse and prose, *The Dynasts* (1904–8). In all he

Thomas Hardy's cottage in Dorset.

wrote over 900 poems, and he is now considered one of the most important poets of the twentieth century. He has influenced later poets such as W. H. Auden and Philip Larkin.

One of the most popular poets of the century was A. E. Housman. He published *A Shropshire Lad* in 1896, and over the next twenty years it became a best-seller; it was the volume of poetry most read by the soldiers in the First World War. Again his subject is nature, but Housman is also the poet of emotional loss, and his themes of being alone found echoes in many other writers of the twentieth century. His *Last Poems* were published in 1922 and his *More Poems* were published in the year of his death, 1936. His forms are traditional rather than modern, but his simplicity, his emotion and the beauty of his descriptions of nature have made him popular despite all the changing fashions in poetry:

That is the land of lost content, [1]
I see it shining plain,
The happy highways [2] where I went
And cannot come again.

(A Shropshire Lad)

[1] happiness   [2] main roads

W. B. Yeats began his poetic career in the 1880s, and was an important literary figure until his death in 1939. Probably more than any other writer, he shows in his poems many of the changes which were happening in the world he lived in. He was Irish, and was closely involved in the struggles for independence, especially the Easter Rising in 1916 when Irish nationalists fought unsuccessfully against the British. Sixteen Irish leaders were shot. 'Easter 1916' is one of the best-known poems, with the famous refrain 'A terrible beauty is born.' Yeats is the poet of this paradox, writing about the wars and revolutions which shook the world. 'The Second Coming', published in 1921 in the volume Michael Robartes and the Dancer, gives an image for the twentieth century as clear as Matthew Arnold's image of the nineteenth century in 'Dover Beach':

Things fall apart; [1] the centre cannot hold;
Mere anarchy [2] is loosed [3] upon the world,
The blood-dimmed [4] tide is loosed, and everywhere
The ceremony of innocence is drowned;
The best lack all conviction, while the worst
Are full of passionate intensity. [5]

[1] do not remain together   [2] simple lack of respect for the government
[3] released   [4] darkened with blood   [5] very strong feelings

Yeats wrote over twenty volumes of poetry in his long career, as well as many plays. He was very important in the revival of Irish writing, especially drama, in the early years of the century, known as the Celtic Revival, and his plays were staged at the famous Abbey Theatre in Dublin. He described himself as among 'the last of the Romantics' in 1931, and wrote some of the best poems about growing old, although one of his best-known poems, 'Sailing to

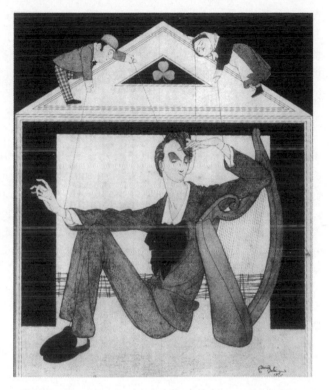

W. B. Yeats and the Irish Theatre, a painting by Edmund Dulac.

Byzantium', describes Ireland as 'no country for old men'. From love poems to poems of political crisis, the range of Yeats's work makes him one of the great poets of the century.

*

The changes in values at the turn of the century meant also that poets looked for new ways of saying things and used new kinds of language in their works. One result of this was the Imagist movement in the early years of the new century. It was a reaction against Romanticism. T. E. Hulme was an important figure in this movement. He wrote that he wanted a new kind of poetry, 'cheerful, dry and sophisticated' [sophisticated = clever]. His own poetry consists of short sharp images, for example, of sunset, or of the moon at night. In this poem 'Above the Dock' Hulme describes the moon at night hanging in the sky above a ship:

Above the quiet dock in midnight
Tangled[1] in the tall mast's corded height,[2]
Hangs the moon. What seemed so far away
Is but a child's balloon, forgotten after play.

[1] mixed among   [2] the high supports for sails, and their ropes

Hulme wrote very little, as he was killed in action in the First World War. But his essays were important, especially *Speculations* [theories] (1924); he was one of the first Modernists. His philosophy and the poems of the Imagists changed the way modern poetry was written. The American Ezra Pound edited the first anthology, *Des Imagistes* [The Imagists], which was published in 1914. The poems are images of a scene of a mood, such as this one by Pound himself from his 1916 book *Lustra*:

The apparition[1] of these faces in the crowd;
Petals[2] on a wet, black bough.[3]

[1] appearance   [2] parts of a flower   [3] branch

The Georgian poets were a group whose work appeared in five volumes called *Georgian Poetry* between 1912 and 1922. They named themselves after King George V. Many of the most famous writers of the time are among them: Rupert Brooke, John Masefield (who later became Poet Laureate), D. H. Lawrence, Siegfried Sassoon and Robert Graves. The Georgians cannot be seen as a movement: the books simply contain the work of the best young poets of the time. Brooke is perhaps the most typical: his 'The Old Vicarage Grantchester' [vicarage = home of a churchman] (1912) is one of the last poems to look back to an older, possibly happier way of life:

Say, is there Beauty yet to find?
And Certainty? and Quiet kind?[1]
Deep meadows[2] yet, for to forget
The lies, the truths, and pain? . . . oh! yet

Stands the Church clock at ten to three?
And is there honey still for tea?

¹ gentle innocence   ² grassland

But for the poets of the early years of the century, the certainty they looked for was about to end. With the First World War, the old world ended, and things were never the same again.

FIRST WORLD WAR POETRY

The First World War was called 'the war to end all wars'. In fact it was just the first of many wars in the twentieth century, which was a century of wars all over the world. It was, however, the first war in which the soldiers from the lower classes could read and write – and they wrote home describing the horrors and the uselessness of the war they were fighting. A new range of words entered everyone's language: 'no-man's-land' is one example. No-man's-land describes a piece of land between two sides in a battle which both sides agree to keep safe and not to enter.

The poets who wrote about the war from their own experience did not try to make the soldiers into heroes. 'The poetry is in the pity' wrote Wilfred Owen. This is very different from the heroism of Tennyson, or the epic poetry of war. In another poem, Owen uses a famous Latin line to question the values of war: *Dulce et decorum est pro patria mori* – 'It is sweet and correct to die for your country.' In the First World War it was no longer such a good thing, and Owen's irony about the war gave a new tone to modern poetry. Poems like 'Anthem for Doomed Youth' [song for youth without hope], 'Strange Meeting' and 'Futility' are elegies for a dead generation, poems about the wasteland of modern war:

Was it for this the clay ¹ grew tall?
– O what made fatuous sunbeams² toil³
To break earth's sleep at all?
                              ('Futility' 1918)

¹ soil (in the Bible, the first man was created from clay)
² useless light of the sun   ³ work

Like so many other soldiers, Wilfred Owen was killed in the war, and most of his poems were published after his death. Rupert Brooke also died in the war not long after writing these famous lines:

> If I should die, think only this of me;
> That there's some corner of a foreign field
> That is forever England.
>
> ('The Soldier' 1915)

*Many poets described the
horror of the First World
War very clearly.*

Edward Thomas was a poet of nature. He describes the effects
of the war on the English countryside in 'The Team's Head-Brass'.
His best-known poem 'Adlestrop' is rather like a poem by Brooke
as it describes a moment which can never return.

Many other poets described the war in detail. Isaac Rosenberg,
for example, in 'Dead Man's Dump' describes the dead bodies and
the horror of war very clearly. He was only twenty-eight when he
died; Brooke was the same age; T. E. Hulme was thirty-four;

Edward Thomas was thirty-nine; Wilfred Owen was only twenty-five. A generation of poets and other artists died in the war. The shock to those who survived was great, and in many ways the years that followed the war were a time when people tried very hard to come to terms with and to accept this shock.

Siegfried Sassoon survived the war, and went on to write poetry and prose for many years. But the best of his writing is about the war. Poems like 'The General' [army leader] (1918) were among the first to criticize the way the war was planned. This kind of criticism soon extended to all levels of society. The poem criticizes the leaders of the country who have let down the ordinary soldiers and even directly caused their deaths. The final line describes the general's failure:

> 'Good morning; good morning!' the General said
> When we met him last week on our way to the line.[1]
> Now the soldiers he smiled at are most of 'em dead,
> And we're cursing his staff for incompetent[2] swine.[3]
> 'He's a cheery old card,'[4] grunted[5] Harry to Jack
> As they slogged[6] up to Arras with rifle[7] and pack.
> . . .
> But he did for them[8] both by his plan of attack.

[1] where fighting happens in a war [2] not able to do things properly
[3] pigs [4] pleasant person [5] speak roughly, making noise like a pig
[6] walked in a tired way [7] gun [8] killed them

Another survivor, Edmund Blunden, was the editor of Owen's poems when a collected edition was published in 1931. Blunden's own volume *Undertones of War* (1928) is one of the most detailed accounts of life in the trenches, seen from the distance of a few years after the war had ended.

T. S. Eliot

T. S. Eliot is considered by many critics to be the most important poet in English of the twentieth century. Like so many other writers he was an outsider – he was born in St Louis, Missouri, in America and came to live in England before the First World War. Ezra Pound (also American by birth) encouraged him in his writing, and his first volume was published in 1917. This was *Prufrock and other Observations*. It contains one of Eliot's best-known poems 'The Love Song of J. Alfred Prufrock' which was first published in 1915. This poem shows Eliot's way of writing – he uses images, fragments and memorable phrases to build up a broad picture of the character, his anxieties and his time. The first image is well known. It compares the experience of evening to a sick person in hospital who lies unconscious:

> Let us go then, you and I,
> When the evening is spread out against the sky,
> Like a patient etherized[1] upon a table.

[1] given gas to bring sleep

T. S. Eliot

The poem is about time, and wasted time, and how the different inner parts of the character of Prufrock grow old and see his life become more and more meaningless:

> I have measured out my life with coffee spoons.
> I grow old . . . I grow old . . .
> I shall wear the bottoms of my trousers rolled.

In 1922 T. S. Eliot published *The Waste Land* and, ever since, it has been considered the most important single poem of the century. It takes the ideas of time, and waste, already found in 'Prufrock' and extends them to all societies, all times and all cultures. It is a poem full of references to other texts, and is very complex, with a wide range of intellectual reference. Many people have found it difficult, but Eliot wanted the poetry of the time to reflect the great new difficult problems of the age, the problem, above all, of the fragmenting of emotion, experience and society after the First World War.

It begins with an echo of Chaucer's Prologue to *The Canterbury Tales*. Chaucer writes of the sweet showers of spring, using April as the month which brings the coming of spring, but Eliot changes that positive idea with the words 'April is the cruellest month.' The poem then goes on to describe London, and the image of all the poem is of wastelands, deserts – the same kind of futility as was found in Wilfred Owen, and indeed in the final lines of Matthew Arnold's 'Dover Beach' more than fifty years before. The image of the wasteland has come to be one of the most common images of modern times, and Eliot's poem has been discussed and examined by a great many critics.

Eliot's later poetry also comes out of crisis, especially *Four Quartets* [quartet = music for four instruments or singers] (1935–42). He joined the Anglican church, and wrote the verse drama *Murder in the Cathedral* (1935) for performance in Canterbury Cathedral. This was the beginning of a new wave of verse drama, which continued after the Second World War.

Eliot's concern with time is seen again in the opening lines of the first of the *Four Quartets* 'Burnt Norton' (1935):

Time present and time past,
Are both perhaps present in time future
And time future contained in time past.

In *Four Quartets* the passing of time is not simply a futile experience but is seen as positive and offers hope of spiritual rebirth.

Poetry after Eliot

The popular new form of art in the early part of the twentieth century was the cinema. Eliot's technique of moving quickly from one scene to another, is sometimes called cinematic. Certainly the quick movement of words and images becomes a feature of modernism. So also is the idea of time – time is questioned again and again; in the same way, memory and reality are questioned, and new visions and expressions of reality are presented.

There is a definite separation between high culture and popular culture in the 1920s. Texts like *The Waste Land* were deliberately difficult in the range of references and in the modern techniques used. Novels by writers like James Joyce and Virginia Woolf were also considered intellectual, and the world of literature began to become a limited one, for educated readers who could catch all the references and discuss the texts they had read.

Of course, many poets still wrote in traditional ways – perhaps Robert Graves is the most important. He continued to write until the 1980s, and became one of the great lyric poets of the century, taking little notice of the fashions of intellectual poetry. The poetry of Norman Cameron, a close friend of Graves, continued the work of the early Imagists, but Cameron did not achieve wide recognition in his own lifetime. John Masefield was very popular, especially for poems of the sea. This is the beginning of one of his best-known poems, 'Sea Fever' (1902): 'I must go down to the sea again, to the lonely sea and the sky.' Walter de la Mare, who wrote many poems for children, was another writer who did not follow the fashions of high culture, and remained popular for well over fifty years.

*

In the 1930s, the poets who followed Eliot brought a new political tone into modern poetry. W. H. Auden, Stephen Spender, Louis MacNeice and C. Day-Lewis are often considered together as a group known as the Thirties poets. All of them continued to write for many years, but in the 1930s their way of looking at the modern world and their way of introducing political views into their works was new. The Scottish poet Hugh MacDiarmid had begun writing left-wing political poetry with *A Drunk Man Looks at the Thistle* [thistle = flower that is the symbol of Scotland] in 1926. He continued to use the language of Scotland and his own communist political ideas in his poetry for many years, but was never accepted as part of mainstream English literature. But the left-wing point of view was very much part of thirties writing. As the world moved towards the Second World War this serious tone was an important change.

Another important change in the 1930s was that the poets talked of modern subjects like electricity pylons, public opinion and the way the world was at the time. 'Look, stranger, on this island now,' is the beginning of one of Auden's best-known poems, 'Seascape' from 1936. It asks the reader to look at the modern world as if it were for the first time. Stephen Spender's poem 'The Pylons' describes how large electricity pylons cross the countryside. They are the landscape of the future:

> Now over these small hills they have built the concrete[1]
> That trails[2] black wire:
> Pylons,[3] these pillars[4]
> Bare like nude,[5] giant girls that have no secret.

[1] hard material used for building   [2] hangs in a line
[3] supports for electric wires   [4] supports for buildings
[5] without clothes

All these writers had a view of the political changes which were happening in the 1930s, and observed developments in Germany, and the Civil War in Spain (1936–9). At the end of the 1930s Auden left Britain to live in the United States and continue his career there. In 'Spain' (1937) Auden had written 'today the struggle' – and much of his writing, and the writing of the others in the Thirties group, has this suggestion of future pain rather than hope:

> Tomorrow for the young the poets exploding like bombs.
>
> ('Spain')

This came true as the world moved rapidly towards war for the second time in the century.

W. H. Auden

8 The Contemporary Period: 1939 to Today

Setting the Scene

The end of the Second World War in 1945 did not make the world a peaceful place. When atomic bombs were dropped on Hiroshima and Nagasaki in Japan in 1945, people understood that the whole world could end at any moment. There was now a Cold War between communist countries and the West which ended only in the late 1980s. The United States of America entered the First World War in 1917 and the Second World War in 1941. Each time it was on the winning side. Victory helped the USA to become the major economic and cultural force in the world.

The Second World War helped to break up the British Empire and made the country think carefully about its place in the world. During this time British influence grew weaker. Nationally, too, the country had begun to break up in many different ways and there have been many contrasts in British life in the years after the war. There have been contrasts between London and the regions, between England and the other countries of Britain (Scotland, Ireland and Wales), between the wealthier south of England and the poorer north of England, between white British and black British people, between employed and unemployed, and between optimistic years (1960s and 1980s) and more pessimistic years (1970s and 1990s). A war also continued in Northern Ireland between Catholics and Protestants, and many British soldiers died there between the 1960s and 1990s.

But during these years many people have become wealthier and have had a better standard of living which has let them travel more in Britain and other countries and let them own their own homes. Free time has increased and more people watch television as a main source of information and entertainment. More books are now read by more people than ever before.

The Novel

Although poetry was the most memorable literary form to come out of the First World War, the novel was the form which told the stories of the Second World War. Partly this was because mass media, newspapers, cinema and radio had changed the way information (and entertainment) were given.

Of course many of the writers who wrote about the war had already begun their careers before the war. Henry Green, for example, had written his first novel, *Blindness*, at the age of twenty-one in 1926. Green's novels, *Party Going* (1939), *Caught* (1943) and *Loving* (1945) are among the best to be published during the war. His style is simple and symbolic. *Party Going* describes a group of rich people waiting at a station, but their train is delayed by fog; *Loving* is a story of class difference set in a country house in Ireland during the war. In his seemingly simple stories, Green manages to contain a lot of observation and meaning. After the war, Green went on to write several novels including *Nothing* (1950), which is almost entirely written in dialogue form.

Graham Greene wrote some of his most important novels in the 1940s. *The Power and the Glory* (1940) has a Catholic theme, about a 'whisky priest' in Mexico, and his faults as a man and a priest. *The Heart of the Matter* (1948) is set in West Africa, and again the hero has problems of faith and honour: his name is Scobie, and he represents the typical Greene hero and the problems of the ordinary man. Of another character in the novel, Greene's third-person narrator says 'He felt the loyalty we all feel to unhappiness – the sense that that is where we really belong.' This sense of unhappiness and uncertainty is typical not only of Greene but of many other novelists of the second half of the twentieth century. Greene's later novels, from *The End of the Affair* (1951), about love in wartime, to *A Burnt-out Case* (1961), which many people consider his best novel, all explore regions of human unhappiness in many different areas of the world.

For many readers the Irishman Samuel Beckett is the writer who best shows this human sadness. He is best known for his plays, but his novels are also very important. Beckett was a close

BRITISH AND IRISH WINNERS OF THE NOBEL PRIZE FOR LITERATURE

1907	Rudyard Kipling (1865–1936) *Kim, The Jungle Book, Stalky and Co*	1948	T.S. Eliot (1888–1965) *The Waste Land, Four Quartets*
1923	W.B. Yeats (1865–1939) *Michael Robartes and the Dancer, The Tower*	1953	Winston Churchill (1874–65) *The Second World War*
		1969	Samuel Beckett (1906–89) *Waiting for Godot, How It Is*
1925	G.B. Shaw (1856–1950) *Heartbreak House, Saint Joan, Pygmalion*	1983	William Golding (1911–93) *Lord of the Flies, Rites of Passage*
1932	John Galsworthy (1867–1933) *The Forsyte Saga*	1995	Seamus Heaney (1939–) *Death of a Naturalist, North*

friend and helper of James Joyce, but his novels are quite different from Joyce's. From *Murphy* (1938) through to *How It Is* (1961) Beckett uses first-person narrators to describe the interior feelings of lonely souls. His tone is comic and his language very exact: he lived for many years in France, and very often translated his own works from the French in which he first wrote them, in order, he said, to help make the language clearer. Despite the atmosphere of loneliness and futility in all his writings, there is always a positive aspect, and survival is always important in Beckett's work. One of his late pieces, a very short novel, is called *Imagination Dead Imagine* (1966) – it shows that as long as there is imagination there is life. One of the most famous lines in Beckett is the last words of *The Unnamable* (1960) when the main character says:

> Where I am, I don't know, I'll never know, in the
> silence you don't know, you must go on. I can't go on,
> I'll go on.

Samuel Beckett won the Nobel Prize for Literature in 1969.

Evelyn Waugh, like Graham Greene, became a Catholic. In his wartime trilogy *Sword of Honour*, written well after the end of the

Left: Brideshead Revisited, *by Evelyn Waugh, describes an upper-class family and its decline in modern society.*

Opposite: *'Big Brother is Watching You.' A scene from the film of George Orwell's novel,* Nineteen Eighty-Four.

war, between 1952 and 1961, he gives a satirical, well-observed, picture of the British upper classes at war. Waugh's *Brideshead Revisited*, published in 1945, was one of the most successful novels of its time. It describes an upper-class family, its Catholic religion, and its decline in modern society. As always with Waugh, there is humour, as well as a tone of regret in the description of the decline and fall of the old values and codes.

Possibly the best single novel about the Second World War is *The River Line* (1949) by Charles Morgan. A novel of action and personal relationships, it uses the present in contrast with the past, which is the war, to give a psychological and moral insight into its characters' behaviour. Where the poetry of the First World War was very personal and emotional in its descriptions of the war, most of the novels about the Second World War have a certain ironic distance, which gives them a quite different feel and quality.

*

The novels of George Orwell always have a political intention. As a socialist Orwell believed in equality. In the thirties he had written several works including the novels *Keep the Aspidistra Flying* [aspidistra = common English house-plant] (1936), with themes of culture and money, and *Homage to Catalonia* [homage = act of respect] (1938), about his experiences in the Spanish Civil War. Orwell's best-known works are *Animal Farm* (1945) and *Nineteen Eighty-Four* (1949). The first is a fable where the animals free themselves from their masters and take over Manor Farm. But gradually they become more and more like their masters had been. It is a satire against the political systems which Orwell had seen develop in the 1930s and 1940s. In *Animal Farm*, after the rebellion, the animals say that all animals are equal. Here he describes some of the animals who have become powerful:

> And a moment later, out from the door of the
> farmhouse came a long file[1] of pigs, all walking on
> their hind[2] legs . . . And finally there was a tremendous
> baying[3] of dogs and a shrill crowing[4] from the black
> cockerel[5] and out came Napoleon himself . . . with his
> dogs gambolling[6] around him.
>   He carried a whip in his trotter.[7]

[1]line   [2]back   [3]loud barking   [4]loud music made by a bird
[5]male chicken   [6]running and jumping   [7]pig's foot

Later the animals create another saying. It is: 'All animals are equal but some animals are more equal than others.' Orwell believed that socialist and communist societies could become dictatorships in which ordinary people were not free.

Nineteen Eighty-Four is similar to Huxley's *Brave New World* in some ways. It describes a future world (in 1984) when the political system has total control over people. The menacing power of this system can be seen in the words 'Big Brother is Watching You' which are displayed in every public place. Orwell also wrote many essays, and gave many radio broadcasts, usually giving a political insight into English society and culture.

THE NOVEL IN THE 1950S AND 60S

Each decade introduces different ways of writing. In the 1950s a new generation of writers began to appear, with new subjects and concerns. Angus Wilson is in some ways the most traditional of the new writers, but his way of looking at society is unusual for he gives space to middle-aged characters, and to outsiders (he is particularly good on homosexual characters). His novels are full of ironic observation, and follow Dickens and Thackeray rather than any modernist trend. *Hemlock and After* [hemlock = poisonous plant] (1952) was his first novel; *Anglo-Saxon Attitudes* (1956), *The Middle Age of Mrs Eliot* (1958) and *No Laughing Matter* (1967) are his best-known works.

The voice of the lower classes is heard in novels by Colin Wilson, John Wain and Alan Sillitoe. The young men are now

Angry Young Men, perhaps with a university education, as in Wain's *Hurry on Down* (1953), perhaps frustrated in their working-class environment, as in Sillitoe's *Saturday Night and Sunday Morning* (1958). They are all outsiders – and this is the title of Colin Wilson's most famous book, *The Outsider* (1956). Wilson's outsider hero is a man of genius who is not understood, and his struggle is typical of the 'existential' crisis of the 1950s generation. The fifties brought many outsiders into literature. It is not an age of success, but a time of struggle towards success.

The most successful comic novel of the fifties was Kingsley Amis's *Lucky Jim* (1954). It was one of the first novels to have a university setting – this later became very popular in the novels of Malcolm Bradbury and David Lodge. Amis's hero Jim Dixon shows the comedy of being an outsider trying to fit into the new world he has struggled to reach. As the title suggests, this outsider has better luck in his fights with authority than most outsider heroes. Amis's later novels continue to have a comic style, but his main characters grow older as the author does – and *The Old Devils* (1986), for example, is a study of old age.

His later novels include *The Biographer's Moustache* (1995) and *You Can't Have Both* (1996). The publication of Amis's letters in 2000 coincided with the publication of the autobiographical work *Experience* by his son Martin, also a very successful novelist – the different attitudes of father and son illuminate many of the differences in their novels and in society towards the end of the twentieth century.

Among the women writers who became famous in the fifties, Muriel Spark and Doris Lessing show different ways of writing about society. Spark's style is witty and subtle. Her novel about old people *Memento Mori* (1959) shows more comedy than Amis on the same theme. Her story of a school teacher *The Prime of Miss Jean Brodie* (1961) is her best-known work, also known as a play, as a film and as a television series. The novel describes the life of Jean Brodie, a school teacher in Edinburgh, Scotland, who is in her prime, the best years of her life. She is an excellent and inspirational teacher but she chooses pupils for special attention and favours them, calling such pupils her 'crème de la crème' [the very best, the cream of the cream]. The novel explores her influence on these girls. The influence is both good and bad, and Spark comments wittily on the dangers of obsessive behaviour. The novel is traditional in form and structure, but *The Driver's Seat* (1970) is much more experimental. It describes a woman who has a death-wish, and is written throughout in the simple present tense. Her later work, such as *A Far Cry from Kensington* [a far cry = a long way] (1988), *Loitering with Intent* [loitering = waiting around] (1995), *Reality and Dreams* (1996) and *Aiding and Abetting* [abetting = helping with criminal acts] (2000) brings a new theme of memory and loss, and shows Spark's development as a writer of social comedy, again with a focus on female characters.

Doris Lessing is more politically and socially concerned than Spark. She was brought up in Africa, and her early stories and novels are set there. The series *Children of Violence* (1952–69), moves from Africa to England, and moves forward in time to the year 2000. In the five novels the story of Martha Quest is told, and is one of the best growing-up stories about a young woman in modern literature. Lessing also wrote *The Golden Notebook* (1962) which brings together politics and psychology. *The Golden Notebook* presents the four experimental notebooks of the writer Anna Wulf who is in crisis in her domestic life, is unable to write as she wants and whose political beliefs are uncertain. In each notebook she explores her experiences in different styles and from different points of view, but they are fragments which she finds difficult to bring together into a whole. Anna suffers a breakdown but recovers, finding new freedom with an American lover, becoming more independent in her politics (she joins the socialist British Labour party) and producing new creative work. The novel, especially its section 'Free Women', is seen as an important feature in the description of women's independence in the twentieth century. Doris Lessing also wrote a science fiction series *Canopus in Argos: Archives* [archives = records] (also five novels, between 1979 and 1983). After the 1960s, she wrote about the ways in which society and the individual personality are falling to pieces. A recent novel *Love, Again* (1996) is a story of love and passion set at the end of the nineteenth century.

Barbara Pym seems at first sight more traditional than Lessing or Spark, but her simple love stories of lonely women are full of

William Golding

humour and sadness. She has been compared to Jane Austen in her awareness of the sexual pressures of society and the comic observation of male and female behaviour. Her first novel was *Excellent Women* (1952). *Quartet in Autumn* (1977) is sometimes considered her best work. Her work was mostly forgotten between 1963 and 1977, but Pym became famous and very popular in the three years before her death in 1980. Readers now found her stories of loneliness and lost love realistic, rather than romantic, and Pym's reputation is assured. Barbara Comyns wrote several novels about her own poor background, such as *Our Spoons Came from Woolworth's* (1950), but her fable of the plague in a village, *Who Was Changed and Who Was Dead* (1954) is one of the strangest novels of its time.

Only the novel *Lord of the Flies*, by William Golding, also published in 1954, touches similarly unusual themes. In this novel a group of boys on a desert island return to the savage state. It shows the animal in all of us, and caused great shock when it was first published.

In this scene from *Lord of the Flies* Golding describes the boys as they begin to behave and act like wild men in a savage tribe:

Ralph hit out; then he and what seemed like a dozen
others were rolling over and over, hitting, biting,
scratching. He was torn and jolted,[1] found fingers in his
mouth and bit them.

[1] knocked

Golding was one of the great story-tellers of his time, always
exploring in his novels the things which form human behaviour. In
The Inheritors (1955) he went back to prehistory to do this. In his
final great trilogy of sea novels, starting with *Rites of Passage*
[events marking important points in life] in 1980, he went back to a
sea voyage in the early nineteenth century – again using a society in
a small group like the boys on the island, and told the story of how
the whole society coped with all the pressures of a long voyage.
William Golding won the Nobel Prize for Literature in 1983.

Iris Murdoch also published her first novel in 1954. This was
Under the Net, a comedy. Most of her novels, however, are more
philosophical than comic. They have a wide range of themes, and
show that serious novels can still become best-sellers. Among her
best-known works are *The Bell* (1958), and a novel about the Irish
rebellion in 1916, *The Red and the Green* (1965). Perhaps her best
work is from the 1970s, when she wrote *The Black Prince* (1973),
A Word Child (1975) and *The Sea, The Sea* (1978), which many
people consider her best novel. Murdoch is always concerned with
philosophical and moral problems of good and bad, right and
wrong, art and life, and the nature of truth. Her final novels
included *The Message to the Planet* (1989), *The Green Knight*
(1993) and *Jackson's Dilemma* (1995).

The colonial setting for the novel appears again in the 1950s
in *The Malayan Trilogy* (1956–9) by Anthony Burgess. Burgess
went on to write such novels as *A Clockwork Orange* (1962), a
novel of violence which became better known as a film. This novel
and *Earthly Powers* (1980) show Burgess's fascination with
language, with music, and his very large themes. His range of
themes, ideas and subjects is greater than that of almost any other
writer of his time.

Edna O'Brien

In the 1960s more women writers became famous. Margaret Drabble has written many novels, usually with female leading characters. She follows her characters through their education and on to their careers and family relationships. Her early novels include *A Summer Bird-Cage* (1963) and *The Garrick Year* (1964). Her trilogy about the 1980s, *The Radiant Way* [radiant = bright], *A Natural Curiosity* and *The Gates of Ivory* [ivory = smooth white bone from an elephant] (1987–91), is one of the clearest descriptions of that decade, and the political attitudes shown at that time. *The Witch of Exmoor* (1996) takes a different direction, looking at family, madness, closeness and distance in a tragicomedy of the end of the century.

Edna O'Brien is perhaps the best-known woman writer from Ireland. Her early stories of poor girls, *The Country Girls* trilogy (1960–63), show the contrast between sensual desires and a Catholic background. Ireland has always produced important writers. In the 1960s, William Trevor became known both for his short stories and for novels such as *The Old Boys* (1964). His later Irish novel *Fools of Fortune* [fortune = destiny] (1983) shows the effects of the continuing problems of the people of that country. Trevor's novel *Felicia's Journey* (1994) won the Whitbread Prize and became a successful film. It tells the story of a young Irish girl who has been abandoned by the father of her child – her journey is the search to try to find him in England. *Death in Summer* (1998) is a novel about the return of figures from the past and their influence on the present.

Jean Rhys wrote her first novels in the 1920s and 1930s, but she was rediscovered in the 1960s when she published *Wide Sargasso Sea* (1966). It is set in the 1830s, and gives the story of one of the characters of Charlotte Brontë's *Jane Eyre* – the first wife of Mr Rochester. With this novel Jean Rhys became an important figure in women's writing.

The genre of the detective novel has produced many women writers in the twentieth century. The best known is Agatha Christie, with her detectives Hercule Poirot and Miss Marple. Others include Dorothy L. Sayers, and her detective Lord Peter Wimsey. More recently, P. D. James, whose detective is called Adam Dalgliesh, has taken the genre into more serious areas. Ruth Rendell has written many novels featuring Inspector Wexford, and many other psychological thrillers. Margaret Yorke, Minette Walters and Joan Smith are also among the best known of today's women detective story writers. Among men writers, Julian Symons, Edmund Crispin, H. R. F. Keating (whose detective is Indian) and Reginald Hill are perhaps the best known. Television versions of the novels have brought success to many writers, including Colin Dexter, with his detective Inspector Morse.

The Morse novels are set in Oxford: a strong local setting is becoming an important feature of many new detective novels. Reginald Hill sets many of his stories in the north of England. Ian Rankin has written more than a dozen detective thrillers from *Knots and Crosses* (1987) to *Set in Darkness* (2000), featuring Jack Rebus, set in present-day Edinburgh in Scotland. Christopher Brookmyre uses a Glasgow detective, Jack Parlabane, in some of his thrillers, such as *Quite Ugly One Morning* (1996) and *Country of the Blind* (1997). His *Not the End of the World* (1998) is a comedy thriller about extreme religious views and the millennium.

*

The short story has continued to be popular, and many of the best-known writers of the century, from Samuel Beckett to Doris Lessing, have written in the form. The writers who are better known for their short stories rather than any other kind of writing include the Irishman Sean O'Faolain. His first volume of stories was published in 1932, and his *Collected Stories* almost fifty years later, in 1981. V. S. Pritchett had been writing for even longer: his first stories were published in the 1920s. He wrote many kinds of books, including novels and travel books, but it is his short stories which are best remembered. They are collected in two volumes of *Collected Stories* published in 1982 and 1983.

THE NOVEL FROM 1970

The novel in the 1970s took several directions. The four main directions were: the focus on foreign and local, regional voices; more female voices; the academic or campus novel; and the coming of the kind of fantasy known as magic realism.

Novelists born outside Britain, or of foreign origins, have brought a new range of experience into the modern novel. Kazuo Ishiguro's background is Japanese and his first novel *A Pale View of Hills* (1982) uses this setting. His best-known work is *The Remains of the Day* (1989) which, like the earlier novel, uses the past and an examination of guilt and responsibility to examine the present. The main character is a butler, Stevens, who has been present at some historic occasions, but his master was a traitor. By the end of the novel, Stevens finds he has lost more than he has gained through his faithful service. *The Remains of the Day* won the Booker Prize, and was later successfully filmed. *The Unconsoled* (1996) is a long mysterious novel about a piano player, which was generally not well received. *When We Were Orphans* [orphan = child without parents] (2000) uses a detective story form to explore questions of identity.

Timothy Mo also mixes cultures in his novels: *Sour Sweet* (1982) uses Chinese immigrants in England to show the conflicts

A scene from the film of Kazuo Ishiguro's novel, The Remains of the Day, *1993.*

of modern Britain; *An Insular Possession* [insular = island] (1986) and *The Redundancy of Courage* [redundancy = uselessness] (1991) show some of the historical conflicts behind today's situation.

Hanif Kureishi in *The Buddha of Suburbia* (1990) looks at immigration from India and the difficulties of living in a new culture. He also wrote the film *My Beautiful Laundrette* [laundrette = self-service laundry] (1984) which successfully illustrated similar problems among young people. *The Black Album* (1995) and *Intimacy* (1998) combine personal stories of family break-up and social concerns of racial difference. Ben Okri, from Nigeria, set his prize-winning novel *The Famished Road* [famished = hungry] (1991) in that country.

Two writers of Caribbean origin, Caryl Phillips and David Dabydeen also return constantly to their origins in their writings. Phillips's *The Final Passage* (1985) is about a young Caribbean

CRITICAL WINNERS OF THE BOOKER PRIZE

The prize is awarded by a panel of judges to the best novel by a citizen of the United Kingdom, the British Commonwealth or the Republic of Ireland. It was first awarded in 1969, and after 25 years 'A Booker of Bookers' prize was given to *Midnight's Children*, the Booker Prize winner in 1981. So far there have only been 11 female winners out of 34. (Authors marked * are mentioned in this book.)

1969	P.H. Newby	*Something to Answer*	
1970	Bernice Rubens	*The Elected Member*	
1971	V.S. Naipaul	*In A Free State*	Tr
1972	John Berger	*G*	
1973	J.G. Farrell	*The Siege of Krishnapur*	Ire
1974	(two winners)		
	Nadine Gordimer	*The Conservationist*	SA
	Stanley Middleton	*Holiday*	
1975	Ruth Prawer Jhabvala	*Heat and Dust*	In
1976	David Storey	*Saville*	
1977	Paul Scott	*Staying On*	
1978	Iris Murdoch*	*The Sea, The Sea*	
1979	Penelope Fitzgerald	*Offshore*	
1980	William Golding*	*Rites of Passage*	
1981	Salman Rushdie*	*Midnight's Children*	In
1982	Thomas Kenneally	*Schindler's Ark*	Aus
1983	J.M. Coetzee	*Life and Times of Michael K*	SA
1984	Anita Brookner*	*Hotel du Lac*	
1985	Keri Hulme	*The Bone People*	NZ
1986	Kingsley Amis*	*The Old Devils*	
1987	Penelope Lively	*Moon Tiger*	
1988	Peter Carey	*Oscar and Lucinda*	Aus
1989	Kazuo Ishiguro*	*The Remains of the Day*	
1990	A.S. Byatt	*Possession*	
1991	Ben Okri*	*The Famished Road*	Nig
1992	(two winners)		
	Michael Ondaatje	*The English Patient*	Can
	Barry Unsworth	*Sacred Hunger*	
1993	Roddy Doyle*	*Paddy Clarke Ha Ha Ha*	Ire
1994	James Kelman*	*How Late It Was, How Late*	
1995	Pat Barker*	*The Ghost Road*	
1996	Graham Swift*	*Last Orders*	
1997	Arundhati Roy	*The God of Small Things*	In
1998	Ian McEwan*	*Amsterdam*	
1999	J.M. Coetzee	*Disgrace*	SA
2000	Margaret Atwood	*The Blind Assassin*	Can

girl's struggles on the island of her birth and in the new (to her) island of England. *A State of Independence* (1986) tells of a British West Indian, Bertram Francis, who returns to his home to celebrate the end of colonial rule, but is disappointed with what he finds. *Cambridge* (1991) is the story of a slave who ironically bears the name of the English city of Cambridge. In *The Nature of Blood* (1997) Phillips links stories of prosecution, race and memory in an epic story.

Dabydeen, originally from Guyana, has written two novels bringing together themes of art and slavery: *The Counting House* (1996) and *A Harlot's Progress* [harlot = prostitute] (1999), which starts from an eighteenth-century painting by William Hogarth to examine the role of black people in England. *Disappearance* (1998) uses an image of the cliffs of the south of England crumbling and falling apart as a metaphor for the state of England. David Dabydeen is also a poet, and used the paintings of Turner as a title for a long poem in 1994.

Sam Selvon was the first writer of West Indian origin to write novels and stories using the new variety of English, London Caribbean English, in such novels as *The Lonely Londoners* (1956). The story of this novel's main character, Moses, is continued in *Moses Ascending* [rising] (1975) and *Moses Migrating* [moving to another country] (1983), in which Moses returns to Trinidad.

Of the younger generation of British writers, Martin Amis (son of Kingsley Amis) started his career with shocking novels on sexual themes (*The Rachel Papers*, 1973 and *Dead Babies*, 1975). But in the 1970s and 1980s Amis showed that he is one of the best social observers of his generation. *Success* (1978) and *Money* (1984) show the emptiness of modern values and *London Fields* (1989) is a comic view of morals and murder in the television age. *Time's Arrow* (1991) moves backward in its narration of the Second World War and its effects on the present. Amis returned to several of his familiar themes in *The Information* (1995), but broke new ground with *Night Train* (1997), which uses the police novel as a framework for a serious examination of innocence and guilt, power and responsibility. *Heavy Water* (1998) is a collection of stories which shows how Amis experiments with language and themes.

Julian Barnes in *A History of the World in 10 1/2 Chapters* (1989) gives an unusual view of history; *Flaubert's Parrot* (1984) looks at the great French nineteenth-century novelist from a new point of view. This change of point of view is typical of many new writers. Ian McEwan, for example, in *The Child in Time* (1987) uses the loss of a child to look at the values of a modern couple. McEwan won the Booker Prize for his short novel *Amsterdam* (1998), a slight piece about love and death. Many people considered *Enduring Love* (1997) the year before to be his masterpiece. It is a painful novel about love and obsession, much more powerful than *Amsterdam*, but perhaps less immediately appealing. Graham Swift in *Waterland* (1983) uses an area of eastern England, known as the Fens, to examine past and present in a complex and rich family story. Both writers use new and unusual situations to present very modern questions. In 1996 Swift won the Booker Prize for his novel *Last Orders,* a novel about a group of friends journeying to Canterbury and telling stories as they go. The book echoes Chaucer's *The Canterbury Tales.*

Anita Brookner's novels usually present a single woman, living unhappily. *Hotel du Lac* (1984) became very successful and won the Booker Prize. It goes against the line of more feminist writing, for her characters do not rebel against society, but often simply accept their lonely situation. In *Hotel du Lac* the heroine does, however, make a major decision: *not* to get married on her wedding day. Brookner's 'spinster' novels have continued with *A Friend from England* (1987), *Fraud* [cheating] (1992), *Altered States* (1996) and her nineteenth novel *Undue Influence* (1999) which gives readers her youngest heroine and is a story of a generation of women who are unexpectedly lonely. Fay Weldon is sometimes seen as a feminist, but sees herself as a female novelist rather than as a feminist writer. Her books usually have a female main character, and are realistic, often comic examinations of modern life. *Praxis* (1978) and *The Life and Loves of a She-Devil* (1983) are among her best-known books. *Letters to Alice on First Reading Jane Austen* (1984) is a book which makes the case for reading and for literature in a most attractive way. *Big Women* (1997) is about a female publishing house, *A Hard Time to Be a Father* (1998) is a collection of stories which looks at male and female issues from different points of view and *The Godless of Eden* (1999) is a collection of articles and opinions on the same subjects.

Jeanette Winterson is openly gay, and her novels are strongly positive on female themes. *Oranges Are Not The Only Fruit* (1985) is her best-known work. This was followed by *Written on the Body* (1992) and *Art and Lies* (1994) among others. *The World and Other Places* (1998) is a powerful collection of stories and is daring in its themes and styles. *The Power Book* (2000) is a novel set in the world and conventions of E-mail. The novels and short stories of Susan Hill are more traditional in form. She is a story-teller, and her books range from sympathetic observations of old age, to the First World War *Strange Meeting* (1971) and the delicate love story *Air and Angels* (1991). *The Service of Clouds* (1998) is a moving story of death, love and memory.

The academic novel, or campus novel, became popular among readers who had been to university, and could recognize many of the issues discussed. *The History Man* (1975) by Malcolm Bradbury was a great success. Its hero, Dr Howard Kirk, is a university teacher at the new plate-glass University of Watermouth. He is an ambitious academic who uses his wife, his academic colleagues and his students so that we question who he is and what he really believes in. Bradbury wrote *Stepping Westward* (1965) about an English professor in America and *Rates of Exchange* (1983). David Lodge, in *Changing Places* (1975) and *Small World* (1984), makes comedy out of academic work exchanges and, in his Catholic novels, such as *How Far Can You Go?* (1980), raises religious and moral issues which are not often found in the modern novel.

John Fowles wrote several very successful novels in the 1960s and 1970s. *The Collector* (1963), *The Magus* (1966, reworked in 1977) and *The French Lieutenant's Woman* [lieutenant's = army officer's] (1969) made him world famous. Fowles examines how the story is told, how the reader reacts, and plays with the forms of the novel: *The French Lieutenant's Woman*, for example, seems to be a Victorian novel, and offers two possible endings. This was seen as very new at the time, although it had been done a century before, by Thackeray in *The Newcomes*, for example.

Another kind of magic is found in the novels of Angela Carter. *Nights at the Circus* (1984) and *Wise Children* (1991) are called magic realist novels as they move beyond the usual limits of the novel and the story, bringing in a new range of experiences. Magic realist novels have a strong plot, but day-to-day realistic events mix with unexpected events which cannot be explained and which appear to belong to a dream, fairy-story or myth. Angela Carter died in 1992 soon after the publication of *Wise Children*.

Alasdair Gray's very Scottish novel *Lanark* (1981) also has many features of magic realism. Gray is one of the most adventurous of Scottish writers, and such books as *The Fall of Kelvin Walker* (1985) and *Poor Things* (1992) examine the differences between being Scottish and being English, often with a historical but comic tone. *A History Maker* (1994) moves into the future of Scottish history, telling a story of border wars in 2220, echoing the kind of Scottish history found in the novels of Sir Walter Scott from the nineteenth century. James Kelman, in such very realistic novels as *A Disaffection* (1989) and *How Late It Was, How Late* (1994), gives a new view of Scottish language and society.

A. L. Kennedy came to notice with her first collection of stories *Night Geometry and the Garscadden Trains* (1991), which won several prizes. She has followed that with novels such as *Looking for the Possible Dance* (1993), an account of a train journey from Glasgow to London, which brings in the heroine's entire life story, *So I Am Glad* (1995), a further collection of stories and a new novel *Everything You Need* (1999).

Janice Galloway's first novel *The Trick Is to Keep Breathing* (1989) uses her own experience to tell a story of being depressed and alone. *Foreign Parts* (1994) is a happier account of two girls travelling in France in search of the past. Jackie Kay is a black Scottish poet whose first novel *Trumpet* (1998) won several prizes. It is the story of a female musician who pretended to be a man, and the consequences for her wife and son.

Several writers strengthened their reputations in the 1990s. Peter Ackroyd has written many novels, almost all of which use London as a setting, both historically and socially, exploring the history, the myths, the architecture and the literature of the city.

Hawksmoor (1985) uses the history and architecture of churches, *The House of Doctor Dee* (1993) is about the Elizabethan magus who inspired Shakespeare. *The Last Testament of Oscar Wilde* (1983) makes fiction from the true life story of the late Victorian playwright. *Dan Leno and the Limehouse Golem* (1994) takes the story of the murderer Jack the Ripper and places it in the context of the theatre of the time. *Milton in America* (1996) is a more recent novel. Ackroyd is also a successful biographer of such figures as William Blake, T. S. Eliot and Charles Dickens.

Beryl Bainbridge's novels on historical themes, *Every Man for Himself* (1997) about the sinking of the *Titanic*, and *Master Georgie* (1998) about the Crimean War almost won her the Booker Prize. She has won every other major award since her first novels appeared in the 1970s. Among the most successful are *The Bottle Factory Outing* (1974) and *Injury Time* (1977). These are not historical, but are carefully observed portraits of the poorer people of society who become highly sympathetic as she describes them. By transferring her observation to historical contexts Bainbridge brings a new approach to the novel, exploring forgotten aspects of character.

Pat Barker began her career with *Union Street* (1982), a novel of working-class women. *Blow Your House Down* (1984) is about a city threatened by a serial killer, and the reactions, especially of women to the crisis. It was with her trilogy of the First World War that Pat Barker reached immense critical and popular success. *Regeneration* (1991), *The Eye in the Door* (1993) and *The Ghost Road* (1995) take a very untraditional approach to the masculine games of war, and provide new insights into the great tragedy of the war which marked the whole of the rest of the twentieth century. *Regeneration* became a film, and the other novels won the Whitbread and the Booker Prizes respectively.

Roddy Doyle wrote several very popular novels based in his home town of Dublin – *The Commitments* (1987), *The Van* (1991) and *The Snapper* (1990) all became hit movies. *Paddy Clarke Ha Ha Ha* (1993) tells the story of a child damaged when his parents parted, and won the Booker Prize. *A Star Called Henry* (1999) is a historical examination of the Irish fight for independence in the early years of the twentieth century – it is the first of a planned series of three books.

Louis de Bernières achieved great popular success with several novels with very exotic settings. Three are set in South America and combine 'magic realism' with satire and political themes: they are *The War of Don Emmanuel's Nether Parts* (1991), *Senor Vivo and the Coca Lord* (1992) and *The Troublesome Offspring of Cardinal Guzman* [offspring = child] (1992). These won several prizes, but it was *Captain Corelli's Mandolin* [mandolin = a kind of musical instrument like a guitar] (1994) which had the greatest success, becoming one of the biggest selling novels of the decade. It is set in Greece during the Second World War and is an epic story of love and suffering.

Iain Banks writes fiction and science fiction, sometimes using the name Iain M. Banks for the latter. His *Espedair Street* (1987) is one of the best novels about pop music. *The Crow Road* (1992) became very successful on television – it is a story of modern Scotland. *The Business* (1999) is a wide-ranging epic about the power of money and business. William Boyd began his career with *A Good Man in Africa* (1981), a comic novel of the end of colonialism, and followed it with *An Ice-Cream War* (1982) also set in Africa and *Stars and Bars* (1984) set in the USA. *The New Confessions* (1987) and *Brazzaville Beach* (1990) are epics in terms of historical and anthropological themes. More recently his novels have been set in other places such as the Philippines (*The Blue Afternoon* 1993) and finally in London, *Armadillo* (1998).

Salman Rushdie is perhaps the best-known writer to have brought together east and west in his writings. *Midnight's Children* (1981) won the Booker Prize when it was published and later was named the Booker of Bookers, the best novel of the past twenty-five years. It is a celebration of India and its independence, a rich mixture of characters and plots with realism and fantasy, comedy and pathos. *Shame* (1983) was similarly successful in its handling of a Pakistani setting and themes. Later Rushdie's work caused great controversy, but with *The Moor's Last Sigh* (1995), which brings together Asian and European concerns, his reputation recovered, and he is now considered one of the most important writers of his generation.

Irvine Welsh's *Trainspotting* (1993) became one of the best-known novels of the 1990s. Set near Edinburgh, it is a novel of the AIDS and drug culture and became a hugely successful stage play and film. It is written in the dialect of Edinburgh, and started a fashion for realistic novels of strong language and powerful social criticism. Welsh's best novel is *Marabou Stork Nightmares* (1995), which moves between an African setting and Scotland, and between a troubled childhood and adult suffering. His *Filth* (1998) is about police corruption in Edinburgh and is in many ways a parody of the successful detective novels of Ian Rankin which are also set in that city.

Poetry

Poetry after the war included many works by W. H. Auden, who by then lived in America. His long poem *The Age of Anxiety* (1948) in many ways gave its name to the period. The war had not been heroic, and the mood afterwards was not of victory, but of change: the old class system in Britain was ending, the younger generation made themselves heard, and new scenes of realism came into literature.

The poets of the 1920s and 1930s continued to write during and after the Second World War. T. S. Eliot's *Four Quartets* was completed with 'East Coker', 'The Dry Salvages' and 'Little Gidding' between 1940 and 1942. In many ways these were the most important poems of the Second World War. The poets who died during the war did not produce work of such greatness as the soldiers of the First World War. But the poetry of Keith Douglas and Sidney Keyes is the poetry of war. Douglas's *Selected Poems* came out in 1943, before his death in 1944; his best poetry is in *Alamein to Zem Zem* (1946). Keyes too had published a couple of volumes before his death; his *Collected Poems* was published in 1945.

In this poem by Keith Douglas called 'Vergissmeinnicht' (the German word for a flower called forget-me-not) the poet finds on the body of a dead German soldier the picture of a girl with the message 'forget-me-not':

For here the lover and the killer are mingled[1]
Who had one body and one heart,
And death, who had the soldier singled[2]
Has done the lover mortal[3] hurt.

[1]mixed [2]chosen [3]fatal

Dylan Thomas, who had started publishing poetry in the 1930s, was in many ways the most important new voice of the 1940s. His language is rich and colourful, his images complex, and his view of nature bright. He goes beyond the fear of death:

After the first death there is no other.
('A Refusal to Mourn' in *Deaths and Entrances* 1946)

Do not go gentle[1] into that good night.
(in *Collected Poems* 1952)

[1]without resisting

Dylan Thomas's home in Laugharne, Wales.

His play for voices, *Under Milk Wood*, was broadcast on radio in 1954, and remains a classic work, bringing sound and sense together in a new way.

R. S. Thomas was a different kind of Welsh poet. He was a priest, and closer to the poetry of George Herbert than to any twentieth-century writer. But the country in Thomas is full of problems, illness and difficulty. Only the relationship with God can give meaning to such a life.

John Betjeman became Poet Laureate, and was a very popular figure. His *Collected Poems* (1958/1962) was a best-seller, as was his autobiography in verse, *Summoned by Bells* [summoned = called] (1960). His poems, written from the 1930s to the 1970s, often have a gentle sense of humour, as in this poem about the war, and an ugly English town:

> Come friendly bombs and fall on Slough,
> It isn't fit for humans now.
>
> ('Slough')

For the poet Philip Larkin the poetry of Betjeman was important because it was Betjeman 'who restored direct intelligible communication to poetry'.

The poets of the 1950s are often considered together as The Movement. But in fact the name has little real meaning, since most of the poets did not consider themselves part of any group. Thom Gunn wrote about motorbike boys, and similar new figures in society, in *Fighting Terms* (1954). He then moved to California where he has continued to write, publishing *The Man with Night Sweats* (1992), which takes AIDS as its main subject. *Boss Cupid* (2000) is a collection about survival and achievement, mixed with sadness and memory, inspired by Cupid, the God of Love. With it Thom Gunn has gone beyond the AIDS tragedy and describes eternal human passions and desires.

Elizabeth Jennings, in *A Way of Looking* (1955), showed a new way of writing, as well as looking, with clear description, often ironic in its attitudes. Jennings often writes of personal pain. Donald Davies and D. J. Enright are figures from the 1950s who have continued to write important poetry. But the main figure through the 1960s to the 1980s was Philip Larkin. His poems seem very simple, but are very carefully written, and contain many of the sharpest observations of that age. His tone is ironic, sad and witty:

> Life is first boredom, then fear.
> Whether or not we use it, it goes,
> And leaves us what something hidden from us chose,
> And age, and then the only end of age.
> ('Dockery and Son' in *The Whitsun Weddings* 1964)

Larkin is capable of writing positively too, as in some of his poems about churches, and the loss of natural things, although there is always a feeling of doubt:

> . . . to prove
> Our almost-instinct[1] almost true:
> What will survive of us is love.
> ('An Arundel Tomb' in *The Whitsun Weddings* 1964)

[1]almost acting without conscious intention

Stevie Smith also used humour in her poems. They are unusual observations of society – 'Not Waving But Drowning' (1957) is her best-known poem. Sylvia Plath became famous after her suicide in 1963 for her poems of pain and suffering. Her first volume was *The Colossus* (1960). 'Daddy' talks about her relationship with her father. Her novel *The Bell Jar* (1963) is also autobiographical. This is an example of the tone of most of her work:

> Dying
> Is an art, like everything else.
> I do it exceptionally[1] well.
>   ('Lady Lazarus' 1963)

[1]extremely

The language of modern poetry is often the language of dialect and slang. Tony Harrison is from Leeds in Yorkshire, and many of his poems use local settings and language: *V* (1985) caused controversy because of its language as he used many vulgar words

Stevie Smith

in the poem. Harrison refused to be considered for the Poet Laureate appointment after the death of Ted Hughes, and wrote controversially about it. His most recent collection is called *Laureate's Block and other occasional poems* (2000). At the time of the success of the popular music group the Beatles in the 1960s, the Liverpool Group of poets became famous. Of these, Roger McGough has continued to produce popular light verse which takes poetry to a wide audience.

Northern Ireland has produced a number of important poets: Seamus Heaney is the best known. His volumes, such as *Door into the Dark* (1969) and *North* (1975) bring local politics and history together in strong and effective verse. *Seeing Things* (1991) shows how Heaney can bring past and present, reality and imagination together in a single vision. Heaney won the Nobel Prize for Literature in 1995, the first Irish poet to do so since W. B. Yeats in 1923. He then published *The Spirit Level* (1996) which tries to show the balance of all things in Heaney's vision, bringing together politics, family history and spiritual well-being. *Opened Ground* (1998) collected his poems from between 1966 and 1996, and the translation of *Beowulf* (1999) brought him great popular and critical praise. Tom Paulin, Paul Durcan and Paul Muldoon are among the other writers from Northern Ireland who describe the continuing problems and difficulties of that region.

In Scotland the poetry of Edwin Morgan has become well known. He often uses 'concrete' forms, making the shape tell the story, but also writes lyric poems of simplicity and beauty. His *Collected Poems* was published in 1990 and his *New Selected Poems* in 2000. He won the Scottish writer of the year prize for his volume *Virtual and Other Realities* (1997). Carol Ann Duffy is one of the more exciting young poets. *Selling Manhattan* (1987) and *Mean Time* (1993) are among her volumes. Her collection of poems representing female voices through the ages *The World's Wife* (1999) was a critical and popular success. In England, Geoffrey Hill uses the history of his own area, the West Midlands, to write about the present and the past. *Mercian Hymns* (1971) is his best-known work. More recently, Simon Armitage in *Zoom!* (1989) and *Kid* [young person] (1992), and Glyn Maxwell with *Tale of the Mayor's Son* (1990), *Out of the Rain* (1992) and *Cloudcuckooland* (1997) have brought young regional voices into poetry.

Ted Hughes became the Poet Laureate after John Betjeman. He is a poet of nature, often writing about animals and birds such as the hawk and the crow. His *The Hawk in the Rain* (1957) and *Crow* (1970) are among his best-known volumes. For Hughes the crow becomes a symbol of the violence of nature. *Season Songs* (1976) and *Moortown* (1979) are among his later works. In his well-known poem 'Hawk Roosting' Hughes goes inside the mind of a hawk which enjoys the act of destroying things and people. It seems a symbol of a world from which all moral values have disappeared:

> I kill where I please because it is all mine
> My manners are tearing off heads, the allotment[1] of
>   death.

The sun is behind me.
Nothing has changed since I began:
My eye has permitted no change.
I am going to keep things like this.

[1] placing

Hughes reached great popular success in the year or two before his death. *The Birthday Letters* (1997) looked back at his relationship with the poet Sylvia Plath. With the publication of letters and journals from 2000 on, a more balanced view of that relationship will be possible. Hughes's *Translations from Ovid* (1998) also won several prizes and took the Latin poet into the best-seller lists.

Andrew Motion is one of the most important of the younger generation of poets. His first volume *The Pleasure Steamers* [steamers = boats] (1978) led to several others, including *Dangerous Play* (1985), *Love in a Life* (1991) and *Saltwater* (1997). Motion is one of the few poets who successfully write longer poems. He is also the biographer of Philip Larkin, John Keats and Thomas Wainewright. After the death of Ted Hughes, Motion became Poet Laureate in 1999.

James Fenton is highly regarded for his well-observed, often documentary poems. He has written in the Philippines, and in Cambodia, and many of his poems have political themes as a result. *The Memory of War and Children in Exile* (1981) brings together his poems from 1968 to 1981, and *Out of Danger* (1993) is his most recent work.

There are many poets from the old Commonwealth countries, who are now part of British writing: Fred d'Aguiar and David Dabydeen from Guyana are among the best-known of these. D'Aguiar's *British Subjects* [citizens] (1993) is an ironic collection moving between the Caribbean and Britain. Dabydeen's *Turner* (1994) looks at paintings and images of how black people have been treated and seen by white people. Benjamin Zephaniah was born in Birmingham, was brought up in Jamaica and Britain, and is well known as a performance poet. He regularly reads his poems at poetry festivals as many of his poems are written to read aloud. Among his works are *The Dread Affair* (1985), *Talking Turkeys* (1995) and *Funky Chickens* (1996).

Drama

After T. S. Eliot's *Murder in the Cathedral* in 1935, there was a short period when poetic drama became popular. Eliot's plays, such as *The Family Reunion* (1939) and *The Cocktail Party* [cocktail = alcoholic drink] (1950), were very successful. Christopher Fry was the other main poetic dramatist. His plays include the medieval romance *The Lady's Not For Burning* (1949) and *Venus Observed* (1950). Terence Rattigan's plays were not poetic. They enjoyed great success, especially in the 1940s and early 1950s, with audiences who shared their middle-class background and concerns. *The Winslow Boy* (1946) and *Separate Tables* (1954) are two of his most successful plays, both on themes of honour and justice.

During the 1950s a new kind of drama began to reach the theatres of Europe. There were two new trends in drama in the 1950s – absurd drama and social drama. Absurd drama began in France in the 1940s and reached Britain with *Waiting for Godot* by Samuel Beckett in 1955. The term absurd was first used by the critic Martin Esslin to describe the new kind of drama, which showed how meaningless life was. Esslin has now decided the term was wrong, and has tried to find another way of describing these plays – however no suitable name has been found, apart from the adjective Beckettian, from the author's name.

In *Waiting for Godot*, the two main characters, Vladimir and Estragon (often seen as tramps, although not in the text), spend their time waiting for Godot to appear. Godot never appears. The characters therefore have to fill the time as best they can, and the tragicomedy is about how they do this. So the themes are time, waiting and the repeating of day-to-day actions:

VLADIMIR:	That passed the time.
ESTRAGON:	It would have passed in any case.
VLADIMIR:	Yes, but not so rapidly.
	Pause
ESTRAGON:	What do we do now?
VLADIMIR:	I don't know.
ESTRAGON:	Let's go.
VLADIMIR:	We can't.

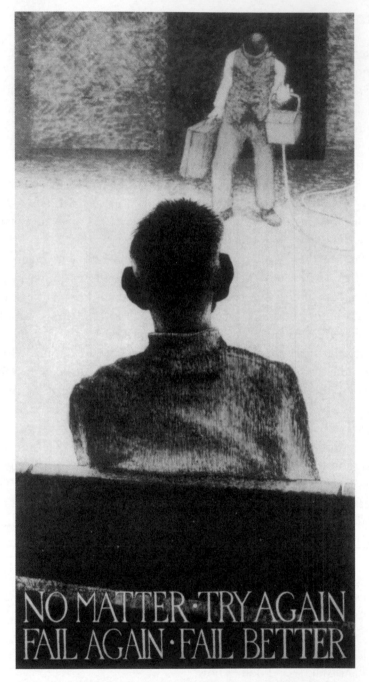

Samuel Beckett directing his play Waiting for Godot *in 1984.*

ESTRAGON: Why not?
VLADIMIR: We're waiting for Godot.
                                    (Act I)

Beckett's later plays continue with these themes. He reduces the number of characters, and makes the setting smaller: in *Endgame* (1958) two of the characters live in dustbins; in *Krapp's Last Tape* (1958) the only character lives his past and his present with the help of a tape-recorder. This process of reduction, known as minimalist drama, reaches its extreme in *Breath* (1969) which lasts about thirty seconds, has no characters, and has only rubbish on stage, the sounds of two cries and a long breath. This Beckettian minimalism has come to be seen as one of the strongest symbols of modern life. It continues, in many ways, T. S. Eliot's image of the wasteland, the strongest literary image of the first half of the century.

The new social drama of the 1950s brought into drama the young generation after the war, often from the lower classes. The most famous play of the time was *Look Back in Anger* by John Osborne, staged at the Royal Court Theatre in London in 1956. The play has lost a lot of its strength now, but at the time the hero, Jimmy Porter, the original angry young man, made a huge impression on audiences. He represented the concerns of the younger generation, the need for society to change, and for new values in the modern world. But he is angry because he can find no values for which he can fight:

JIMMY: I suppose people of our generation aren't able
    to die for good causes[1] any longer. We had all that
    done for us, in the thirties and forties, when we were
    still kids[2] . . . there aren't any good, brave causes left.
    If the big bang does come, and we all get killed off, it
    won't be in aid of[3] the old-fashioned, grand[4] design.

    [1] beliefs worth supporting or fighting for   [2] children   [3] to help
    [4] great

Jimmy also attacks the middle- and upper-class people who govern the country, referring to his brother-by-marriage, Nigel:

Look Back in Anger, *1956, by John Osborne, was the most famous play of its time and made a huge impression on audiences.*

JIMMY: . . . The Platitude[1] from Outer-Space – that's brother Nigel. He'll end up in the Cabinet[2] one day, make no mistake. But somewhere at the back of that mind is the vague knowledge that he and his pals[3] have been plundering[4] and fooling everyone for generations.

[1] dull saying without originality   [2] one of the highest offices of government   [3] friends   [4] robbing

Osborne's later plays presented other angry young men such as Martin Luther in *Luther* (1961), set at the time of the Reformation in Europe in the sixteenth century. *A Patriot for Me* [patriot = a person who loves his or her country] (1965) is in a different style: it is an epic play, set in Austria just before the First World War, about homosexuality and power.

Arnold Wesker's plays, especially *The Kitchen* (1959) and the Wesker trilogy (1958–60), brought the phrase kitchen-sink drama into use. Wesker often uses family settings, as in his trilogy, to examine social and class issues. In *The Kitchen* he uses a restaurant kitchen; in *Chips with Everything* (1962) the setting is the Royal Air Force.

Harold Pinter became known for his comedies of menace, like *The Birthday Party* (1958) and *The Caretaker* (1960). Like Beckett, Pinter creates a world of his own and, again, a special adjective has been invented to describe it – Pinteresque. This world is full of silences, distrust and hidden violence. He likes to use a small group of characters in an enclosed space, and explore the tensions and conflicts between them. But as in the plays of Beckett, there is always comedy just below the surface, too. *The Homecoming* (1965) and *Old Times* (1971) are full-length plays with more than one act, but many of Pinter's best plays are in one act: *The Dumb Waiter* (1960) and his masterpiece, *Silence* (1969) are among these. More recently *Mountain Language* (1988), *Moonlight* (1993) and *Celebration* (2000) showed that Pinter is still one of the masters of modern drama.

The following lines from Pinter's *The Dumb Waiter* show two characters, Ben and Gus. They try to control each other with words. They sound as if the words are used instead of violent actions:

BEN: Go and light it.
GUS: Light what?
BEN: The kettle.
GUS: You mean the gas.
BEN: Who does?
GUS: You do.
BEN: (*his eyes narrowing*) What do you mean, I mean the gas?

In the 1960s, for a short time, Joe Orton showed that the tradition of English comedy from Oscar Wilde to Noël Coward was continuing. Orton's plays made comedy out of dangerous themes: death and bank robbery in *Loot* [stolen money] (1966); psychoanalysis, sexual identity and questioning of authority in his final play, *What the Butler Saw* (1969). It is evidence of how different the playwright's ways of seeing and presenting life on stage was that, yet again, the playwright's name has become an adjective: Ortonesque means strange, anarchic, a twisted yet comic view of life. Joe Orton's death, when he was murdered by his lover at the age of thirty-four, brought a notable career to an early end.

In 1966 Tom Stoppard's play, based on two characters from Shakespeare's *Hamlet*, called *Rosencrantz and Guildenstern Are Dead* became a great success. Ever since, Stoppard has written comedies which play with intellectual themes, philosophy and art. In *Travesties* [parodies] (1974) the writer James Joyce and the revolutionary Lenin are among the characters; in *Jumpers* (1972) acrobats and philosophers share the stage, with a love story as background. Stoppard's *Arcadia* [ideal place] (1993) plays with the idea of knowledge, and the impossibility of knowing much. Stoppard also co-wrote the highly successful film *Shakespeare in Love* (1998).

Stoppard's kind of intelligent comedy uses theatre in new ways: it is theatre of ideas in comic style. The plays of Peter Shaffer also explore large intellectual ideas: *The Royal Hunt of the Sun* (1964) is set in the South American Inca Empire at the time of the European conquest; *Equus* (1973) uses a boy's passionate relationship with horses to explore sexual and psychological mysteries. *Amadeus* (1980) is perhaps Shaffer's best-known play. It is about Wolfgang Amadeus Mozart and, as in all Shaffer's best work, it touches on great themes. Shaffer's plays explore the edges of experience in an adventurous way which is almost the opposite of the minimalist style of Beckett and Pinter.

Alan Ayckbourn has written more than fifty plays, all of them comedies from *Relatively Speaking* (1967) to *Comic Potential* (1999), *Home* and *Garden* (2000). Most of his plays have been very successful in the theatre, both in the provinces (he has his own theatre in Scarborough, in the north of England) and in London. Possibly the commercial success of the plays, such as *Absurd Person Singular* (1973) and the trilogy *The Norman Conquests*

(1974), has meant that the plays have not had critical recognition. But they are adventurous in their use of space and dramatic techniques, and present a wide range of emotions and family situations. Ayckbourn's more recent plays (he writes one a year) have become darker and more serious, handling themes like mental breakdown, attempted suicide and violence in society. *Woman in Mind* (1986) and *Henceforward* [from now on] (1988) are among these plays. Alan Ayckbourn is now considered to be one of the most accurate writers about middle-class life in Britain of the present day.

Political drama has not usually been popular in Britain, but the plays of Edward Bond in the 1960s and 1970s brought a new political tone into the theatre. *Saved* (1965) is a realistic drama of social conflict, with a memorable scene of the killing of a baby which caused great controversy. Bond also reworked Shakespeare's *King Lear* as *Lear* in 1971. This assured his reputation for violent drama. His play about Shakespeare himself, *Bingo* (1973), gave a different view of Britain's greatest dramatist, seeing him as an unhappy man who thought of himself as a failure.

The plays of David Hare have documented Britain in the 1980s and 1990s. *Knuckle* (1974) and *Plenty* (1978) were among his first successes. *Licking Hitler* (1978) was a play for television about the Second World War. *The Secret Rapture* [rapture = great pleasure] (1988) was seen as a criticism of 1980s Thatcherite politics, and is part of a trilogy which is among the major dramatic achievements of recent years. The other plays in the trilogy are *Racing Demon* [demon = devil] (1990) about the church, and *Murmuring Judges* [murmur = speak unclearly] (1991) about the law. *Amy's View* (1997) became Hare's most successful play. Written for the famous British actress Dame Judi Dench it is a play of memories and fantasy. *Via Dolorosa* (1998) is a one-man play which Hare performed himself in London and New York, giving an account of his experience of a visit to Israel in the steps of Christ. His most recent work is *My Zinc Bed* (2000).

Caryl Churchill is the best-known woman dramatist of the 1980s and 1990s. Her *Top Girls* (1982) and *Serious Money* (written in verse, 1987) are severe comments on the concerns with roles, social position and money in the 1980s. *The Skriker* [female spirit

Caryl Churchill

of nature] (1994) is an exploration of myth and mystery from a female point of view. Timberlake Wertenbaker, with *Our Country's Good* (1988) and *Three Birds Alighting on a Field* [alighting = landing] (1992) brings an exciting female voice into modern drama. Through the 1990s she continued to explore female themes in plays like *The Break of Day* (1995), which is a kind of companion piece to Anton Chekhov's *Three Sisters*, the influential Russian drama from 1903. Wertenbaker often uses classical Greek myths in a modern context: her radio play *Dianeira* (1999) uses the ancient Greek dramatist Sophocles' play *Women of Trachis* as its inspiration to look at the theme of women's anger and rebellion. Like Caryl Churchill, she writes about all of society, with wide themes.

The 1990s brought a number of strong masculine voices into the theatre. Patrick Marber is one of the most significant of these voices. His *Dealer's Choice* (1995) is set in the masculine world of card games, and *Closer* (1997) is the first play to bring Internet sexual relations to the stage. Two Irish plays achieved huge worldwide success, Martin McDonagh's *The Beauty Queen of Leenane* (1996) and *The Weir* (1997) by Conor McPherson. Both are gentle plays with a lot of talk, but reveal hidden depths in their examination of the tensions under the surface of relationships.

East is East (1996) by Ayub Khan-Din was a major achievement – it is the first play to show the problems of a Pakistani family who have settled in the north of England. It became a huge success all over the world, and then a very successful film, the first popular comedy to handle such delicate subjects as marriage between the races, arranged marriage and homosexuality.

Theatre is very much alive in the popular comedies of John Godber. *Bouncers* (1987) and *Teechers* [teachers] (1988) show his cabaret style, with small groups of actors playing many parts. His plays are usually set in the north of England, as are many of the plays of Alan Bennett. Bennett's first play, *Forty Years On* (1968), is set in a public school but his television plays, such as *Talking Heads* (1988), show a wide range of characters and settings. These were six monologues spoken by people who are alone and Bennett shows a talent for social observation that is both comic and sad. The monologues are a modern version of the kind of dramatic monologue which Victorian poets like Robert Browning had used. *The Madness of George III* (1991) is a historical drama which later became a successful film. *The Lady in the Van* (1999) shows his relationship with his dying mother and with another old lady who lives in an old van in his garden.

Michael Frayn's *Noises Off* (1982) was one of the most successful comedies of the 1980s. It is a pure farce, which has no social message, although Frayn's other plays, such as *Benefactors* [helpers] (1984), his novels and his translations show him to have a wide range of intellectual and artistic concerns.

Television drama has a huge audience: many millions, rather than the few hundred people in a theatre. Therefore, difficult or controversial themes on TV can cause a lot of argument. Dennis Potter was the best-known serious television dramatist. From the *Nigel Barton* plays (1965) on political themes, he extended television's range in many controversial works such as *Pennies from Heaven* (1978) and *The Singing Detective* (1986).

Alan Bleasdale is the most popular serious television dramatist. His *Boys from the Blackstuff* (1983) was about working men and the problems of looking for a job in a rapidly changing society. More than a thousand years after *Deor's Lament* the subject is still the same. Some things never change, although the time, the place and the society have changed greatly. Literature shows us some of these constants, and some of the changes.

c. 690s –730s	First translation of the Bible into Anglo- Saxon: the *Lindisfarne Gospels*. Old English poem *Beowulf.*	*In the beginning was the Word.* St John's Gospel
c. 1190 1380s–90s 1477 1485	First named authors: Layamon, *Brut* Chaucer, *The Canterbury Tales* Caxton brought printing to England Malory's *Morte d'Arthur* published	*In a cheerful style he then* *began / At once to tell his tale.* Chaucer
1560s 1598–1607 1611	*Gorboduc*, an early tragedy, and *Gammer Gurton's Needle*, a comedy Shakespeare's major works: *Hamlet* (1600) First generally accepted modern English Bible, the *Authorized Version*	*All the world's a stage.* Shakespeare
1709	First Copyright Act protects the new professional authors. Journalism: *The* *Tatler* started by Steele, followed by *The Spectator*, edited with Addison	*No man but a blockhead ever* *wrote except for money.* Johnson
1737 1740 1749	Censorship of the theatre Best-selling epistolary novel: *Pamela* by Richardson Success of Fielding's *Tom Jones*	*I describe not men, but* *manners; not an individual,* *but a species.* Fielding
1812 1814	The first international best-sellers: Byron's poem *Childe Harold's* *Pilgrimage* Scott's novel *Waverley*	*I need a hero.* Byron
1859 1867	Books that changed the world: Darwin, *On the Origin of Species* Marx, *Das Kapital* (published in England)	*I have called this principle …* *Natural Selection.* Darwin
1922 1939	Eliot's poem *The Waste Land*, and Joyce's banned novel, *Ulysses*; the 'novel to end all novels'. *Finnegans Wake* by Joyce	*Things fall apart; the centre* *cannot hold.* Yeats
1955	Beckett's *Waiting for Godot* first performed in England	*You must go on, I can't go on,* *I'll go on.* Beckett
1956 1960	Osborne, *Look Back in Anger* Lawrence's banned novel from the 1920s, *Lady Chatterley's Lover*, first published in England	
1968	Theatres Act ended censorship (since 1737)	

Important Events

1 The Beginnings of English: Old and Middle English 600–1485	**410**	Romans began to leave Britain
	664	Whitby conference; Roman Catholicism became the official religion throughout England
	829	Egbert of Wessex became the agreed leader of the seven English regions, which earlier were separate states: apart from Wessex, the others were Mercia, Northumbria, East Anglia, Essex, Sussex and Kent
	1016–42	Danish invaders ruled England
	1066	The Norman Conquest: the monarchy became French. William, Duke of Normandy, was from the same family as the English king, Edward the Confessor, but English landowners did not want a French king and had chosen Harold, son of Godwin
	1170	Thomas à Becket, the reforming Archbishop of Canterbury, was murdered in the cathedral by Henry II's soldiers
	1189	King Richard I 'the lionheart' came to the throne; he was closely involved in foreign wars, including the Middle Eastern 'Crusades' (which continued into the late thirteenth century)
	1204–15	The unpopular King John lost land in Normandy (1204); he resigned a lot of political power in England with the Magna Carta (1215)
	1210	English colonization of Ireland began
	1282	Wales united with England
	1314	Battle of Bannockburn: Scotland defeated England, which had wanted to unite Scotland, as well as Wales, with England
	1338–1453	The Hundred Years War against France, ending in defeat for England
	***c.* 1348**	'The Black Death' strikes England
	1362	The English language becomes the official language of the Law Courts
	1381	The Peasants' Revolt: a demand for workers' rights
	1382	First translation of the Christian Bible into English, by John Wyclif
	1400	Death of Chaucer: *The Canterbury Tales* left unfinished

1415	Battle of Agincourt: England's high point in the Hundred Years War. King Henry V made English the language of the court instead of French
1455–85	The Wars of the Roses: followers of the Duke of York (the white rose) and the Duke of Lancaster (the red rose) fought for the right to be king

2 The Renaissance 1485–1649

1485	Caxton published Malory's *Le Morte d'Arthur*
1490s	The great decade of discovery: Christopher Columbus (Italian, but paid by Spain) was the first European to discover the American continent, in 1492
c. **1500**	The Dutch philosopher and religious reformer Erasmus published his views on humanism – stressing the importance and supreme value of mankind in daily life and in relationships with God. For the first time in Europe, the power and even the existence of God could be questioned
1521	King Henry VIII given the title Defender of the Faith by the Pope
1534	The Act of Supremacy: Henry VIII founded a new Protestant church in England
1558	Loss of Calais, England's last possession in France
1571	Opening of the London Stock Exchange. England's capitalist economy grew very quickly around this time, with large overseas trading interests
1576	Opening of London's first theatre, The Theatre
1577–80	Sir Francis Drake's first voyage around the world
1584	Sir Walter Raleigh set up Virginia, the first English colony in America
1587	Mary, Queen of Scots, executed
1588	The Spanish navy (the Armada), sailing against England, was defeated
1592–4	London theatres closed because of plague
1594	Foundation of the Bank of England
1600	England's foreign trade continued to spread, with the foundation of the East India Company. This lasted to 1858, when England colonized India
1600	Shakespeare: *Hamlet*

	1603	King James VI of Scotland became king of England, as James I
	1605	The Gunpowder Plot. Catholics, led by Guy Fawkes, attempted to blow up the parliament buildings, in a protest against the official Church of England
	1611	The *King James* or *Authorized Version of The Bible*
	1620	The Pilgrim Fathers – Protestants – left for America
	1623	The *First Folio* (first edition) of Shakespeare's plays
	1629	King Charles I ended the power of his parliament and ruled alone
	1642–8	Civil War: Parliamentarians (Roundheads) defeated Royalists (Cavaliers), and the king was executed in 1649. Britain was a republic from 1649 to 1660
3 The Commonwealth and Restoration 1649–1713	**1660**	Restoration of the monarchy – King Charles II
	1665	The Great Plague: the majority of the people of London die
	1666	The Great Fire of London; Christopher Wren was appointed architect for the rebuilding of the city
	1667	Milton: *Paradise Lost*
	1678–84	Bunyan: *The Pilgrim's Progress*
	1688	The unpopular Catholic monarchy of James II was sent into exile. Party politics and serious religious conflicts (especially in Ireland) date from this time
	1694	Bank of England founded
	1707	Scottish and English parliaments united
	1712	Pope: *The Rape of the Lock*
4 Augustan to Gothic 1713–89	**1713**	End of the War of Spanish Succession, which had involved most of the countries of Europe
	1714	The Elector of Hanover came to Britain as King George I
	1715	First Jacobite Rebellion: the son of King James II claimed the throne of England and led Scottish and Catholic forces against the English
	1745	Second Jacobite Rebellion led by Bonnie Prince Charlie, grandson of James II

	1751	Gray: *Elegy Written in a Country Churchyard*
	1754–63	Wars with France: important British gains in India and Canada – the beginning of Empire
	1775	The invention of the steam-engine, by the Scotsman James Watt, led to a rapid rise in cities and industries (the Industrial Revolution)
	1776	The American Declaration of Independence
5 The Romantic Age 1789–1832	1789	The French Revolution: this led to the founding of a new republic in France in 1792
	1793–1815	The Reign of Terror in France, followed by the Napoleonic Wars (from 1804); France's aims for supremacy in Europe were finally defeated at Waterloo (1815)
	1798	William Wordsworth and Samuel Taylor Coleridge: *Lyrical Ballads*
	1801	Ireland politically joined to Britain
	1814	Scott: *Waverley*
	1814	Invention of the railway engine by George Stephenson
	1819	The Peterloo Massacre: government forces violently put an end to a protest for workers' rights
	1819	Keats wrote his most famous poems
	1824	Trades unions were recognized by the British government
	1829	Unfair treatment against Catholics made unlawful
6 The Victorian Period 1832–1900	1832	The First Reform Act: voting rights for men extended
	1836	Dickens: *The Pickwick Papers*
	1837	Victoria became queen
	1848	The Year of Revolutions: many revolutions in Europe
	1848	Karl Marx and Friedrich Engels: *The Communist Manifesto*
	1850	Death of Wordsworth; Tennyson became Poet Laureate
	1851	The First World Fair (the Great Exhibition) was held

in the Crystal Palace, specially built in Hyde Park, London. The Great Exhibition is widely regarded as the high point of British imperialism

1854–6	The Crimean War: the first war reported in daily newspapers
1857–8	The Indian Mutiny; Britain moved the running of the colony from private control into government hands
1859	Darwin: *On the Origin of Species*
1861	Death of Prince Albert, the husband of Queen Victoria
1861–5	The American Civil War. War between the Southern and the Northern States led by President Lincoln
1868	Foundation of the Trades Unions Congress
1870s	Britain leads international communications with the development of postal services and telephone communications (the Italian inventor of the telephone, Giuseppe Marconi, worked in England)
1870	Education made law for children aged five to thirteen
1871–2	Eliot: *Middlemarch*
1876	Queen Victoria declared Empress of India
1895	Wilde: *The Importance of Being Earnest*
1899–1902	The Boer War, in South Africa

7 The Twentieth Century to 1939

1901	Death of Queen Victoria
1907	Kipling first British winner of Nobel Prize for Literature
1912	Defeat of the Liberal government's Irish Home Rule bill; growth of the Labour party
1914–18	The First World War
1916	The Easter Rising in Ireland; many protestors against British rule were executed
1922	Irish Free State (Eire) was formed but a northern region of the island remained British
1922	Eliot: *The Waste Land* and Joyce: *Ulysses*
1929	Worldwide financial failure began in the United States
1933	Adolf Hitler came to power in Germany

8 The Contemporary Period: 1939 to Today	**1939–45**	The Second World War
	1940	Winston Churchill (aged sixty-six) became leader of the British National government
	1945	New Labour party government: many major industries placed under state control
	1946	Foundation of the free National Health Service in Britain
	1947	Britain gave independence to India – most of Britain's overseas possessions became independent in the late 1950s or 1960s
	1948	The Jewish state of Israel formed
	1954	Golding: *Lord of the Flies*
	1955	Beckett: *Waiting for Godot* (first performance in English)
	1956	Osborne: *Look Back in Anger*
	1964–70	London became the worldwide capital of youth culture – especially music, clothes and design
	1969	US spacemen Armstrong and Aldrin landed on the moon. This was the end of a 'space race' with the USSR, begun with the Soviet spaceman Yuri Gagarin who was the first man to travel in space in 1961
	1969	Beckett wins Nobel Prize for Literature
	1973	Britain joined the European Common Market (European Union)
	1979	A new Conservative party government stressed an economy and culture led by money
	1983	Golding wins Nobel Prize for Literature
	1989	End of communism in eastern Europe; capitalism begins to extend east
	1997	Tony Blair's New Labour wins General Election
	1999	Ceasefire agreement between all sides in N. Ireland

Extra Words

These words are the extra words that do not appear in the Penguin Readers' level 6 vocabulary list, the cultural terms or the literary terms. You should look up the meaning of these words in your dictionary if you do not already know them.

abortion
acrobat
albatross
alligator
anarchy/anarchic
anthropological
ape
aspect
avenge

beloved
bliss
brutish

cabaret
Capitol
circulate
circus
climax
coffer
colonel
compromise
compulsory
conclude
conflict
conscience
contemporary
context
controversy/controversial
convention
corrupt/-ion

decadent
defect
deformed
depression
despair
destiny
diminish
dragon

drawing room
driveth

emblem
eternity/eternal
execute
execution
exile

fantastic
farewell
fascination
feminine
flatter
focus
forge
found/-ation
fragment
fraternity
frustrated
futile/futility

generation
genius
giant
gloom/-y
glory/glorious
grail
greed

harmony
headstrong

iceberg
immigrant/immigration
immortal
incest
insight
inspire/inspiration, -al
institution

intellect
interlude
invade/-r/invasion

laissez-faire
legend/-ary
legislator
leviathan
liberty

magus
maid
mainstream
manacles
masculine
mask
massacre
masterpiece
menace/menacing
merchant
merry
minimalism/minimalist
miracle/miraculous
mock
monster

obscene
obscure
obsess/-ed, -ion, -ive

paradox
parson
passion/-ate
plague
plough
prejudice
prime
primitive
profane/-ness
professor

241

prosecution
psalm
psalter
psychoanalysis
punctuation
pylon

rake
rape
refresh
reign
revival/revive
revolt
revolutionary

sacrifice
savage
scandal/-ous
secular

sensual/-ity
sentiment
shepherd
slough
solitary
sparrow
species
spectator
squire
stress
structure
subtle
successor
suicide
superhuman
supernatural
supreme/supremacy
symbolic
sympathy

tame
theme
throne
tolerate
traitor
trench
tribe

unite/uniting
updating

vague
vanity
venerable
vow
vulgar

wasteland
weep

Cultural Terms

Abbey	large and important church. In the past, the centre of a **monastery.**
academic	an academic is someone who teaches and studies in a university or college.
act	an act is a law made by **parliament.**
AIDS	a very serious disease which means that the human body cannot resist infections.
Anglo-Saxon	Anglo-Saxons lived in England from the fifth century to the Norman Conquest in 1066. The word is also used today to describe members of the English race or societies and cultures which have been influenced by the English.
angry young men	a term used to describe the generation of young men in the 1950s who protested against society. They appear as characters in novels and plays in the 1950s.
apocrypha	stories which are not believed to be true.
archbishop	*see* **bishop**.
aristocrat/ aristocracy	people who belong to families with a very high social position. Some aristocrats have special titles like **lord** or earl.
best-seller	a book which is very popular and which sells lots of copies.
Bible	the holy book of Christians.
bill	a bill is a plan for a law which is considered by members of **parliament**.
bishop	bishops and archbishops are leaders of the priests in the Christian church.
Boer	a Boer was a white South African who originally came to South Africa from Holland.
bohemian	one who does not accept the morality or conventions by which most people live.
butler	the most important male servant in a house, normally the house of an **aristocratic** or very rich family.
Calvinism	is a form of **Protestantism** based on the works of the Swiss-based writer Jean Calvin. The stress is on good and evil. Calvinism is particularly strong in Scotland.
capitalism	capitalism is an economic system in which property and businesses belong to individuals and not to the state. The main aim of the individuals is to make a profit.

Catholic   a Catholic is a Christian who believes that the **Pope** is the leader of the Christian church.

Cavalier   the name of a supporter of King Charles I before and during the Civil War (1642–9). The **Puritans**, who supported Oliver Cromwell, were called Roundheads.

CD-ROM   a device for reading or recovering information on a computer. The initials mean 'Compact Disc – Read Only Memory'.

Celt/-ic   Celtic people or Celts are those who are connected with the people and culture of Scotland, Wales and Ireland.

censor/-ship   books or plays are censored when the government of a country instructs that all or parts of them cannot be published or performed.

charter   document which explains or gives **rights** in a democratic state. (*See* **Chartist** below.)

Chartist   a political group which tried to win better **rights** for workers in the early nineteenth century.

chivalry   the word 'chivalry' describes behaviour, usually by men towards women, which is especially polite. In medieval times chivalry was a moral, social and religious way of life.

cold war   a cold war happens when two or more countries do not actually fight each other but are politically and economically very unfriendly. A cold war existed until recently between the USA and the former Soviet Union.

colony   a colony was a place where a foreign country told the people how they should be governed. This policy, largely by western **capitalist** nations, was called colonialism.

Commonwealth   the period from 1649 to 1660 when Britain was a republic led by Oliver Cromwell. The term is also used to describe countries, usually former colonies, which together form a loose political group. For example, India, Nigeria, Australia and Singapore are members of the British Commonwealth.

communism   communism is a social and political system in which property and businesses belong to the state rather than to individuals. The goods and wealth of a communist society are divided among all the people.

conquer   take over any country and replace its political systems. William of Normandy (King William I) is always called 'the Conqueror' and his defeat of Britain is called 'the Norman Conquest'.

conservative   a conservative is someone who values traditions and dislikes change. The Conservative party is a political party in Britain which supports **capitalism** and is against state control of society.

court   people who live in or around the home of the king or queen live at court. Such people include **nobles** and officials. Courtly behaviour is extremely polite behaviour.

Creation   this word, normally with a capital C, refers to the way in which the **Bible** describes that the world was made by God.

dandy   the word 'dandy' refers to a man of fashion who thinks a lot about his own personal appearance.

Dark Ages   the period in Europe from about AD 500 to 1100.

democracy   a political system in which people vote for the leaders of the country. Something which is democratic is something which is based on the idea that everyone shares it equally.

Depression   period when money loses value, leading to bad conditions in **capitalist** states. The Great Depression began in New York in 1929.

dialect   a variety of language spoken by people from a particular group or region.

dictator/-ship   a dictator is a political leader who does not accept opposition in the country he controls.

double standards   when one group of people is allowed greater freedom of behaviour than another then double standards are said to operate.

duke   an **aristocrat** similar to an **earl.**

emperor/empress   a leader of an empire. An empire is a number of countries which are ruled by one country.

empire   *see* **emperor/empress.**

Enlightenment   a period in Europe in the eighteenth century where people believed that science and reason would improve human life and human society.

escapism   the word 'escapism' used to describe ideas, or films or stories which allow you to think about pleasant things and not about the unpleasant things in life.

Fall   the **sin** of Adam as described in the **Bible**.

fascism   **right-wing** political ideas which are based on government by one strong leader and on control of the state are described as fascist.

feminist   a feminist believes that women should have equal rights with men.

gay   a person who is gay is homosexual, that is, he or she is sexually attracted to people of the same sex.

guild   an organized group of people all of whom do the same job and have the same interests.

highbrow   a person who has an interest in intellectual and artistic matters.

homosexual   *see* **gay.**

humanist   a humanist believes in the goodness of human beings and that happiness can be found on earth.

humanity   all human beings, especially in the way they think. *See* **humanism/-ist.**

illuminated manuscripts   *see* **manuscript.**

imperialist   an imperialist believes in the power of **empire.**

irrational   not using logical thought or reason. *See* **rational.**

Jacobite rebellions   in 1715 and 1745 the Catholic descendants of King James II (1685–8) tried to win power. The name Jacobite comes from James. The leader of the 1745 rebellion was Bonnie Prince Charlie, Charles Edward Stuart.

knight   in medieval times a knight was a person of noble birth who normally served a king. In modern times in Britain a knight can be created by the **prime minister** to reward important work for the country. A knight can put 'Sir' in front of his name.

Labour   a political party which believes in **socialist** ideas, in particular that people's life and work should be controlled by a state which will try to make things more equal for everyone.

lord   *see* **noble.**

manuscript   a written text; sometimes a text written by hand. Illuminated manuscripts are medieval manuscripts with gold, silver and coloured designs.

mass media   ways in which people are entertained and informed, for example, television, newspapers, radio.

medieval   the period in history normally between the years 1100 and 1500.

middlebrow   neither stupid nor very intelligent. An average person's level of taste or understanding.

monarch   a monarch is the ruler of a country or state, for example a king or a queen. Monarchs normally rule because of the family into which they are born or marry.

monastery/monk   monks are men who reject a sensual life in order to live by religious ideals. Their communal home is called a monastery.

nationalist   a nationalist is someone who has a deep pride in their own country, often political in nature.

Nobel Prize   several Nobel Prizes are given each year for important work in science, medicine and literature. There is also a Nobel Prize for World Peace.

noble   a person who has a very high social position, for example an **earl** or a **lord**.

nun   a woman who has rejected a sensual life, and lives with other women in order to serve God.

pacifist   a pacifist is a person who refuses to fight in wars because they believe that war is morally wrong.

paradise   another word for heaven, a place where Christians believe that people go after they die.

parliament   the people of a country vote for the members of a parliament. The parliament makes the laws for that country.

pilgrim   a religious person who makes a journey to a holy place.

plate-glass university   a new university, built in Great Britain in the 1960s. Many of the windows in the buildings are made with large, flat pieces of glass.

Pope   the leader of the **Catholic** church.

prime minister   the leader of a government of a country.

prostitute   a prostitute is a person who has sex with other people and who is paid by them for this work.

Protestant   a Protestant is a Christian but, unlike a **Catholic**, does not accept that the **Pope** is the head of the Christian Church. The head of the British Protestant Church is the king or queen of the country.

public school   a private school which charges for pupils to study there.

Puritans   a religious group in the sixteenth and seventeenth centuries. The Puritans worked to make religious life simple and basic.

rational/-ism   based upon reason and logical thought rather than for example emotion or religious belief. *See* **irrational**.

reform political change

Reformation a religious movement which resulted in the foundation of **Protestantism**.

Renaissance a period in history which began in Italy in the fifteenth century, when art and literature aimed for the high ideals of ancient Latin and Greek culture.

repent to regret something bad which you have done. The word is often used with a religious meaning, for example to repent of **sins**.

Restoration The Restoration (1660–1713) was the period in British history after the return of Charles II as King of England, after the **Commonwealth**.

restore put back something that was there before. *See* **Restoration** above.

Resurrection Christ's rising from the dead.

right-wing a word used to express ideas which are closely linked with **capitalism** and **conservatism**.

rights rights are basic things which every citizen in a country should have, for example, a right to vote, a right to a home, a right to education.

Roman Catholic *see* **Catholic**.

Royal Air Force the military organization of Britain which is involved in air defences and battles in the air.

sermon a talk given by a religious person, usually in a church and which usually has moral advice.

sin human behaviour which breaks the law of God.

socialist a socialist believes that society should be organized so that everyone is treated more equally and has equal opportunities.

Stock Exchange a place for buying and selling shares, which are units of ownership in a public company.

subculture the way of life of groups that are considered outside society in some way – motorbike boys and **gays** are often considered part of a subculture.

terrorist someone who uses violence in order to obtain political demands.

testament another word for 'will', what you give to others when you die. Also, the name of the two main sections of the **Bible** (the Old Testament and the New Testament).

Thatcherite based on the ideas and political philosophy of Margaret Thatcher who was prime minister of Britain from 1979 to 1990.

the West the part of the world which includes Western Europe and the USA (normally written with a capital letter).

Trades Union trades unions are groups of workers who join together to protect their **rights**. The Trades Union Congress (TUC) represents all trades unions.

utilitarian a philosophy by which society is organized for the good of the greatest number of people.

Utopia a society in which everyone is happy and everything is perfect. An anti-Utopia is a society in which everyone is unhappy and nothing is perfect.

viking north-European people from Norway and Denmark who made explorations by sea in the period from about AD 800 to 1200, and affected the culture of countries they invaded. For instance, the name Normandy comes from 'Norsemen', an alternative name for vikings.

whisky-priest a priest who has become an alcoholic.

working class a group of people in a society who work with their hands. They normally have a low social and economic position.

Literary Terms

absurd a term describing texts, normally drama texts, which show a world that has no meaning, and which can leave a reader or audience with a feeling of despair.

act (of a play) a play is divided into parts which are usually called acts. Most plays have between three and five acts. Acts are further divided into **scenes**.

adaptation/adapt to adapt something is to write it in another medium. For example, a writer may adapt a play for television or a novel for the cinema.

aestheticism a form of art and literature in which the art and the beauty of art exists only for itself.

allegory usually a simple story which has a deeper meaning below the surface. People and places in the story can symbolize deeper ideas.

alliteration alliteration happens when the same letters are repeated in a pattern of sounds, especially at the beginning of words and in poems. 'Full fathom five thy Father lies' is an example of alliteration.

allusion a reference to the words and forms of other writers.

anapaestic a poetic **foot** with two short **stresses** followed by one long stress. *See* p. 116.

anonymous (the identity of the author is) unknown.

anthology collection of literary works, usually poetry, by different authors.

anti-hero the opposite of a traditional hero whose personal qualities contrast with the bravery, skill and strength of the hero.

Augustan a period of English literature at the end of the seventeenth and the beginning of the eighteenth centuries. The writers took their name from the **classical** Latin age of the Roman Emperor Augustus (27 BC–AD 14).

autobiography *see* **biography**.

ballad a poem which tells a story. It has a regular rhythm and was usually also sung to music.

biography a biography is a book about someone's life. An autobiography is a book about your own life.

black comedy a **comedy** in which serious and sometimes tragic problems are also explored.

blank verse	poetry written in lines which normally have five main **stresses** and which are usually written in an **iambic pentameter** pattern (*see* p. 116).
burlesque/ burletta	forms of **comic** theatrical entertainment, usually with music, and often making fun of more serious drama.
caesura	a break or pause in a line of poetry, usually in the middle of a line.
campus novel	a novel set in a new university and with university teachers and students as main characters.
canto	**epic** poems and long **narrative** poems are divided into cantos. Cantos can be compared with chapters in a novel.
chorus	in **classical** Greek drama a chorus tells the main story and is present during the action.
classic	*see* **classical** below. The word is also used to mean something of major importance.
classical	writing which is influenced by ancient Greek and Latin literature.
comedy	a text in which amusing things happen and which has a happy ending.
comic	*see* **comedy** above. The word implies the intention of making people laugh.
concrete poetry	poems in which the shape of the words on the page help us to understand the meaning.
copyright	the legal right of authors to receive financial benefit from their works.
couplet	two lines of verse which **rhyme**. A heroic couplet is a pair of rhyming lines written in the rhythm of an **iambic pentameter** (*see* p. 116).
critic	a critic makes comments and judgements on a work of literature. His work is to criticize, i.e. to give an opinion, which may lead readers to further discussion.
dactyllic	a **foot** in poetry with one **stressed syllable** followed by two without stress (*see* p. 116).
definitive edition	an **edition** of a text which is agreed by experts to be as close as possible to the text which the writer intended.
dialogue	dialogue happens when two or more people speak with each other. Dialogue is written in poetry, **prose** and drama. **Monologue** is a speech by one person only.
diction	the language chosen by a writer, usually by poets. Poetic diction is usually a special, formal choice of words,

including items which are only found in poems. 'Steed' (horse) and 'main' (sea) are examples of poetic diction.

documentary a novel or a play which is based on real events such as newspaper stories, legal reports, official reports or facts about the lives of real people.

dramatist a writer of plays (drama), also called a playwright.

edit *see* **edition** below. To edit is to make texts easier to read, often by reduction, but also by the whole process of giving more information to the reader.

edition books are printed in different editions. Second or following editions usually contain changes to the text.

elegy an elegy is a poem in which the death of a hero or of a way of life is described. An elegy is usually a poem written about great sadness.

epic a long **narrative** poem which describes the actions of gods, or heroes in a society. Epics can have a national purpose.

epistolary in the form of a series of letters.

essay **prose** writing which discusses ideas and in which strong views are argued. An essayist is one who writes essays.

existentialism a modern belief that individuals live in a world without God and without meaning and are responsible for their own actions.

fable a fable is a story which tries to teach something. It can be based on a **myth** or a legend.

fairy story a story in which there are supernatural events. Fairy stories usually have happy endings.

fantasy a text in which characters and events are imagined. Some may even be very obviously based on dreams.

farce texts, usually plays, which aim to make people laugh in a very basic way. **Plot** is more important than character in farce; the comedy is normally physical rather than intellectual.

fiction a work in **prose**, normally a novel or short story. The word suggests that the character and events in the story are creatively and imaginatively described.

foot *see* p. 116.

free verse *see* p. 116.

genre a type of literary art: **epic, tragedy, melodrama, satire** are literary genres.

gospel   relating to the works of Matthew, Mark, Luke and John in the Biblical New Testament. The word also implies truth, which cannot be challenged.

great tradition   a term used by the English critic F. R. Leavis and others to describe a group of English novels. The novels raise important moral questions. Writers in the great tradition include Jane Austen and George Eliot.

heroic couplet   *see* **couplet**.

hexameter   verse written in lines with six **feet**. (The word means six measures in Greek.)

hymn   a religious poem, usually set to music.

iambic pentameter   *see* p. 116.

image   an image is a picture in words; imagery describes several word pictures which also involve different **metaphors** and **similes**.

impressionism   impressionism is the novelist's or poet's description of the inner life of a character. It is close to **stream of consciousness**. The term can also be used to describe a writer's personal response to the world.

index   part of a book, usually at the end, which is an alphabetic list of names and subjects, and where in the book they can be found.

inscape   the essential character of an object. This feature is particularly important in the poetry of G. M. Hopkins.

irony   a text which is written with irony has a second meaning which is often the opposite of the first meaning. The reader is intended to understand the second meaning.

lament   a poem or song expressing sorrow or regret.

lexicographer   person who explains the meaning of words; a writer of dictionaries.

limerick   a form of short verse in five lines, usually **comic**, with the **rhyme scheme**, *a a b b a.*

lyric   originally a lyric was a poem which was sung and the word today still refers to the words of popular songs. A lyric poem is now any short poem that does not have a **narrative**.

magic realism   magic realism is a kind of writing that contains events which are unexpected and which cannot be explained. Many magical realist texts combine dreams, **fairy stories** and **rhyme**.

manuscript   the written-down words of a book before it is published.

masque   a poetic drama in which songs, dance and music are combined.

masterpiece   the very best work of an author, or the best example of work from a particular period.

melodrama   a play or a story in which events are exaggerated in order to make it exciting.

metaphor   a metaphor describes something by comparing it to something else. For example 'she is a mouse' is metaphoric (*see* **simile**).

metaphysical   metaphysical is an adjective used to describe the poetry of a group of seventeenth-century poets (for example, Donne, Marvell, Herbert) whose language, **imagery** and verse forms were very original.

metre   *see* p. 116.

mock (heroic/epic)   a style used by a writer to make an unimportant subject seem heroic. A mock-heroic style can satirize the subject (*see* **satire**).

mock romance   a text which is not a real romance and in which the romantic subject matter is satirized (*see* **satire**).

monologue   a speech by one person in a poem, play or novel.

movement   a development in literature in which several writers write in a similar style or about similar themes.

myth   a story which is normally not true and in which supernatural beings play important parts. Writers often create myths so that they can help us better understand the world and the creation of the world.

narrative/narrator   a narrative is another word for story; a narrator is someone who tells a story. Authors can use narrators to tell their stories, in their poems or novels.

naturalism   a kind of writing in which hard social realities are described. The term is often used together with **realism**.

ode   a **lyric** poem with a complex structure in which someone or something is praised.

pamphlet   a short book with thin paper covers. The form has been used by writers to give political and religious views. Many pamphlets are written about the problems of the time.

paperback   book with soft covers, usually much cheaper than the same books which have a hard cardboard cover.

parody   in a parody something, or someone, is imitated so that people will laugh at it.

pastoral	writing that is about country life in which the natural world is described as ideal.
patent	a government authority. Patents protect originality, but give the state more control. Legally, a patent cannot be copied for profit.
pathos	a quality in a work of art that is intended to create feelings of sadness or pity.
patron	in the past a patron gave money to authors to help them continue writing. The act of what would now be called sponsorship is called patronage. Only recently, patronage has become a negative word, meaning the use of writers to make wealthy people appear more pleasant than they really are.
performance poet	a poet who reads poetry to an audience in public places such as theatres.
playwright	*see* **dramatist**.
plot	the series of events which happen in a novel or a play or a **narrative** poem.
Poet Laureate	this is a title which is given to the poet who is officially appointed by the king or queen to be the national poet.
preface	an introduction which comes before a book or play.
proscenium arch	*see* **stage**.
prose	prose contrasts with verse. It describes language written in a usual form, not as poetry.
quotation	to quote something is to use the words of another person, normally in order to approve what they have written or said.
realistic	a realistic work is a work which tries to show human life as it really is.
refrain	these are lines in a poem which are repeated, often at the end of a **stanza**.
rhetoric	a text in which language is used to persuade someone to accept a particular point of view.
rhyme royal	a **stanza** form with seven lines, each with ten syllables. The lines rhyme *ababbcc*.
rhyme (scheme)	a rhyme is two or more words with the same sound ('sun' and 'done'/'go' and 'though' are rhymes). A rhyme scheme is a pattern of rhymes.
rhythm	the movement of the sound of a piece of writing but most obviously in poetry.

romance a story which usually contains love and adventure.

saga a saga is a **narrative** about famous heroes or famous families or about kings and soldiers.

satire a text in which people or ideas are socially criticized.

scene a scene is part of an **act** of a play.

science fiction texts, usually novels, which stretch the imagination. Science fiction is usually set in other worlds or even planets. Frequently they are set in the future.

simile a simile describes something by comparing it to something else using the words 'like' or 'as', for example 'He fought like a tiger' (*see* **metaphor**).

slang a very informal and often vulgar use of language.

soliloquy a speech in a play in which a character, usually alone on stage, tells the audience about his or her thoughts and feelings.

sonnet a poem of fourteen lines. There are two main forms of the sonnet: the Petrarchan sonnet and the Shakespearian sonnet. The Petrarchan sonnet has a **rhyme scheme** *abbaabba cdcdcd*; the Shakespearian sonnet has a rhyme scheme *abab cdcd efef gg*. Sonnets are divided into an octet (eight lines) and a sestet (six lines).

spinster novel a novel which is based on the experiences of a spinster, an unmarried woman.

spondaic *see* p. 116

spy novel a novel, which is usually a **thriller**, and which involves main characters who obtain secret information about other countries or organizations.

stage a thrust stage is one where the audience surrounds the actors on three sides. Otherwise the stage is behind the proscenium arch (*see* illustration on p. 37).

stanza a group of lines of poetry which have a **rhyme** pattern.

stream of consciousness the description of the flow of inner experience through the mind of a character, usually in a novel. It is also described by the term 'interior **monologue**'.

stress in lines of poetry, a **syllable** which carries the heaviest part of the rhythm (*see* p. 116).

subtitle a second title given to a book. For example, *Tess of the D'Urbervilles* A Pure Woman. 'A Pure Woman' is the subtitle.

syllable   each sound in a word. For example, this word has three syllables: syl- la-ble.

thriller   a novel or play which has an exciting plot. It is written in order to excite and even to frighten the reader (*see* **spy novel**).

thrust stage   *see* **stage**.

tone   the choice of language by writers which expresses their attitude to things.

tragedy   a text, usually a drama, in which themes are treated seriously, a hero or heroine usually meets some disaster, and which has an unhappy ending.

tragicomedy   a novel or play in which features of **comedy** and **tragedy** are mixed.

trilogy   a group of three plays or novels which are linked by the same theme or the same characters.

triple-decker   a term for long novels in the Victorian era. These often were published in magazines, then collected in three volumes for publication as books.

trochaic   *see* p. 116

wit   the use of language in a very clever and amusing way.

word play   creative uses of language in which, often, double meanings are made.

Author Index

(Numbers in *italics* refer to illustrations.)